Contents

vi *Contents*

Acknowledgements

This book arose from a review of research on poverty and social exclusion that was commissioned by the ESRC in 1992. I would like to thank the ESRC for their support for this work, and for a short update in 1994. My thanks are also due to Graham Room and Carol Walker, who collaborated in the original review, and to Helen Sims, for her help with the subsequent study.

Most of the theoretical part of the book was developed during two visits to the Centre for Social Policy Research (ZeS) at the University of Bremen. I am very grateful to Claus Offe, Winfried Schmähl, Rainer Müller and Stephan Leibfried for making these visits possible. I owe most to the many colleagues and students with whom I had discussions and seminars, and especially to Michael Breuer, Thomas Faist, Maciej Zukowski, Dita Vogel, Sabine Horstmann, Sven Giegold, Faith Dasko, Holger Backhaus-Maul and Susanne Angerhausen.

As always, I consulted with a very helpful circle of friends, who were generous with their comments and criticism. I would specially like to thank Robert van der Veen, Martin Hollis and Maurice Roche for their help. I am also grateful to colleagues at Exeter, Aalborg and elsewhere for collaborative work that was stimulating and valuable, notably Jon Arnold, Johannes Andersen, Bjørn Johnson, Martyn Jones, Marcus Redley, Zdeněk Konopásek and Lars Torpe.

Finally, I would like to thank Jean Packman and other friends for making my travelling lifestyle possible, and for all the support and cheer they offered over the past three years. Special thanks are due to Nigel Parton, Phil Makin, Helen Masson, and above all, to Gill Watson, without whom it would be quite impossible for someone with a stone-age grasp of technology to pursue a postmodern life strategy. Her work in producing the text, from handwritten drafts posted in all corners of Europe, has been heroic.

1

Introduction: The Great Exclusion?

One of the most striking features of the past two decades has been the deterioration in the living standards of the worst-off members of all kinds of societies. This has been most marked in the poorest countries of the Third World, whence the horrors of mass starvation have haunted the television screens of the comfortable world. But it has also been a new and shocking phenomenon in the Second World – the former communist countries – where until 1989, 'many were cold but few were frozen' (Glasman, 1994, p. 212). And in almost all the prosperous countries of the advanced industrialized First World, the proportion of national income going to the worst-off has fallen, while numbers claiming social assistance have risen everywhere except in Japan (Seeleib-Kaiser, 1995).

Yet this century is ending with very little optimism that these problems can be quickly remedied, and remarkably little consensus – among social scientists, politicians or lay people – about the nature, causes or likely future course of poverty. Welfare states have delivered only part of what they promised. The orthodox academic view emerging in the 1990s is that spending on the social services in the advanced industrialized countries – even the USA and UK, after their market-minded regimes of the 1980s – has emerged relatively unscathed from two decades of retrenchment (C. Pierson, 1991; Klein, 1993; P. Pierson, 1995).

In these rich countries, they still redistribute between 10 (Japan) and 35 per cent (Sweden) of Gross National Product, but not in such a way as to protect the poor from reliance on means-tested benefits, or to secure anything near what used to be called 'full employment'. In the developing world, international financial institutions (the World Bank and International Monetary Fund) have required much larger cuts in public sector provision as part of new conditional loans to heavily indebted economies, with correspondingly greater hardships for their poorest.

All this has coincided exactly with the resurgence of free-market Utopianism as a political creed. The idea of a self-regulating market as the basis of a global order first appeared with the Industrial Revolution in Britain and, in the next century, effectively accomplished the transformation of all societies (Polanyi, 1944). By the 1870s there was indeed a kind of world order, sustained by the balance of power between the leading European states, the gold standard of convertible currencies for international exchange, and forms of governance that seemed to be moving in the direction of free-market liberalism. But by 1939 this whole global institutional structure had been transformed again, via economic and social protectionism, through imperialism and territorial rivalry among the European states, class conflict, and the consequent collapse into nationalism, totalitarianism and world war. After 1945, few people foresaw a return to a market-driven world order, as new institutions seemed to provide more effective ways of regulating trade and international relations, as well as domestic economies.

The new wave of free-market Utopianism arose in the Anglo-Saxon countries, whose strongly individualistic liberal traditions saw wealth and poverty in terms of the resources available for participants in a competitive economic and political environment. In the 1980s, the New Right sought to dismantle barriers to 'flexibility' in exchanges between individual actors with a gung-ho optimism that this would make all but the seriously incompetent better off. In the 1990s, the debate has shifted; as millions have become poorer, unemployment has remained stubbornly high, crime rates have risen, and all kinds of other problems (homelessness, single parenthood, truancy, drug abuse, suicide) have multiplied, the focus has moved on to individual pathology. In the USA, the poor have become a target for remoralization through coercion; it is good populist politics to recommend 'orphanages' for the children of 'welfare mothers', so that the mothers can be set to work for their keep (Gingrich, 1994).

In Continental Europe, these principles are coming to be cautiously adopted, as befits institutional systems that have by tradition been more concerned to 'combat social exclusion' than to target poverty. The defining characteristics of European welfare states are that they both redistribute more resources and do so within systems of hierarchically ordered social-status groupings, whose relationships are regulated through the state. The poor are of concern because they have been relegated from these systems, by falling out of the labour market or the family, on which institutionalized social inclusion is based. It is not only for political correctness that in France the poor are referred to as 'les exclus' (roughly 'the outcasts'). But even in the 'softer' welfare states, such as the Netherlands, Denmark and Belgium, social inclusion is increasingly pursued by compulsory measures for 'activating' or 'inserting' those who have fallen through the net (Adriaansens and Dercksen, 1993; Petersen and Søndergaard, 1994; Pacolet and Debrabander, 1995).

These developments in the 1990s represent something of a convergence between two traditions. The Anglo-Saxon liberal tradition emphasized *poverty* as a natural condition, governed by scientific laws of population and resources. It was concerned with policies to remove institutional barriers to the disciplinary effects of these laws on individuals in a competitive environment (M. Dean, 1991, p. 85). In the original theories of this tradition, such as those of Malthus (1798), the poor were seen as beings who would learn the principles of economics only through pain: 'hunger will tame the fiercest of animals; it will teach decency and civility, obedience and subjection, to the most perverse' (J. Townsend, 1786, p. 57). The Continental mercantilist tradition, governance and policy were concerned with *social exclusion* and 'the conservation and utilization of human beings as valued resources of the state [so that] their end is not the positive

enhancement of life but the augmentation of the national estate'
(M. Dean, 1991, p. 34). In this tradition, the poor were more like
sheep and cattle to be farmed (regulated and provided for as
part of the creation and conservation of natural wealth) than
wild animals to be tamed. Esping-Andersen's distinction between
liberal Anglo-Saxon and conservative Continental welfare states
indicates the persistence of these traditions over more than two
centuries (Esping-Andersen, 1990).

The starting-point of this book is that neither of these two
intellectual and political traditions has so far produced a convincing analysis of how poverty and social exclusion are related
under present-day conditions. The aim of the book is to develop
such an analysis. What has to be explained is why these phenomena have reappeared in prosperous countries, and grown in poor
ones, at this particular time; and why neither the deregulatory,
free-trade policies of market-minded governments nor the more
protective and solidaristic systems of European states have hitherto been able to check their growth.

The liberal tradition analyses poverty in terms of competitive
interactions under scarcity, and the problems of collective action
arising from these. The Continental tradition analyses social
exclusion as a problem in the regulation of the human resources
of the state. Hence it is hardly surprising that the theory of
poverty and social exclusion has hitherto dealt mainly in the
dynamic between markets and states. What has been missing has
been a more comprehensive view of how groups form, organize
and act collectively in pursuit of their interests, and how vulnerable individuals come to be excluded and marginalized in such
interactions.

Poverty has been a feature of all modern societies, but so has
the attempt to provide inclusive systems to protect the poor.
Since both inclusion and exclusion are universal features of
social formations, the task is to devise models that capture the
mechanisms and rationales through which people with few
resources are either enabled to contribute and to make some
claims on others, or pushed outside to fend for themselves. It is
also to reveal and compare the social costs associated with these
processes.

The present era of expanding transnational exchanges and shrinking global time and space has also seen a reduction in the ability of nation states to protect their citizens from economic risks (Held and McGrew, 1994). Theory on poverty and social exclusion has hitherto been only partially successful in relating these phenomena. I shall also try to develop an analysis that explains how globalization and the transformation of states are affecting the living conditions of vulnerable individuals, groups and communities.

This opening chapter introduces the major theses of the book, and relates them to the current theoretical debates in the social sciences. Now, as in the early nineteenth century when the analysis of poverty was first developed, the issue raises fundamental questions for the understanding of society and its governance.

COLLECTIVIZATION AND FRAGMENTATION

Any theory that seeks to explain the relationship between individual need and social exclusion must necessarily analyse the economics of human collectivities. Individuals are most vulnerable when they have fewest personal capacities and material resources, and especially when they face the hazards of childhood, old age, sickness, disability or handicap. But none of these deficits and risks necessarily threatens their survival so long as they enjoy the protections afforded by membership of an inclusive group, that co-operates productively and redistributes its product. Conversely, of course, a social formation that protects its vulnerable members may do so by exploiting or oppressing other members, notably women, who might be better off under some other, more liberal, individualistic regime.

The question raised by poverty is therefore how human beings, interacting under conditions of scarcity in all kinds of collectivities (from households to nation states) come to include some vulnerable individuals and exclude others from the benefits of membership – and at what costs to the rest of the members. This is best analysed, I shall argue in this section, as an *economic* question.

Aside from the traditions identified in the opening section it is understandable that the analysis of poverty and social exclusion should focus on the dynamic between markets and states. Modern forms of poverty (and discourses about them) emerged in parallel with the capacities of political systems to organize for new forms of civil governance, rather than simply for criminal justice and war. In England, for example, these new capacities were triggered when the enclosure movement enabled landowners to improve the productivity of their agriculture by evicting the rural populace from their settlements and commons (Polanyi, 1944, ch. 3). By the end of the sixteenth century, a national system of local government (the Poor Law) was established to regulate the social disruption caused by economic 'improvement'. At the end of the eighteenth century, the more dramatic dislocations of the Industrial Revolution were countered, first by local innovations for wage supplements and compulsory work for benefits ('workfare') under the Speenhamland system, and then (in 1834) by legislative and administrative reforms that largely structured the new institutions of national and local government.

De Swaan (1988) has analysed the parallel developments that took place all over Europe, from the late medieval period to the creation of welfare states, in terms of a progressive process of collectivization. The *exclusions* required to create private property (where previously there had been communal production) implied a need to *include* the dispossessed. Poverty amid 'improvement' meant want in the presence of an economic surplus; hence there were new – albeit limited and conditional – entitlements for the poor under conditions of exclusion (de Swaan, 1988, p. 14). Once interdependence between haves and have-nots was structured into local collective systems (as much to settle, pacify, control and subordinate the poor as to provide for their needs), these had to be co-ordinated, first regionally and then nationally, to deal with problems of mass migration, crowding and disorder. De Swaan went on to develop a comprehensive theory of collectivization as a response to the dilemmas faced by interdependent but uncoordinated actors in large industrial societies, such that eventually all the advanced capitalist countries had collective, nationwide and compulsory arrangements to deal with social welfare issues affecting their whole populations.

But de Swaan's theory only tackles half the task I have set myself in this book. It is of limited value in explaining the re-emergence of poverty in our times, when the mass solidarities established through welfare states are being broken into narrower mutualities, as the better-off turn to private insurance, and the poor fall into public assistance, or down through that into reliance on each other. I shall argue that what is needed is a *theory of groups* that explains how individuals choose to join together in associations of all kinds (from households to communities), excluding outsiders from the goods that they supply to each other. In such a theory, private property does not necessarily imply exclusivity alone, since most 'private' resources are owned by associations (families, firms, financial institutions); they are thus both inclusively owned and used, and exclusive of other would-be owners and users. Similarly, most collective (or 'public') goods (including the benefits and services of the welfare state) are partially exclusive, because most non-nationals, and often some citizens also, are not entitled to receive them, and therefore not included. This applies even to defence, the classic 'public' good, which would be of little value if it extended to hostile states.

Because of this ambiguity in the nature of almost all goods (that they are private from some perspectives, and collective from others), a theory based on the interaction between markets and states will not be adequate for the analysis of poverty and social exclusion. What is needed is a theory that explains how groups organize themselves to include some members and exclude non-members, and above all how people with few resources, or facing high risks, fare in such social interactions. In other words, a theory of poverty and social exclusion is necessarily an *economic theory of exclusive groups* (how people interact in relation to their economic risks, capacities and resources), and this is what the book will set out to develop.

The study of the economics of groups is now well established, but it has so far been little applied to issues of social policy, except in a rather cavalier way by public-choice theorists, as a kind of coda to their prescriptions on competition policies and the virtues of markets (Buchanan, 1978, 1986d; T. Wilson, 1985). The seminal works in this tradition were both published in 1965. Mancur Olson's *The Logic of Collective Action: Public Goods and the Theory of Groups* set out to explain how individuals overcome the strong disincentives to acting in their collective interests, when each will receive only a small part of the joint benefits of such actions, and when each will be equally tempted to 'free ride' on the efforts of others. Hence public goods, from which no one in a group can be excluded, will tend to be undersupplied – and the undersupply increases with the size of the group (in a small group it may be worth one member's while to provide the goods for the group as a whole, but in a large group each member knows that his or her individual contribution will make little difference to overall provision). Olson showed how, in a stable political system with a market economy, 'distributional coalitions' or 'collusions' (monopolies, cartels, trade union closed shops, lobby groups) could overcome these collective-action problems by the use of compulsion and selective incentives. In this way they could organize themselves to capture 'rents' (returns greater than those needed to keep resources in their place: that is, greater than the incomes arising from their marginal costs) and hence bring about allocations of resources that were advantageous for themselves, but sub-optimal (inefficient or inequitable) for society as a whole. In other words, by restraining competition among members and excluding non-members from the field, business cartels and unions could act against the interests of unorganized or disorganized firms and workers; and by gathering members and exerting pressure, lobby groups could likewise draw resources away from more productive (and hence more socially beneficial) uses.

James Buchanan's 'An Economic Theory of Clubs' (1965) analysed the provision of a whole range of goods through interactions that are intermediate between markets and political allocations. His example was of a swimming pool, jointly supplied by members of a club to each other, but with a fence around it to exclude non-members, making its use non-rivalrous among a limited number who contribute to maintenance costs, but avoiding the disutilities of congestion by others, who do not contribute. But the same analysis could apply to any good or bundle of goods that could be supplied to a limited membership through some technological form of exclusion, even to technically private goods (McGuire, 1972) such as health insurance (Breuer, 1995). As Bill Clinton has found to his cost in the USA, if health insurance plans are able to select only good risks and exclude bad ones, non-profit organizations find it difficult to supply health insurance to vulnerable people at low cost, and government finds it difficult to mobilize political support for a redistributive national health service. Thus interactions within exclusive clubs have repercussions for the population at large which are very similar to Olson's account of collective action by 'collusive' producer groups.

Both these analyses have been extensively developed in subsequent literatures – Olson's in the elucidation of collective-action problems in political economy, and how institutions can help groups to overcome them (North, 1990; Coleman, 1990); and Buchanan's in 'club theory', a branch of the literature of public choice and public finance (Starrett, 1988; Mueller, 1989). Both developments contribute to the explanation of how individuals choose to act in groups, how members are selected and non-members excluded, how contributions are assured, and how competition between members is restrained. All this is of obvious relevance to social policy, and especially to the analysis of how vulnerable people come to be excluded from an equitable share in the collective security, cultural life and material resources of their societies; yet it has not been applied in any systematic way to these issues. This is the main project of this book; the theoretical groundwork is laid in chapter 2.

What is at stake here is the action of exclusive groups in welfare states, as well as in societies in transition from command economies, and in less developed countries. The perspective allows social policy issues to be addressed by analysing the interaction between individual choices and strategies, the formal systems, policies and rules of governments, and the informal norms and practices of groups (Breuer, Faist and Jordan, 1994). All this has been lacking in theory on poverty and social exclusion, for reasons that will be explored in chapter 3.

Such a theory should be able to handle both the explanation of how large-scale collective systems of social protection were established in the rich countries in the hundred years after 1880, *and* how these are currently being fragmented through the exit of the better-off into private schemes, and the exclusion of the poor. It should be able to analyse how social security schemes in Europe have now been divided between social insurance that is *positively* related to income (the more you earn, the more you benefit) and a growing social assistance sector which is *negatively* income-related (the more resources you have the less you can claim); and why welfare claimants are currently being demonized in the United States. The theory is particularly suitable for explaining the economics of diversity, pluralism and polarization in social relations – all tendencies associated with 'late modernity' (Giddens, 1991) or 'post-modernity' (Bauman, 1992; Smart, 1991). Even as *globalization* accelerates – transnational exchanges of goods, capital, people, information, culture, pollution and crime; greater interdependence of spheres of decision-making previously treated as separate, such as foreign and domestic policy (Parry, 1994); and the emergence of transnational institutions, such as G7 and the European Union – new opportunities and incentives are created for groups to organize and pursue common interests, or protect themselves from common threats.

All such collective action has certain common features, but there are important differences between closed and open groups. What is common to all is that the rules and structures of groups – right up to the level of states and international regimes (Zürn, 1995) – restrain members from mutually frustrating competition with each other, and mobilize them for successful competition with non-members. Group rules are able to achieve this by internalizing some of the costs of the goods they supply to each other (positive interdependencies among members) and externalizing other costs (negative externalities for non-members).

Closed groups ('clubs') may take the form of professional networks, formed to capture a specific market or government grant: luxurious condominiums, elite schools or health facilities, where benefits stem from prestige and snob-value as well as actual amenities; 'lifestyle groups' such as counselling, environmental or emotionally supportive self-help organizations, where they arise from the re-enforcement of shared values; or mutual protection groups, such as immigrants taking collective action to counter racist or xenophobic attacks. But they may even take the form of drugs subcultures or criminal gangs, where what is shared is the high risk associated with activities giving large short-term returns. As an extreme example, HIV-positive men (who are immune from imprisonment in Italy) have been operating as gangs of bank robbers there (BBC Radio 4, *Today* programme, 9 August 1995). All of these restrict membership to exclude others who would crowd, pollute, deplete, water down, free-ride, spy, betray or compete away these advantages.

Open groups exert pressure to redistribute resources, or change the rules governing production or distribution, or resist changes to such rules. These are what Olson (1965) calls 'inclusive groups' because the costs of recruiting extra members are very low, and outweighed by the benefits. They include political parties, social movements and lobby groups of all but the most elitist or subversive kinds (these last two operate as exclusive clubs, because of sharing high costs or high risks). They are therefore open to poor people, though as is well known their rate of joining such organizations is low, because the selective incentives provided to attract members are seldom those most relevant to their needs.

It may seem surprising that the starting-point of my analysis of poverty and social exclusion is derived from public-choice theory, notoriously associated with criticisms of the welfare state, and the advocacy of Utopian global free-market deregulation. But – as I shall argue in chapter 2 and illustrate throughout the book – this perspective has the great merit of allowing alternative uses of resources to be compared, and the costs associated with various forms of social interaction to be revealed and evaluated. I shall show that this perspective on the analysis of interaction in exclusive groups reaches some surprising conclusions when applied to poverty and social exclusion – conclusions that are very different from the ones proclaimed in leading public-choice theorists' policy prescriptions, and that reveal the perverse incentives, moral hazard and unintended consequences of market-minded reforms of the social services.

However, there are also disadvantages (costs) in this, as in every other method; 'Nothing is for nothing', as public-choice theorists never tire of telling us. One advantage is that, because it studies human interdependency as a phenomenon associated with the indivisibility of some resources, the costs of allocating goods for exclusive use, the absence of competition in their supply, or the gains from co-operation and exclusion, it allows all social interactions (the material and the moral economy) to be analysed within a single framework (Buchanan, 1968; 1986b). A disadvantage is that it can obscure issues of power, subordination and discrimination, and how these are resisted. This will be the subject of the next section.

THE FEMINIZATION AND RACIALIZATION OF POVERTY AND EXCLUSION

The perspective outlined in the previous section allows poverty and social exclusion to be explained in terms of group interactions aimed at maximizing value and minimizing costs. But there are two very important dimensions where poverty and social exclusion are *not* necessarily related to the *economic* potentialities and vulnerabilities of individuals – sex and skin colour. There is a huge and growing literature, both theoretical and empirical, that documents and analyses the ways in which material disadvantage in the advanced industrialized countries is concentrated among women (Zopf, 1989; Goldberg and Kremen, 1990; Millar and Glendinning, 1991) and members of ethnic minorities (W. J. Wilson, 1987; Eggebeen and Lichter, 1991; Aponte, 1991). In the USA, the shift from optimism about how the poor could gain from free-market liberalization to authoritarianism about the social obligations of welfare claimants has focused on black women. Although the extent to which the debate about 'morality and the underclass' is racialized is variable in other countries, there is disturbing evidence, from Continental Europe as well as from Britain, that appeals to traditionalist 'family values' and crude racism have been linked, and have achieved significant electoral support (Bovenkerk, Miles and Verbunt, 1990).

One major challenge for the perspective that I am adopting in this book is thus whether it can encompass these aspects of poverty and social exclusion. It might therefore be useful to sketch, right at the outset, the approach to these issues that I shall be adopting.

Since the whole aim of my analysis is to explain the *dynamic relationship* between the material disadvantages of the poor and the advantages of the better-off as the outcome of social interactions (rather than simply to describe a 'tendency' towards relative inequalities), it is of prime importance to recognize and take account of the historical and cultural dimensions of social exclusion. My analysis will be partial and misleading if it does not encompass developments in the structures and relationships of households and kinship networks, and how these interact with labour markets and state systems. Furthermore, it must take account of the enormous significance of citizenship in determining an individual's level of resources, since membership of a rich, developed polity alone guarantees an income beyond the dreams of the vast majority of citizens of less developed economies. Hence both migration and the exclusion of would-be immigrants are of great relevance to the dynamics of wealth and poverty (Bauböck, 1991).

However, it is also important not to lose my focus on the *economic* basis of inclusion and exclusion if my analysis is to be coherent and comprehensive. The aim is therefore to identify the economic processes by which gender- and 'race'-based poverty and social exclusion have evolved from, and are still produced by, group interactions. A full account of such processes would require a very long book, but in this section I shall give a brief résumé of the approach taken here.

The history of economic development has involved uneven and largely unpredictable shifts: from small and often nomadic social formations (hunter-gatherers) who shared almost all they were able to supply, working and living as a collective unit; to smaller, territorial, agricultural formations (peasant households) participating in local communal systems of reciprocity and redistribution, under the authority of a political – but usually not a territorial – sovereign (Spruyt, 1994); to yet smaller and much more mobile units (nuclear families), whose members interact in labour markets with complex divisions of labour, within sovereign states providing a wide range of goods to their citizens. But these changes have by no means occurred through peaceful evolution. Throughout history, the process of change from one system to another has involved war, the destruction of a cultural heritage, and the subordination of one part of the population by another.

The two countries *least* invaded and fought over by foreign armies in the modern age both illustrate this clearly. Britain (more accurately England) has not been 'conquered' since 1066, yet its ruling class and institutional system still bear many of the marks of the Norman invaders almost a millennium later, while its ethnic mix of inhabitants bears witness to its 'success' in conquering and colonizing territory in every part of the globe, and compulsorily incorporating their inhabitants within the world economic systems of industrial production and trade over which it presided in the nineteenth century. The population of the United States reflects the outcome of European colonization and immigration, the warlike seizure of 'free land' from the native inhabitants, the coercive transportation of huge numbers of African slaves, and more recent migrations from Central and South America and South-East Asia. The American Constitution was written by white, colonialist, slave-owning men, who had just been victorious in a war to secure their independence.

Thus social relationships, like many of the property holdings of the rich, are largely the historical legacy of violence and subordination rather than the outcome of a strikingly efficient form of economic organization, in evolutionary competition with others. Except in the most remote environments that are least hospitable to human habitation, the habitats of nomadic hunter-gatherers have been ruthlessly expropriated for 'more productive' uses, and their ways of life destroyed (as is still happening in the Amazonian rain forest). Even when natural ecological systems have remained intact, other methods of subjugation have been practised – for instance, the forcible resocialization of children. As recently as the 1950s, the Canadian authorities pursued policies of compulsorily removing children from native people in order to provide them with full-time education in boarding schools, a practice that prevented these children from learning to survive in their environments or communities (Armitage, 1975).

By the same token, the peasant economies of Asia, Africa and Central America were transformed by colonial regimes that taxed or harassed their inhabitants into new forms of production (mines and plantations), and were structured for exploitation by, and dependence on, the industrialized economies of the colonial powers, leaving them with long-term disadvantages after decolonization. This process has given rise to the dynamic of migration from these economies towards the rich countries, who attempt to counter the trend by increasing restrictions on immigration, and special categories of time-limited and conditional residence, giving reduced rights, and heightened insecurity and vulnerability to those who are able to enter (Hammar, 1990).

Within this chaotic story of forced subordination and the destruction of traditional social units, or their exclusion from access to the cultural and material resources of their traditional communities, there were nevertheless certain long-term continuities of development. In the Ancient World of classical Greece and Rome, the sphere of production was the private household, consisting of a master and his dependants (wife, children and servants, slaves), all under his patriarchal authority (Gorz, 1988). The public sphere was that of collective decision-making (politics), in which freemen participated (Farrar, 1992), and from which all those condemned to labour (the dependent members of households) were excluded. Thus patriarchy as domestic and economic authority was the system of subordination of women, servants *and* slaves, and hence the common source of all these forms of exclusion from the collective institutions of government, political authority and the public sphere (Nye, 1987, ch. 5; Hudson and Lee, 1990, ch. 1).

Patriarchal authority continued to provide the basis for domestic subordination in European societies right up to modern times; it was even transferred to the public sphere as the source of justification for absolute monarchical power, the Divine Right of Kings (Filmer, 1680). Thus it was only when the patriarchal claims of lordship and kingship were challenged (by free cities in Italy and northern Europe in the late Middle Ages, and by coalitions of nobility, bourgeoisie and artisans in the Netherlands, Britain and elsewhere from the end of the sixteenth century), that new justifications and forms of governance could develop.

Women's subordination in households was thus historically linked with that of servants (employees) and slaves, and the economic dependence of all three groups to their political exclusion. Erickson's (1993) painstaking research shows that in England, although families in the seventeenth and early eighteenth centuries spent as much on educating girls as boys, and although women inherited *more* moveable property than men (to compensate for primogeniture in the bequest of freehold land), 'married women's legal disabilities put them in the same category with idiots, convicted criminals and infants'; that 'there are ways in which women were treated as a form of property' (of their husbands); and that 'in the seventeenth century a number of women (and a very few men) protested that women were treated as little better than slaves' (pp. 232–3).

So long as households (whether of poor peasants, more prosperous handcraft workers, or wealthy merchants and nobles) remained the basic economic units – for production as well as consumption – emancipation was hardly achievable, despite the great increase in texts, many privately or secretly published, advocating the rights of women and, later, of workers and slaves, during the eighteenth century. So it was the Industrial Revolution that broke up the economic system of household production, by drawing women (and children) into factories, by concentrating large numbers of workers in new urban centres, and thus created a *public* sphere of economic activity, in which they could take collective action through associations, trade unions and political parties. It also created new possibilities for individual rights, group formation and political mobilization. In the case of slavery, technological changes and the growth of trade altered the incentives and opportunities, and made the practice unprofitable except in the specific conditions of large plantations in certain environments, a state of affairs that divided American society, and led to the Civil War between the liberal, industrialized northern states, and those whose economies were still based on households and slavery in the South.

Thus the economic processes of commercialization, and later, industrialization, allowed new opportunities for individual and collective action for emancipation from 'the idiocy of domestic life'. But it also led to new social formations and political movements in which the three categories of dependants, formerly with common interests in changing the rules and forms of governance, now had potentially divergent interests. As wives and mothers, women remained within the domestic system for a large part of their lives, and this gave them common interests with their male partners within the wider economy. Women in better-off households, even though they might remain subordinates, and have personal incomes much closer to – or lower than – those of workers (and hence, latent interests in socialization or redistribution of resources), also had a stake in current allocations, through their partners' assets.

The position of the recently emancipated slaves in late nineteenth-century America also illustrates this potential divergence. Even when they left the South and moved to work in factories in the industrializing northern states (as millions did), they did not find themselves in the same situation as white workers. To give just one ironic example, by the end of that century about two-thirds of American-born white people over the age of 65 were receiving federal pensions, arising from service in the Civil War (de Swaan, 1988, p. 204). African Americans found themselves excluded, right from the start, from collective systems that gave more security and higher income to white workers; they found common interest instead with new immigrants from eastern and southern Europe, and took forms of collective action, in line with these interests, that shaped American municipal and national politics in the first half of the twentieth century (Ward, 1989, chs 5 and 6).

In Europe, too, the interests of white working classes and black immigrants diverged, which led to group formation and strategic collective action. These dimensions of social interaction, group formation and collective organization will be further analysed in chapters 2, 4 and 5. The aim is to explain how women and black people are especially vulnerable to poverty, through the workings of exclusive groups. Although discrimination and subordination have longstanding cultural origins, outlined in this section, the specific dynamics of inclusion and exclusion relating to gender and 'race' can be analysed in terms of the economic perspective that is the basis of this study.

GROUPS AND COMMUNITIES

A second possible objection to the perspective to be adopted in this book is that it emphasizes the instrumental, utilitarian, calculative elements in human interactions, and neglects their moral and social dimensions. This is particularly topical in the American and British political contexts, since opposition to free-market Utopianism now takes the form of appeals to 'community', at least to the same extent as calls for collective action through the power of the state. The notion of community implies that social relations cannot and should not be understood in purely economic terms. The aim of this section is to clarify the nature of such claims, and briefly to relate the sociology of group interaction to the economic theory that will underpin my analysis.

This book explains poverty-related social exclusion in terms of the economics of collective action in groups of all kinds. Put crudely, poor people are excluded because they cannot make the relevant contribution, and thus lose the benefits of membership. But 'community' constitutes a kind of unconditional inclusion that seems to transcend such economic factors. Hence it requires careful analysis as a possible focus for counter-exclusionary collective action.

According to the communitarian critique of liberal individualism and utilitarianism, whether or not economically vulnerable people are included in social formations is a moral, not an economic, issue. Poverty is related to exclusion through the workings (or failures) of systems of moral obligation; where these pre-scribe sharing, caring and contribution, those facing highest risks are sheltered by the collective action of the group. This applies to every social formation, from families to nations. In the latter it is citizenship, as a form of common membership, that supplies the necessary social obligations for inclusion.

As its basic units of account, economic theory takes rational, calculative individuals, who have preferences that they can order consistently in making their decisions, and who are motivated to get the best returns from their actions and choices, in terms of those preferences, in social interactions with others. It also assumes that they will treat others as similarly motivated, that they will deduce the preferences and strategies of others from their actions, and hence that they will plan and pattern their own choices on the basis of how others will respond to theirs. Such assumptions represent a stern abstraction from human reality (Hargreaves Heap et al., 1993); hence the conclusions from eco-nomic theory must constantly be tested and criticized in the light of evidence from sociological research.

Public-choice theory extends these assumptions beyond exchange in markets (where they are already controversial) to non-market situations. In perfect markets, because of the large number of individuals supplying and demanding goods, there is a *price* which allows all to transact exchanges without reference to interactions that are happening elsewhere. Each transaction will influence prices, but no single one of them will influence them enough for the parties involved to be motivated to behave stra-tegically in their exchange. Thus markets are said to 'harmonize' the diverse preferences of millions of individuals, because they tend towards an equilibrium in the demand and supply of goods, and do so without the conscious effort of any participants (they are moved by an Invisible Hand).

Public-choice theory analyses decisions by economically ratio-nal actors about goods that cannot (for reasons to be analysed in chapter 2) or should not be marketed in this way. Some criti-cisms of its methods rest on the accusation that its assumptions are highly artificial in non-market contexts (Etzioni, 1988). Others argue that it has a largely covert moral agenda of its own;

its theories are disguised prescriptions for actions and policies that are narrowly self-interested and orientated towards instrumentalist goals; its assumptions therefore become self-fulfilling prophecies (Wolfe, 1989).

According to such critics, all social interactions must be understood in a surrounding (or 'encapsulating') context of norms, cultural practices and social institutions that steer, stabilize and regulate them (Etzioni, 1988, ch. 12). Without an analysis of this context, any attempted explanation will at best be crude, and more probably downright misleading. The 'societal capsule' consists of institutions that are ways of constraining behaviour and shaping interaction, both formal and informal (North, 1990, p. 4). They also separate actions into spheres or subsystems, and thus insulate markets, as the main means of allocating material resources, from collective decision-making and many other interactions. Morality and community (systems of social obligation) existed before and are more fundamental features of social relations than markets, and 'socialize' them for the sake of the common interest. Mutual dependency and social obligation – unlike markets – have to be reasoned about and organized; the 'self regulatory' features of markets are only possible because of the moral order of communities (Wolfe, 1991).

Some authors argue that community arises spontaneously in civil society. According to this view, community contributes the common features that sustain human values in all social formations, without which the substance of a viable mode of life could not be sustained (Polanyi, 1944, chs 4–6). Whereas states require coercive force, and markets the partition of goods, ownership entitlements and the enforcement of contracts, communities emerge from the circumstances of interdependency.

The analysis of community can also be seen as part of a debate between liberal political theorists and their critics. In the variants of liberalism that emerged in the 1970s and early 1980s (J. Rawls, 1970; Nozick, 1974; Dworkin, 1981), the first principle is a strong version of the moral sovereignty of individuals, and the importance of adopting political institutions that uphold this. Communitarians argue that society and its socialization of its members are logically and factually prior to individuals, and hence that all social arrangements are best understood (and all policies best pursued) as attempts to give individuals recognizable common interests in co-operation for the sake of a good shared quality of life (MacIntyre, 1981; Sandel, 1982; Walzer, 1983, 1990; C. Taylor, 1983, 1991). This intellectual debate of the 1980s has entered the practical politics of the 1990s, as governments seek to discover ways to soften conflicts, promote consensus, produce harmony, trust and obedience to rules, and to encourage identification with fellow citizens.

The values and practices of community are of particular relevance to issues of poverty and social exclusion. In the 1980s, market-minded regimes deregulated labour markets, cut back social provision and promoted businesslike structures of financial accountability in the public sector, promising that this would reduce social conflicts as well as improving economic efficiency. More recently, the civil wars in former Soviet republics and the former Yugoslavia, terrorism in Japan and in the heartlands of the USA, and the escalation of social problems in the post-communist countries as well as in the prosperous West, all point towards a sharpening of social conflicts, and especially of intergroup rivalries. Although there is now little political support for the strategy of trying to restore harmony through increased state benefits and services, there is urgent concern to find a new cement for society. Communitarianism is appealing for both left and right; it seems to offer a rather low-price solution – homespun morality, neighbourliness, civic pride and kindly remonstrations (Etzioni, 1993, 1994) – that might remind citizens of their obligations to each other, and restore the sense of membership and common purpose. In no policy sphere is this more appealing than that of poverty, where the 1980s have left a huge legacy of alienated, despairing, dispossessed people, without a clear social role or contribution to make, whose integration into the mainstream through traditional public spending would be vastly expensive, but who threaten to be almost equally socially costly (in terms of crime and deviance, as well as dependence on state benefits and services) if they are left to deteriorate still further.

The new interest in *inclusive* community thus both picks up and challenges the central thrust of this book – that poverty can be understood in terms of interaction within and between exclusive groups. This will be a major theme of chapters 2, 5 and 6, when I analyse how the processes of social exclusion are in turn countered by actions, movements and policies for inclusion of the poor, and how conflicts arise. But for the purposes of this introduction, it seems appropriate to clarify some basic issues about the nature of community, and to explain how the public-choice perspective is relevant for their analysis, despite the strong objections of some communitarians (Etzioni, 1988, ch. 12).

Communitarian social and political theory is often justifiably criticized for inadequate specification of the nature and functioning of the communities on which its analysis and prescriptions rely. In this section I shall therefore try to identify the main elements in a theory of community. In the next I shall analyse the relationship between markets and communities, and in particular the argument emerging from the public-choice tradition that community is in fact a kind of market, and that the only communities worth the name (voluntary exchanges between sovereign individuals) come about exclusively through markets (Foldvary, 1994).

What constitutes the necessary and sufficient conditions for community? There follows an outline of the elements that go to make up apparently spontaneous systems of mutual obligation, sustained by social institutions that enable voluntary interactions of an interdependent and supportive kind, and a consideration of how these relate to inclusion and exclusion.

Morality

Informal constraints on the actions of individuals, into which they are socialized in childhood, and which they then impose on themselves and each other as adults (though not necessarily consistently), seem to be universal features of all human societies. Recent micro-sociological analysis suggests that these stem from the nature of human interaction itself. Meaningful communication is a co-operative accomplishment, the joint construction of mutually comprehensible utterances between active participants in an exchange. Human speech is unique as a code, because it can refer to abstract or distant phenomena (such as God or the late Elvis Presley), but it only succeeds through processes of *reciprocity* in communication. Goffman (1969) showed how communication is embedded in ritual exchanges of social value – 'face' – between members, which are as necessary as the rules of grammar for the successful construction of meaning. Rituals of interaction include taking turns in conversation (Sacks, 1972), conveying understanding, often non-verbally, of what is said, replying when spoken to, and building on the previous utterance. Both the sense of binding moral obligation in social relations and, indeed, the sense of external reality itself depend on the co-operative social construction achieved through such exchanges (Hilbert, 1992). This 'bottom up' analysis of reciprocities in communication contrasts with earlier structuralist accounts of socialization through the rules, roles and norms of formal social relations (Parsons, 1956).

Children (on this alternative account of the origins of social obligation) learn these basic reciprocities unconsciously, as they learn to understand others and make themselves understood. They are also socialized into other unwritten rules of conduct, that are never overtly enforced in the adult world, but seem to occur spontaneously in most societies – avoiding rough bodily contact with strangers, queuing (standing in line for admission to public facilities), offering to share food and drink with visitors, buying one's round of drinks. All these are forms of reciprocity that can be subsumed under a general rule, but few who practise them could frame the rule as a guiding principle.

The forms of morality discussed in more theoretical books on communitarianism, such as virtue, heroism, duty and justice (MacIntyre, 1981), are far more variable between societies and between individuals, both as to standards and to compliance. They are the mere superstructure on that more basic morality, that seems almost spontaneous and unregulated. Basic reciprocity is also *inclusive*; it forms a kind of global culture of humanity that applies in every interaction, imposing certain obligations and constraints on all exchanges. Global tourism and global trade are possible because of this code, and despite cultural differences and language barriers.

Morality, in this sense, is a necessary but not a sufficient condition for community. Without it, no more complex and sophisticated set of social obligations can be put in place because all these have to be collectively decided, interpreted through debate and negotiation, and reinforced by interaction (Larmore, 1987). But on its own morality merely provides the preconditions for any such system, not the substance of a specific community.

Shared activities

There are some activities, in every kind of social formation, where value arises from the fact that others are involved; sharing is a benefit, not a cost. In modern societies these include team games, dances and concerts, religious ceremonies and parties of all kinds. In every known society there are fairs, feasts and festivals – exceptional rather than everyday events, where large numbers of people celebrate collectively (and often drunkenly) – though most also have more sober religious rites of collective worship.

Some shared activities are *capacious* if not fully inclusive in the sense that applies to morality. Mass events like rock concerts, raves and mega-meetings (world sports championships) are examples. Without much regulation, these events seem to generate a kind of spontaneous order – 'peace and love' – despite very large numbers and great cultural diversity. But beyond a certain point, crowding and congestion would risk disorder; hence a *price* is charged, and only a limited number of tickets are sold. Also, the characteristic of such events is their short duration.

However, most shared activities that occur often or continuously involve *common pool resources* – buildings or equipment that are jointly managed, such as sports centres and clubs, allotment gardens, village halls, church buildings, community centres and so on. Even when they are used by a large number of people, and no charge is made, they are managed by a small (sometimes representative, elected) group, with a stake in their use, who conserve and maintain them and impose some constraints on others.

Political theorists have recently become interested in the systems by which such resources are managed, because their success over time seems to contradict a strong theorem of public-choice theory – the 'tragedy of the commons'. Hardin (1968) argued that resources such as common grazing lands that were not in private ownership tended to be over-used, and thus to fall into decay and deterioration, because each user had an interest in trying to get more from their use than was compatible with conservation. But analysis and surveys of empirical studies by Ostrom (1990) and others have shown that this does not occur where there are limited numbers of users with a large stake in the resource, and effective ways of managing and monitoring its use. Singleton and Taylor (1992) point out that the conditions for successful management of common pool resources correspond to Michael Taylor's definition of community (1982, 1987).

It is difficult to conceive of a community (even an electronic network) that does not have some common pool resource for shared activity. The successful management of such a resource involves the creation of a set of mutual obligations regarding its use, and hence a system of governance of a kind. Dryzek (1990) calls such regimes in the management of environmental issues 'discursive democracies', and contrasts them with state regimes that use compulsory power in the name of instrumental rationality and social engineering. But success in such communities involves *exclusion* – the restriction of use to a limited number of members, whose activities can be monitored. Thus if such systems of governance are to provide both necessary and sufficient conditions for communities, they involve the formation and regulation of exclusive groups. This is important for my analysis of poverty and social exclusion.

Redistribution

Another universal feature of all social formations is the redistribution of goods for final consumption. This assertion sounds odd to those raised in the liberal individualist tradition, but it is a truism of human biology and the science of physics. All social formations involve collective activity in *production* and *reproduction* – they would not be social formations if individuals acted alone, and a single individual cannot reproduce another generation. But final consumption is always individual in a certain sense, because eating requires the division of food into pieces that fit into a mouth, rest and shelter depend on the allocation of space in which to stand, sit or lie, and clothing has to be rendered into garments that fit a human body. So even if people work and live together in a group, sharing all activities and resources (as in a commune), each must have *property rights* (claims on the group) for deciding who gets what in terms of final consumption.

Thus all social formations have rules about rights as well as obligations, which determine when, where and how the goods for final consumption will be distributed. These rules are laid down collectively, but result in individual entitlements. This means that they must have a definition of membership, as well as setting out what a member can claim by virtue of contribution, merit, status, need, or any other reason. Contrary to neo-conservative (and increasingly now also neo-labourist) thought, these rights are usually quite independent of the obligations discussed in the previous two sections; there is no close correspondence, for instance, between the obligation to use a village hall with care and respect, and the right to use it for shelter in a thunderstorm or after a domestic fire disaster.

Communal property and daily public redistribution were prominent features of early communities (tribes), because their collectivity was the survival unit. The threat to life itself from the natural environment and from other tribes was such that all individuals were highly vulnerable, interdependent and interactive. Because productive activity and leisure were collective, and what was produced could not be stored, systems for redistribution to individuals were elaborate and overt – rituals of gift-giving, for instance. Such communities had to devise collective means of managing everyday hazards such as sickness, injury and disability. Many modern communities (associations of people living some distance apart, and in some cases never meeting face-to-face) do not have any such rules and rituals of redistribution, though living units (such as families and kinship groups) always do – for example, Christmas and birthday parties.

This implies that redistribution is a sufficient condition for community (all redistributive systems entail a kind of community) but not a necessary condition. Modern property rights in commercial societies take the form of private ownership of material resources, and certain claims against the public authority for benefits and services; communities in the form of voluntary associations redistribute few resources, in comparison with these other rights. Hence poor people cannot usually rely on their rights in the collective resources of communities and voluntary associations (other than families and kinship groups) to redistribute goods for final consumption to them, in the way members of tribes could (Polanyi, 1944, ch. 4). With those exceptions the resources of such social formations mainly take the form of common pool property for shared activity, not money to share among members. The suggestion that non-territorial communities (voluntary associations) should be given a larger redistributive role (Hirst, 1994) will be further discussed in chapters 5 and 6.

GLOBAL MARKETS, EXCLUSIVE COMMUNITIES?

The analysis of community in the previous section suggests a long-term dynamic between such social formations, markets and states. Communities (nomadic or settled groups with more communal than private resources) were systems for production and reproduction, as well as networks of moral obligation and shared activity, in those earliest economies. They included their vulnerable members in systems of redistribution (claims upon the group) because of strong interdependence within an exclusive survival unit. As commercialization has advanced, so the proportion of private property has grown, and living units (first households and then families) have become smaller and separated from working (producing) units. Those without enough private property to survive adverse contingencies still relied on claims from communal resources, but new collective-action problems developed around contributions from private property to such redistributive funds. States solved these problems by requiring contributions through compulsion, and by organizing funds in larger and larger collectivities – the collectivization process (de Swaan, 1988). This leaves communities with a moral and integrational, but little economic, role and implies that this shift was inevitable, given the expansion of markets, and the parallel development of the power of the state.

It also explains the continuing dynamic of economic development in a global system, where the commercialization of social relations gradually subverts the remaining communal systems of the developing world, drawing their members into the sprawling shanty towns surrounding mega-cities, or towards the allurements of the developed countries. On this analysis, the poverty of the Third World is part of the story of the impoverishment and destruction of communities by markets, which can only be countered by compulsory collective action through states, providing systems of redistribution and social protection.

In this section I shall argue that this simple model is misleading. Communities, as social formations with those particular economic functions, were indeed destroyed by the expansion of markets. Attempts to protect them by institutional innovations such as the Speenhamland system (1795) in England failed (Polanyi, 1944, chs 6–9). But the creation of labour markets, new forms of social organization and systems of public provision transformed communities, and enabled new forms, based on mobility, communications technology and new modes of exclusion, to develop. As the capacities of nation states have weakened in recent years, and globalization erodes collective social welfare arrangements, the significance of a new dynamic of social inclusion and exclusion, through residential segregation, increases. To understand this, we need an analysis of the economics of exclusive territorial communities.

So far, the development of states has been discussed in terms of the growth in their capacities for solving collective-action dilemmas over poverty, and the threat to order and security that it posed. But states had a logic of their own, relating to the extraction of revenue from their inhabitants, and the mobilization of those inhabitants, for competition with other states. They developed systems of institutions to conserve and develop national resources to wage war, as in the mercantilism of France under Louis XIV (Zürn, 1995). Through military conquest and mutual empowerment, nation states eventually divided up the globe between themselves, replacing older systems of cities, city leagues and empires (Spruyt, 1994).

What was new and distinctive about nation states was the concept of territorial sovereignty. Previously, feudal lords imposed obligations on their vassals by means of personal bonds and oaths of allegiance, and because these multiple non-hierarchical, non-territorial systems of authority overlapped, organized power had no territorial boundaries. The Holy Roman Emperor and the Pope both claimed universal sovereignty, and fought each other over such claims. Nation states – first France, between the eleventh and thirteenth centuries, then Spain, Portugal, England, Denmark, Sweden and the Netherlands by the seventeenth – established territorial sovereignty; and, in the Treaty of Westphalia (1647), refused recognition to the Hanseatic league, a non-territorial collective-action group of northern European cities, which had previously been strong enough to defeat nation states in war (Spruyt, 1994, chs 3–5).

The nation state (unlike feudal lords or ancient emperors) claimed sovereign authority over all persons and property in its territory, and hence over all the activities that took place within it, and the wealth created there. States claimed the power to determine all property rights, individual and collective, and further, that any rights enjoyed by subjects (citizens) were theirs only by the sovereign power's prerogative (Hobbes, 1651). Against this, liberal theory has always argued for the sovereignty of individuals (Locke, 1698), and liberal political institutions allow a balance between the monopoly of violence and coercion that is held by the agencies of government, the self-governing powers granted to various associations in their domains and the civil and political rights of individual citizens.

As the organizational capacities of governments to levy taxes and provide collective regulation and services expanded, so did the proportion of national income spent through public agencies. Even as the expansion of markets in the first half of the nineteenth century was destroying the old systems of regulation, based on guilds, corporations and local associations, so new central and local government systems were being created to take their place, and this process accelerated in the final quarter of that century, to the disgust of market-minded liberals (Spencer, 1884). More recently, this has been most dramatically illustrated in the Scandinavian countries. By 1990, the Swedish public sector spent almost 70 per cent of GNP; already in 1980, it supported 4.1 million people out of taxes (by employing them or paying them benefits), compared with 2.1 million whose living costs were financed by market activities (Lindbeck, 1995).

But by the 1980s these systems were under pressure. Warlike territorial competition between nationalistic states in the first half of the twentieth century had been followed by 50 years of peace, the rapid expansion of international trade, the growth of new transnational enterprises with enormous wealth, and economic competition between the older industrialized countries and the newly industrializing ones. In this competition, states with very extensive public sectors were seen to do comparatively badly; Sweden slipped from third to thirteenth in the league table of income per head of population between 1973 and 1993, and is now below the average for the OECD countries on this measure (Lindbeck, 1995). As globalization develops, the capacities of states to plan investment and production, to guarantee high levels of employment and social protection – in short, to regulate their domestic economies in the ways that were developed after the Second World War – have been weakened (Held and McGrew, 1994; Zürn, 1995). Whereas in the period between the sixteenth century and the last quarter of the twentieth, success in competition with other economic and political units was strongly correlated with territorial sovereignty and the capacity to raise and spend large revenues, there now arises the previously unthinkable possibility that sovereign states are not the most effective political units for husbanding wealth and protecting societies.

This in turn leads to new interest in transnational institutions and regulatory regimes, and in alternative, smaller social formations, including communities. In particular, it raises the question of how *sovereign individuals* (Locke's primary unit of a contractual political society) would choose to organize themselves under present economic and social conditions, if the territorial sovereignty of states, and their compulsory powers, were absent. Above all, it leads to a questioning of whether the collective-action problems over law and order as a public good (posed by Hobbes, and resolved in favour of a sovereign to enforce the social contract, and to overcome the prisoner's dilemma about trust and cooperation) may yet have other possible solutions.

In economic theory, the undersupply of collective goods is treated as a case of 'market failure', since it arises from the problem of incentives for individuals to supply goods that can be consumed by 'free riders' who do not pay the price needed to cover the cost and yield a profit. But public-choice theory has developed a critique of welfare states that focuses on their tendency to *oversupply* collective goods, because of perverse incentives for politicians, bureaucrats and professionals to expand their patronage and resources, and respond to lobby groups (Peacock, 1979; Buchanan, 1978). Meanwhile, for over a century, a number of unorthodox economists (George, 1879; Heath, 1957; MacCallum, 1970) have pointed out that it *can* pay a landowner to develop a site, providing roads, water supply, waste disposal, communication systems and a range of other public amenities, so long as he or she can charge a rent that corresponds to the value of these improvements. This of course implies that individuals who do not pay this rent can be excluded from the community, arising out of market exchanges, that is thus created. Indeed, many towns in the late Middle Ages (especially in east Prussia and Poland) were built in just this way by feudal landowners, before the creation of nation states in that region (Barraclough, 1984, pp. 254–62).

A community of sovereign individuals, thus established, would have strong incentives to make a new collective contract with the landowner, to ensure that rents were not opportunistically raised, and with each other, to supply such extra services for the community as they, as a self-governing body, deemed desirable. Foldvary (1994) points out that such a 'private community' would be fully consensual: members would only be able to set a contribution rate (tax level) to which all agreed (Wicksell, 1896) – though it would be important within such a system of governance that individuals could be excluded if they did not pay rent or agreed contributions, and that they could move to other communities whenever they chose to do so.

The significance of this apparently counterfactual thought experiment is less as a blueprint for future societies than as a model of what is happening in present-day ones. Foldvary goes on to analyse a number of 'proprietory communities' in the United States, including Disney World in Florida, and several residential districts and towns. Even without the individual sovereignty and free disposal of property that his radical model postulates, the economics of site improvement does encourage developers to establish exclusive communities in which bundles of collective goods are supplied, for shorter or longer periods, in exchange for rent. This gives individuals an incentive structure for sorting themselves into groups, according to their preferences for such bundles of collective goods, and their abilities to pay for them. It corresponds closely to the model proposed by Tiebout (1956) of 'voting with the feet', in which residential areas become, in effect, exclusive territorial clubs, in competition for members.

There is some empirical evidence that the dynamic of 'voting with the feet' is an important part of social polarization in the advanced industrialized countries. Miller (1981) found that districts in California had become more homogeneous in the income levels of their residents over the previous 30 years. W. J. Wilson (1987) presents massive evidence that the exit of educated and successful African American families from the inner-city ghettos has contributed to the concentration of social problems in these districts. In Britain, the acceleration in the sale of council houses in the 1980s has led to a polarization between more desirable estates, and 'sink' estates with high numbers of unemployed people and single parents (Forrest and Murie, 1988a and b). A recent report from Newcastle revealed that a local criminal gang had been hired by the construction firm renovating one such estate for 'private protection' (BBC Radio 4, *Today* programme, 7 June 1995).

This important dimension in the action of exclusive groups in welfare states will be further analysed in chapter 5. It raises fundamental issues about the dynamics of poverty and social exclusion within such societies, and between the developed and less developed worlds. The logic of economic globalization points towards the greater mobility of human beings as well as capital, but land remains rooted to its spot, and its value reflects the history of investments in improvements, and is related to similar investments in the surrounding district. Issues of migration and polarization can only be adequately explained in terms of an analysis of the economics of these processes.

In the late Middle Ages, towns developed an independent status rather like the one envisaged by Foldvary; they governed themselves communally, provided themselves with quite sophisticated collective goods, and organized themselves in leagues for defensive and expansionary action. But they faced perpetual dilemmas about the poor, because they tended to attract migration from the surrounding countryside. New institutions eventually developed to exclude and contain the poor, and regional co-ordination was established, but these problems of migration and polarization have intensified, and have preoccupied public authorities ever since the process of commercialization began. It is estimated that in Germany, as late as the mid-eighteenth century, some 20 per cent of the population still lived in the forests as bands of robbers or beggars, making occasional predatory excursions to the towns (de Swaan, 1988, p. 19). Social exclusion has costs. A major theme of this book will be the processes of exclusion involved in spatial segregation and social polarization, and the costs associated with these interactions (see especially chapters 5 and 6).

EXCLUSION AND THE 'POLITICS OF ENFORCEMENT'

To analyse the social costs of poverty and exclusion, we need a way to address the external consequences of interactions in exclusive groups. In recent years social scientists have developed a particular interest in the positive and negative 'spillovers' from group interaction, but once again such analyses have not hitherto found their way into the study of poverty. In this section I shall introduce this important theme of the book, which will be more fully explored in chapter 6.

A strong argument for including vulnerable people in collective systems of social obligation has always been the costs of crime, disease, disorder and dislocation that would flow from otherwise advantageous exclusion. Hence property rights in conditional and regulatory systems of redistribution grew side by side with the development of exclusive property (de Swaan, 1988, ch. 1). But there is no automatic mechanism through which these costs of exclusion are shared. Like environmental pollution, the external effects of collective action through exclusive groups fall on all, and present a dilemma for the wider community.

In political theory, the study of groups and voluntary associations has focused on how these contribute to efficient governance. The theory of democracy owes much to de Tocqueville's (1835–40) work on American society in the early nineteenth century. He argued that active citizenship and a plurality of voluntary associations give rise to forms of economic and social governance that rely less on coercive enforcement, and generate more co-operation and integration in civil society, than in the Hobbesian model of public authority. The norms, skills and cultures of trust and mutuality *spill over* from such interactions as a form of 'social capital' (Coleman, 1990) that makes democratic self-government possible, and lowers transaction costs in the economy. A recent research study shows a long-term correlation between civic engagement, prosperity and effective democratic government on the one hand, and economic stagnation, social fragmentation and authoritarian enforcement on the other, in the Italian regions (Putnam, 1993).

This contrast between a virtuous circle of civic trust, economic co-operation and social harmony leading to democratic prosperity, and a vicious circle of suspicion, isolation, exploitation and authoritarian backwardness, can no longer be assumed to distinguish First World, advanced industrialized countries from centrally planned or underdeveloped ones. Particularly in the USA, but recently in Britain also, the perception of a deviant and dependent 'underclass', living on crime, practising various kinds of social deviancy and claiming from the labour and property of the rest of the community, has generated a 'politics of enforcement'. This has caused a major shift in policy orientation from 'social justice' through the provision of benefits and services, to the enforcement of work obligations (workfare) and criminal justice sanctions (Hudson, 1993). Spending on enforcement has risen sharply in both countries, and seems set to rise still further in the near future.

What is particularly disturbing about these developments is that they have occurred, at least in part, in response to pressure from organized groups of mainstream citizens (Jordan and Arnold, 1996b). In a society polarized through processes discussed in the previous section ('voting with the feet' leading to exclusive territorial communities), there is much scope for intergroup conflict that escalates and cannot be reconciled by democratic processes; indeed, it may instead provide political 'rents' for populist politicians who gain electoral support by denouncing minorities and welfare beneficiaries. In other words, there may be circumstances in which, as even the strongest advocates of voluntary associations recognize (Hirst, 1994, 53–4; 65–6), group processes spill over as antagonisms and conflicts, which in turn give rise to serious collective-action problems, and high social costs.

Both in the United States and in Britain, the deregulation of labour markets and the implementation of more restrictive regimes in social assistance benefits have been aimed at encouraging or forcing poor people to take available employment at lower wage rates, and at creating a more 'flexible' labour market. In arguing that strong trade unions and legislation on minimum wages and conditions blocked potentially gainful exchanges between employers and unskilled workers, the governments of the 1980s tried to substitute an 'enterprise culture' of small business dynamism for the 'culture of dependency' that they saw as characteristic of welfare states.

But these policies reckoned without the collective resistance of the poor, and the possibilities of collective action by groups who are excluded from the mainstream. Government measures changed the relative incentives of formal and informal activities. They weakened incentives to take unskilled employment, because of the fall in wages and the deterioration of working conditions in such jobs. On the other hand, both opportunities and incentives for various forms of 'informal' activities, including undeclared work for cash while claiming, crime, drug dealing and prostitution, have all grown. For people trapped in deprived 'communities of fate' (Marske, 1991), illegality is often a more secure and rewarding source of income for survival than the new flexible labour market, where extremely irregular employment for below-subsistence wages does not provide the basis for a sustainable way of life (see ch. 4, pp. 148–58).

In chapter 6, I shall argue that the social organization of deprived communities reflects the efforts of their members to compensate themselves for the costs of being excluded from more desirable areas, and from the social interactions that constitute mainstream activity in prosperous societies. Some of these are illegal, and impose direct costs upon the wider community, which in turn leads to the mobilization of mainstream groups against the poor, and to mutually hostile groups, and pressure for policies of enforcement. This is most obvious in the USA, where fears about the 'underclass' have thinly disguised racist undertones. But it has been increasingly evident in Britain, since the moral panics about single parenthood, truancy, crime and drug abuse in the summer and autumn of 1993 drove the government 'back to basics' (Jordan, 1995). The social costs of poverty are reflected in increased spending on enforcement (cancelling out savings in social benefits and services); in increased social conflict, and a decline in the capacities of democratic governance to harmonize interactions and resolve collective-action problems; and in an increase in transaction costs in the economy, because of the erosion of trust and co-operation.

These phenomena raise all the issues that have since preoccupied social scientists who study institutions. Of central concern in these debates has been the question of how both formal and informal constraints are able to steer interactions and save costs by orientating actors towards certain goals in reliable ways

(March and Olsen, 1989). According to North (1990, p. 4), institutions provide the *rules* of interaction (as in the rules of sports and games), while organizations devise and implement the strategies for competition (as in teams who participate). But formal institutional designs intended to produce efficient competition can instead undermine informal norms of tolerance and reciprocity on which all kinds of civic engagement depend. Exclusive groups can come instead to wage antagonistic struggles, using strategies designed to externalize the costs of their members, and impose them upon other groups. This can give rise to a cycle of retaliation that destroys the foundations of a free society. Tocquevillian associations, with their positive spillovers of social capital for democratic governance and economic efficiency, come to be replaced by Hobbesian ones, with negative externalities in conflict and enforcement costs.

Although there are worrying examples of such conflicts in Africa, in the former Yugoslavia, and in the former Soviet Union and Eastern Europe, it is in the United States that the 'politics of enforcement' now finds its most dramatic expression in escalating punishment and coercion, with more than a million citizens in prison, rising numbers of executions, the restoration of chain gangs, and pressure for cruder punishments. In Britain too, a similar development is recognizable, as prison populations increased by 25 per cent in the two years after 1993. A Scottish judge has urged more public participation in sentencing, even if it leads to floggings and brandings (McCluskey, 1994). The liberal traditions that protected the Anglo-Saxon countries from the totalitarianism of the first half of this century may be leading them into new forms of authoritarianism, directed against their own disadvantaged minorities, as we enter the next.

In the USA, these developments are most clearly related to the dynamics of exclusive groups in welfare states, and the fragmentation not merely of the solidarities on which redistributive state services depend, but even of the basic common citizenship that sustains democracies. Suddenly in the mid-1990s, economic insecurity threatens the educated and skilled as well as those with little earning power. The real salaries and wages of college graduates are now falling as rapidly as those of unskilled workers, as large corporations adopt new recruitment strategies based on subcontracting, and dismantle their structures of occupational welfare – pensions, health care, paid vacations – that have been an institutional feature of the American economy since the 1920s. The Republican right has succeeded in channelling this anxiety into blaming disadvantaged minorities: of immigrants, especially Asians and Hispanics, who come illegally and take jobs and services; and of African American welfare mothers, who 'free ride on the welfare cart' and must now be forced to get out and push it (Morone, 1995). Other states seem set to follow the example of California, where an overwhelming majority voted to exclude the children of illegal immigrants from schools, and require such applicants for education and health care to be reported to the authorities for deportation. Opinion polls reveal that most Americans think that social security forms the largest element in federal expenditure, when in fact it stands at 19 per cent, while welfare (public assistance) represents only one per cent of national product.

The fragmentation of the support for social provision into narrowly self-interested groups was well illustrated in the failure of the Clinton presidency's national health insurance plan. The Republican right was able to represent it as a form of government intrusion, forcing good risks to bear the costs of bad. Its opposition to the new programme was based on rejection of all forms of cross-subsidization: why should those with good health prospects pay more to reduce the insurance costs of those at greater risk? Why should suburban whites, with their self-consciously health-orientated lifestyles, join the same insurance group as junkies, gays or the black, inner-city 'underclass'? Its campaign mobilized the economic logic of exclusive groups, the clustering together of like incomes and like risks, and all the most hostile prejudiced assumptions that middle America held about minorities and the poor (D. Stone, 1994).

It also mobilized Americans' increasing mistrust of their government and each other. 'Big government' was portrayed as threatening their rights and their security, on behalf of immoral and unpatriotic values. The bombing of the federal offices in Oklahoma City, at the time of writing believed to be the action of an extreme white supremacist and anti-government paramilitary group, symbolizes the slide into a politics of confrontation between exclusive social formations, enforcement through coercion, and deep mutual mistrust. These negative spillovers from group interactions constitute the reverse side of Tocquevillian social capital as the basis of democracy, which includes the interests of the community in the interests of the group.

CONCLUSIONS

In 1995, the World Health Organization estimated that more than one-fifth of the world's population live in extreme poverty, which is much the largest cause of death in this global perspective. Each year 12.2 million children die for the lack of treatment that could cost less than one US dollar to provide. Life expectancy in the poorest countries is less than half that in the richest (WHO, 1995).

This book seeks to explain poverty in terms of the action of exclusive groups, thus systematically relating these global phenomena to the forms of social exclusion identified in this introductory chapter. Exclusion and inclusion are universal features of social interaction, and institutions serve to structure these processes, through states, markets, communities and voluntary associations. Fragmentation of advanced welfare states and new forms of collectivization through transnational systems, the politics of 'race' and immigration, and the emergence of new intergroup conflicts will all be analysed in terms of the economics of collective action.

2

Interdependency and Collective Action

In the first chapter, I argued that a theory that relates poverty to social exclusion must explain how people interact in relation to their economic capacities, resources and risks, and particularly how they organize themselves in groups to include members and exclude non-members. This chapter lays the theoretical foundations of the analysis that is to follow in the rest of the book.

Seen from the perspective of an advanced industrialized society, most of the inhabitants of the developing world are very poor. They have underdeveloped capacities (in terms of education and training), few resources (in terms of private property rights), and they face high risks (from natural contingencies such as drought, flood and epidemic disease). Yet from the perspective of their own societies, relatively few of them are socially excluded. This is because most of them share in the systems of communal production and consumption (village communities, peasant households) which characterize the social and economic relations of these societies.

It is tempting therefore to see the history of economic development as one of expanding private property rights (driven by the requirements of market exchange), countered in turn by state action to provide public goods (in part at least prompted by the attempt to protect those with fewest private resources, or at greatest risk). But I have already introduced several complications into this straightforward story of exclusive private property and inclusive collective provision, and the analysis of these will be developed in this chapter.

In my alternative story, the basic collectivities of hunter-gatherer societies have gradually been replaced by overlapping, multi-layered social formations, differentiated in increasingly complex ways. The processes by which such collectivities have formed include coercion and subordination (for instance, of women and slaves in households, or of subjects of polities), technological forms of inclusion and exclusion (as in all kinds of 'clubs', including nation states) and self-selection ('voting with the feet', as in residential segregation). Most group interactions involve elements of all three of these processes. The common feature of all kinds of collectivities is that members benefit from restrained competition among themselves, and mobilize for more effective competition with other social formations, whether these be rival nations, firms or football teams.

The task of this chapter is therefore to discover a method for analysing such interactions in terms of individuals' capacities, resources and risks – how collective action through exclusive groups deals with human vulnerabilities, and what its outcomes are for vulnerable people. There is some mileage in the version of development that sees early communal systems as collective survival units that protected their most vulnerable members, and states (ultimately welfare states) as political measures to counter the reduced protection that accompanied processes of commercialization. However, the aim of this chapter is to develop a more complex analysis that explains fragmentation as well as collectivization and, above all, explains new global phenomena of poverty and social exclusion.

To analyse inclusion and exclusion through group interactions it is necessary to use a method that can explain all the dimensions of social interaction (the moral as well as the material economy) within the same framework. Public-choice theory claims to provide such a perspective, because it analyses human interdependencies of all kinds as phenomena associated with the indivisibility of resources, the costs of allocating goods for exclusive use (and benefits of sharing them), or the absence of competition for their supply. It sets itself the basic task of explaining the dynamic between private and public goods in terms of interactions between individuals which are aimed at value maximization and cost minimization (Buchanan, 1968; 1986b).

However, as I shall show in this chapter, the development of public-choice theory has in many ways subverted its own basic assumptions, and its application to the topic of poverty and social exclusion can thoroughly undermine the policy programme to which its leading exponents have committed themselves. This is because more and more ambiguity has developed around the central distinction of the theory, between private and public goods. This ambiguity casts radical doubts upon the framework of institutional reform, aimed at introducing more competition and accountability into formerly public-sector systems, which is the hallmark of this perspective's policy prescriptions.

If – as I have argued – the welfare of vulnerable individuals (including those facing exceptional risks or contingencies) depends upon their rights as members of social collectivities, then the analysis of collective goods is indeed a crucial aspect of the theory of poverty and social exclusion. Public-choice theory seemed to bring an elegant (if somewhat abstract and antiseptic) clarity to this question, and it has been very influential in the social sciences since the 1960s, as a method of explaining political and social interactions of all kinds (Elster, 1986a; Coleman 1990; Hollis, 1994). In this way, an economic perspective has (somewhat imperialistically) conquered large parts of the territory of sociology and political science. (Some would say that – like the hinterlands of Italian city states during late medieval imperial invasions – these domains have surrendered suspiciously easily, or may perhaps have been betrayed by covert conspirators within.)

Although these conquests have elsewhere been fiercely resisted, and the regime of public choice strongly criticized from many sides, I shall argue in this chapter *both* that it still provides the most promising perspective for a coherent and convincing analysis of how poverty relates to social exclusion, *and* that recent developments within its own methods are the best ones for

defeating the simplistic policy programmes of its founding practitioners and their political disciples. The study of the economics
of collective action and collective goods, especially within the
new and more businesslike structures of British and American
welfare states, points towards a radical reinterpretation of many
of the central assumptions and methods of the theory. It also
provides a powerful tool for demonstrating the hidden social
costs of new forms of interaction in exclusive groups in wider
society, as well as in the public sector.

I shall therefore start this chapter by setting out the framework
within which public-choice theorists sought to analyse the optimum distribution between private and public goods in an economy, and hence to explain the economics of interdependence.
I shall go on to show how further work on collective action and
collective goods has undermined important elements of that
analysis. In particular, I shall show how the explanation of both
undersupply of public goods (market failure) and *oversupply* of
public goods (government failure), through which public-choice
theorists sought first to justify the provision of state collective services, and then to limit them to the essential institutions that sustain a competitive market economy, have been subverted by
recent theoretical and empirical research.

All this is necessary for the elaboration of the theory of poverty
and social exclusion that will be developed in subsequent chapters, because the theory of interdependency and collective action
in exclusive groups that I am using to account for poverty and
social exclusion has been developed through this process of trying to refine the analysis of efficient and equitable distributions
between markets in private goods and political exchanges over
public goods. But instead of sharpening the tools for demolish-
ing what it saw as the bastions of political corruption, bureaucratic empire-building, professional restrictive practices, trade
union collusions, and the culture of welfare state dependency,
public-choice theory seems instead to have provided some very
promising tools for undermining much of its own programme,
and for developing a destructive critique of the institutional
reforms that it supported.

Parts of the argument in this chapter are necessarily somewhat abstract and theoretical. For this reason they may have a deterrent effect on some students from politics, social administration and sociology. Conversely, because I will not use the formulae of microeconomic analysis, my analysis may fall short of the rigour demanded by students of economics. These are the perils of interdisciplinary theorizing; I have tried to steer a middle course between them.

PRIVATE AND PUBLIC GOODS

In the liberal, Anglo-Saxon tradition, poverty is defined in terms of individual deficits in material goods for final consumption. If society is conceived in terms of economic and political exchanges in a competitive environment, the key question is then how such deficits in the supply of private goods arise, and how they might be remedied in ways consistent with Pareto optimality (the situation where no further reallocation of resources can make any one individual better off without making another worse off).

In the mercantilist, Continental tradition, social exclusion is seen in terms of systems of mutual obligation between social status groupings, under the regulation of the state. Here the key question is how individuals come to fall (or be pushed) out of such systems of collective inclusion, and how the state can regulate social interactions in such a way as to minimize the social costs of any such exclusions, and maximize the possibility in re-inclusion into collective solidarities.

At first sight, these two traditions deal in incommensurate values – in marketable commodities on the one hand, and human interdependencies on the other. Indeed there has been a long line of social scientific theorists who distinguished between the material and the moral economies, and argued (implicitly or explicitly) that no single theoretical framework could encompass all such interactions (Weber, 1922; Polanyi, 1944; Scott, 1975; Etzioni, 1988). What is therefore distinctive about the public-choice approach (which derives from the liberal tradition, but deals in political and social interactions) is its claim to be able to allocated, and what the optimum supply of each should be. This kind of exercise is by no means straightforward, because of the dynamic nature of the processes of interaction between agents and goods. For instance, in a mixed economy, the garbage generated by private households might be regarded as a collective good (or bad), because of the high costs involved in stopping individuals from dumping it on each other's property, and the lack of competition to purchase or dispose of it. However, given that some agents possess the technological capacity to collect and remove garbage, and the resources to accommodate it, a market in waste disposal might well develop (Starrett, 1988, pp. 40–1). Indeed, one of my ancestors made a considerable fortune in late seventeenth-century Bristol out of just such contracts (Elton, 1994, ch. 2).

But suppose that there is no agent with the necessary technology to collect the garbage, and none with a piece of private land that it is economical to use as a tip, then various consequences follow. First, of course, refuse disposal services will be undersupplied, unless a political decision is made to provide them through a public agency or contract. Everyone will incur garbage accumulation costs (smells, health hazards, congestion) because it is not profitable for anyone to provide this service at an affordable price. This means, secondly, that each household cannot be insulated from the decisions of others. What my neighbours choose to do with their household waste will affect my welfare, and my decisions will affect theirs, even if we both keep the law, and do not dump on each other.

This is an example of interdependency: others' actions enter into my utility function, and mine into theirs, because refuse accumulations have negative externalities (diswelfares or costs that are borne by someone other than the producer of the waste), and successful waste disposal – for instance, an efficient compost heap, or a very convenient hole in the earth's surface – benefits others as well as the prudent or fortunate disposer. Public-choice theorists address these externalities, and analyse how efficient and equitable allocations, which eliminate or compensate for them, can be reached.

It is also an example of market failure, because of the absence provide a single perspective from which to evaluate all exchanges in both these spheres.

As a branch of economic theory, the public-choice approach starts from the assumption that whether or not goods are assigned to a private owner will depend on the costs of excluding others from access to them. Once a system of private property rights can be established, markets will develop in all those commodities where there is enough competition to generate a single exchange rate, or price. When this occurs, each agent can make independent decisions about production and consumption of these goods in terms of their prices, insulated from the decisions of others, so long as no single one of them buys or sells so much as to exert a strategic influence on markets.

Conversely, wherever it is too costly to exclude others by dividing up goods and enforcing private property rights, or whenever goods can be consumed without depleting supplies for other users, private ownership and markets will not develop. Thus the theory of collective goods must analyse other ways in which decisions are reached about the production and consumption of such goods – broadly, in terms of agreements between agents. Since the costs of exclusion vary with technological capacities, and since issues of rivalry and depletion can develop over time (for instance, when some massive technological change introduces new ecological factors, such as a hole in the ozone layer, into the situation), there are always reasons for reassessing the ways in which goods are allocated, and evaluating the efficiency and equity of any particular set of institutions or outcomes (in markets or political systems). Crime, the 'shadow' economy, or a 'black market' may signal that new forms of exclusion and trade have become feasible; alternatively, market failure may signal reasons for collective provision when rivalry no longer exists.

In Buchanan's classic analysis *The Demand and Supply of Public Goods* (1968) he developed his theory from a thought experiment involving two people shipwrecked on a desert island, and the interdependencies that occurred through their interactions. He then introduced complexities to this thought experiment, at each stage analysing the principles according to which goods became excludable and marketable, or collective and politically

that the optimum supply of each should be. This
is by no means straightforward, because of the
of the processes of interaction between agents
stance, in a mixed economy, the garbage gen-
...vate households might be regarded as a collective
good (or bad), because of the high costs involved in stopping
individuals from dumping it on each other's property, and the
lack of competition to purchase or dispose of it. However, given
that some agents possess the technological capacity to collect
and remove garbage, and the resources to accommodate it, a
market in waste disposal might well develop (Starrett, 1988,
pp. 40–1). Indeed, one of my ancestors made a considerable fortune in late seventeenth-century Bristol out of just such contracts
(Elton, 1994, ch. 2).

But suppose that there is no agent with the necessary technology to collect the garbage, and none with a piece of private land
that it is economical to use as a tip, then various consequences
follow. First, of course, refuse disposal services will be undersupplied, unless a political decision is made to provide them
through a public agency or contract. Everyone will incur garbage
accumulation costs (smells, health hazards, congestion) because
it is not profitable for anyone to provide this service at an affordable price. This means, secondly, that each household cannot be
insulated from the decisions of others. What my neighbours
choose to do with their household waste will affect my welfare,
and my decisions will affect theirs, even if we both keep the law,
and do not dump on each other.

This is an example of interdependency: others' actions enter
into my utility function, and mine into theirs, because refuse
accumulations have negative externalities (diswelfares or costs
that are borne by someone other than the producer of the
waste), and successful waste disposal – for instance, an efficient
compost heap, or a very convenient hole in the earth's surface –
benefits others as well as the prudent or fortunate disposer.
Public-choice theorists address these externalities, and analyse
how efficient and equitable allocations, which eliminate or compensate for them, can be reached.

It is also an example of market failure, because of the absence of adequate incentives to induce suppliers to provide garbage disposal services. The public-choice perspective derives a large part of its intellectual coherence and persuasiveness from the principle that there are goods that are distinguishable in terms of these features – indivisibility, non-excludability, non-rivalrousness in consumption, externality and market failure.

Thus human interdependency is studied in public-choice theory not as a matter of moral economy – the ethical allocation of human values – but as a branch of political economy. This approach seems regrettably reductionist – for instance, in treating moral principles as if they were utilitarian preferences – but it has the great advantage of making all kinds of choices (theoretically) commensurate, and thus enabling the dynamic between private and public goods to be analysed, and the overall efficiency and equity of outcomes to be evaluated.

So far the theory says nothing specifically about the processes through which collective goods are supplied. Indeed, the term 'public goods' seems at first sight to imply that they are either owned by no one (as in the case of non-depletable natural resources) or monopolistically provided by the state (as with public provision to remedy undersupply because of market failure). But in practice collective goods are extremely complex and various, and the study of collective action in the public-choice tradition has transformed the analysis of such goods, by shifting attention from their properties – and what differentiates them from private goods – to the processes by which groups act to supply their members with such benefits, and exclude non-members from them.

So long as public goods are regarded as being either freely available natural resources (as in 'the commons', or the unenclosed environments in which hunter-gatherers live) or goods and services allocated by political authorities, poverty is simply a technical issue of redistribution for government, whose task is one of dealing with the negative externalities arising from these circumstances. In the case of a developing economy, periodic crises would arise around droughts, floods and diseases, and their consequent famines, dislocations or epidemics. In an advanced industrialized economy, market processes would constantly give rise to certain inefficient and inequitable outcomes, requiring anticipatory preventive action (such as insurance schemes) or reactive compensation (such as retraining).

But once it is recognized that poverty is closely linked with collective action by exclusive groups, the situation is much more complex. In every society, individuals become vulnerable to poverty when they are excluded from access to certain goods that members of such groups supply to each other through collective action, and when processes of allocation are influenced by the actions of successful organized interests which they cannot join. The analysis of such processes will be the subject of the rest of this chapter.

COMPETITION AND COLLECTIVE ACTION

In the introduction to this chapter, I took it as axiomatic for the analysis of poverty and social exclusion that certain individuals (children, old people, those with sicknesses, handicaps or disabilities, and those with fewest productive capabilities in terms of the technologies available in their societies) are especially vulnerable in social interactions. Their welfare thus depends on co-operation and redistribution in various kinds of social formation, since in open competition with others they would lack the capacities and resources to survive. Inclusive group interactions of various kinds provide the restraints on such competition that allow such individuals to thrive in interdependent collectivities, as we saw in the analysis of community in chapter 1 (pp. 18–27). They also subordinate these individuals (and those who care for them, who are usually women) in systems of social control and moral obligation that provide the substance of that restraint of competition. Inclusion and the restraint of competition imply power; they are forms of collective action (a.k.a. politics). In states, restraints are provided through the action of governments; in households, of course, the personal is political.

The first fundamental contribution to the economic theory of groups to emerge from the public-choice tradition was Olson's *The Logic of Collective Action: Public Goods and the Theory of Groups*

(1965). Olson's starting-point was two paradoxes of collective action. The first was particularly characteristic of interactions in market relations. In such competitive situations, all producers (individuals or firms) have a common interest in the higher price that they could charge if they combined together in a cartel to restrict production; but each individual or firm has a private interest in selling more, up to the point where marginal costs exceed marginal revenues. So if each individual or firm maximizes profits, the profits of the industry as a whole will be lower than they would be if they colluded to restrain competition and thus supply each other with a 'rent'. Similarly, each individual worker shares a common interest in combining together in a trade union closed shop, excluding all competing workers, and thus gaining higher wages and better conditions. But it is in the individual interests of each worker to compete for available jobs at market-determined wages, thus destroying the very rent available through collective action. In both cases, restraint of competition is a collective good that it is in the common interests of the relevant group to supply each other by excluding others and co-operating together, yet the incentives for such action are somewhat inaccessible for the relevant actors. Hence these collective goods, in the form of rents, will tend to be competed away.

The second paradox, closely linked with the first, concerns the nature of externalities and interdependencies. In both these market situations, the common interests of these groups must apparently remain latent, and never be acted upon, because of the special properties of the potential collective good (restrained competition). Each firm and each worker stands to gain from collective action, but the larger the group the smaller the proportion of such gains that will fall to each individual. Furthermore, any sacrifice made by any individual in pursuit of that small gain will benefit the group as a whole. It is therefore rational for a self-interested individual to let others carry the costs of collective action (to be a free rider), since none can be excluded from the benefits. Hence rational individuals will not, unless incentives are shifted, act in the common interests of the group as a whole, and all will lose out. This dilemma of collective action implies that, in a competitive market environment, common interests must remain 'latent', because competition makes them inaccessible. (The exception to this rule concerns small groups, within which it may pay an individual to supply all of the collective good, or individuals may be able to reach binding agreements through negotiation.)

Olson distinguished between producer cartels, where the rents are higher the smaller the number of members (ideally therefore a membership of one, or monopoly), and trade unions, where collective action is aimed at protecting members' wages, conditions and security of employment, and hence depends on including all the workers in the trade. But his analysis points to the similarities between the collective goods that members of both such groups supply to each other when they act in concert to resist the consequences of market competition; and also between these collective goods and the public goods provided by the state. In all cases, the costs of defining exclusive property rights, and hence of limiting the availability of benefits to those who make the relevant sacrifices, preclude a market solution to the problems of co-operation (voluntary exchange), and lead to undersupply. But Olson's conclusions are doubly paradoxical for the theory of private (marketed) and public (politically allocated) goods.

His analysis of the solution to these dilemmas of collective action points to the need for 'selective incentives', including negative sanctions, in order to overcome these problems and achieve intra-group co-operation. As in the case of states supplying public goods, the members of groups that aim to restrain competition within a market environment must offer benefits to each other (from which non-members are excluded) and punishments for those who defect from rules on restraint. In other words, members bind themselves or are bound to agreements, sharing an interest in the compulsory, exclusive and restrictive nature of their association. For the rational individual in any such group, compulsion of other members and exclusion of non-members from the field of competition are necessary conditions for advantageous participation; even though still facing incentives not to contribute individually, he or she rationally wishes all to be forced to do so, since a single defector may compete away all (in the case of firms seeking monopolistic rents) or some (in the case of union closed shops) of the benefits of collective action.

Some terminological confusion may occur here over Olson's distinction between *exclusive* and *inclusive* groups. In market interactions, the size of the available rents (oligopolistic profit or beneficial return to a union closed shop) is fixed, and it pays the group to restrict entry and exit. In non-market interactions, the benefit (in this case, of course, a political, not an economic, rent) may expand as the group grows – though, as we shall see later in this chapter, this varies from group to group. Olson refers to all groups taking collective action for rents in markets as exclusive, and all groups in which it pays to include new members as inclusive.

But in fact all groups are exclusive in one sense. For instance, even though it may pay a political group, campaigning for a policy that is in the common interests of *all* citizens, to recruit every one of them into its membership, such groups are still distributional coalitions in Olson's terms. This is because states are also collective action organizations, restraining competition among their citizens for the sake of more successful competition with other states. Even in this extreme and counterfactual example, the collective gains at stake would only be achieved through exclusion, in the sense that they would not extend to non-citizens, and would actually disadvantage those outsiders, either relatively or absolutely. *A fortiori*, even though it may pay a lobby group to include more members, such a group is only successful in so far as it captures economic gains (through political competition) at the expense of other members of society. Thus Olson's term 'inclusive groups' refers only to incentives to recruit members up to a certain point, defined economically or politically. The logic of exclusion permeates all such interactions.

However, Olson makes it clear that the logic of collective action in his exclusive groups (cartels and closed shops), operating in a *market* environment, works strongly against the very freedoms that are supposed to characterize market exchanges. Not only can such groups overcome the competitive requirements of markets, and hence earn rents; they can and must do so by means of forms of compulsion (under threat of sanctions including, especially in the case of unions, intimidatory violence) that are the very antithesis of the liberal values that markets are supposed to sustain. Except in the rare case where every individual shares an interest in a public good (for example, the sustainability of the global ecological system), collective action is either illiberal or impossible.

The second paradox is even more subversive, and resides within the nature of the collective good described in Olson's chosen examples. In both the cases of producer cartels and labour unions (and also in the lobby groups exerting political pressure for tariffs and subsidies that form his third example), what is at stake is the subversion of the competitive processes that constitute markets. Collective action is rent-seeking behaviour, the collusion of interest groups to undermine the distributions that would occur spontaneously through the Invisible Hand, and thus lead to Pareto-optimal outcomes, in perfectly competitive markets (suitably compensated for externalities).

Interdependence – at least in Olson's examples – arises not from the properties of the goods at stake (for example, non-depletability, non-rivalrousness or non-congestibility) but from members' common interests in the search for advantageous rents, achievable only by successful collusions against those individuals who remain outside the charmed circles of their exclusive interactions. It is fairly obvious that such collective action must inevitably harm the poor, since it represents a kind of conspiracy by the organized against the disorganized. Indeed, Olson's analysis shows, more clearly than any other explanation reviewed so far, how *the vulnerability of the poor lies in their exclusion from membership of rent-seeking, organized groups within a market economy.*

This vulnerability is enhanced by another feature of the interactions analysed by Olson – that social heterogeneity weakens the effectiveness of selective (i.e. social) incentives. Collective action is easier when groups with like incomes and tastes are moved by many overlapping common interests; hence organized groups, seeking maximum agreement to secure concerted action and sustainable strategies, will tend to exclude the poor, a rag-tag category of misfits and losers:

> Everyday observation reveals that most socially interactive groups are fairly homogeneous and that many people resist extensive social interaction with those they deem to have lower status or greatly different tastes . . . In short, the political entrepreneurs who attempt to organize collective action will accordingly be more likely to succeed if they strive to organize relatively homogeneous groups. (Olson, 1982, pp. 24–5)

Furthermore, it is extremely difficult for the poor, themselves a heterogeneous and dispersed grouping, to organize by applying selective incentives; hence 'the vast number of those with relatively low incomes are not in organizations for the poor' (p. 34).

Olson's conclusions about collective 'collusions', developed in his later book *The Rise and Decline of Nations,* are suitably gloomy. Stable, peaceful societies tend to accumulate many such collusive organizations (or 'distributional coalitions') seeking rents; no society exhibits symmetrical organization of all groups, and hence optimizes outcomes through comprehensive bargaining; small groups with large resources tend to gain disproportionate advantages; all special-interest groups tend to reduce efficiency and aggregate income; they slow down decision-making, adaptability and response to change, further retarding the rate of economic growth; they are necessarily exclusive, and seek to limit the diversity of incomes and values of their memberships; the need to regulate them increases the role of government, and leads to administrative complexity, as well as contributing to making political life more divisive (Olson, 1982, p. 74).

Thus in his application of his theory of groups to national economic and social policy, Olson concluded that distributional coalitions were the most significant cause of inequality and discrimination within societies, and tended to slow the rate of economic growth and development. The main aim and function of such exclusive groups, acting within societies of all kinds, was to restrain competition among their members, in order to maximize the benefits from their co-operation, by distorting the (potentially Pareto-optimal) outcomes of gainful exchanges through markets (Olson, 1982, ch. 6). He traced a whole history of cultural restrictive practices – medieval guilds and crafts, Indian castes, endogamy among the British aristocracy, apartheid in South Africa, the dominance of military elites in the banana republics, and most of the framework of welfare states – to organized and institutionalized collusion of this kind. All forms of restraint on market competition, and discrimination in favour of organized groups against the unorganized, were costly for consumers and employers alike, and only by interactions between individuals in unrestrained search of gainful exchanges (free economic and political markets) could they be broken down (Olson, 1982, p. 165).

Whereas most economists concede that free markets generate efficiency except over the distribution of income and externalities, and hence that markets generate inequalities that should be compensated through collective action (state systems of taxation and redistribution), Olson took the radical stance that both efficiency *and* equity can usually be improved by introducing market competition. This was particularly the case, he argued, when restraint of competition was institutionalized through racially or culturally discriminatory practices, as in Indian castes or South African apartheid. Conversely, most government interventions in markets constituted unwarranted and arbitrary redistributions from worse-off to better-off individuals, affording no special protections to the poor; they were the products of lobbying by special-interest groups for their members' benefit, which harmed the least organized and most vulnerable (p. 174). The free movement of capital and free labour markets would, he argued, significantly raise the wages of the poorest, because investment would flow towards the areas with the lowest wage rates.

Olson's conclusions were thus a manifesto for the free-market policies pursued by US and British governments in the 1980s. Above all, he concluded that mass unemployment, the largest *new* cause of poverty to emerge (in the 1970s) from the stability of the post-war era, was mainly the result of the collusive restraints on competition that had been successfully achieved by business cartels, unions and the political pressure of special-interest lobbies. These collective actions by such interest groups blocked potentially gainful exchanges between unemployed workers and employers that would make both better off; hence deregulation was the best policy for the new poor, in the USA and in the more redistributive welfare states of Europe (Olson, 1982, ch. 7).

So Olson traced both poverty and social exclusion to the collective action of exclusive groups and political lobbies, and insisted that it could not be overcome by the redistributive policies of the state. He argued that the only policy programme that could help the poor in any sustainable way was increased competition, to counter the collective actions of such groups; 'the best macroeconomic policy is a good microeconomic policy' (p. 233).

SOCIAL INSTITUTIONS AND EXCLUSIVE GROUPS

The insights and perspectives generated by Olson's (1965) book were highly influential, though the direction in which they have been developed, particularly in the New Institutional Economics (North, 1986) has been somewhat different from Olson's own radical interpretations in his (1982) book. On the one hand, his conclusions on the benefits of free markets have been widely accepted, along with his critique of the consequences of both cartelization and the institutional framework of the social democratic era. But on the other hand, economic and social theorists have shrunk back from the theoretical implications of his analysis of group interactions as restraints on competition. The logical conclusion from this analysis was a Hobbesian one: the state should regard all groups as potential conspiracies against the general welfare guaranteed by the territorial sovereign. It should therefore force them to demonstrate their benefits for the common good, or ban them under threat of penalty (Hobbes, 1651, ch. 22). As is implicit in Olson's title (*The Rise and Decline of Nations*), nation states in his theory constitute the only legitimate source of group power, and the only available countervailing coercive force against the collective action of exclusive groups. The social exclusion of vulnerable people, and their consequent poverty, can therefore only be combated through aggressively market-friendly policies of all kinds, and extreme suspicion of the activities of all organized groups.

The New Institutionalists, whose methods are also derived from the public-choice tradition, take a rather different view of competition and collective action for its restraint, even though their policy conclusions are often very similar. According to North (1990), the analysis of social interaction must start from a distinction between *institutions*, which are designed by human beings to constrain and shape their interactions, and *organizations*, through which they pursue their interests. Whereas North implies that most of the critique of distributional coalitions developed by Olson is validly applied to organizations, he sees institutions as providing necessary conditions for stability in human interactions of all kinds. Institutions are 'perfectly analogous' to the rules of the game in all competitive sports, and organizations to the teams that compete (North, 1990, p. 4). In other words, institutions constrain, steer and structure competition, providing the framework in which it can take place.

North argues that institutions include all formal and informal constraints on interactions, and provide the structures of opportunities and incentives in which competition between individuals and organized groups takes place. Organizations, in turn, structure collective actions, co-ordinating the skills and strategies of the teams competing with each other. 'Organizations include political bodies (political parties, the Senate, a city council, a regulatory agency), economic bodies (firms, trade unions, family farms, co-operatives), social bodies (churches, clubs, athletic associations) and educational bodies (schools, universities, vocational training centres)' (p. 5). Although his analysis is very different in many respects, North shares with March and Olsen (1989) the view that institutions reduce uncertainty and introduce stability into all interactions, by providing a kind of embodied code for decision-making through their rules and social norms, within which these organizations can seek advantage through competitive activities. Each society is constituted through its formal and informal institutions, which define its long-term trajectory of continuity and change, and the advantageous opportunities open to competing organizations. Economic development is thus 'path dependent', the path being institutionally guided. Each national system consists of a 'mixed bag of institutions' (North, 1990, p. 69), some of which increase and some decrease efficiency. North argues that the institutional systems of Western advanced capitalist countries, especially the USA, have tended to increase productivity and investment in skills, and hence, to promote growth and reduce transaction costs, whereas others (in the developing world) have favoured interest groups seeking rents through monopolies, tariffs, subsidies, payoffs and other barriers to voluntary political and economic exchange (p. 67).

The purpose of North's distinction between institutions and organizations is clearly to differentiate between those forms of restraint on competition which enhance all forms of (market and non-market) voluntary exchange, by promoting trust and co-operation in social interactions, and reducing reliance on third-party enforcement, and those forms which – as Olson emphasizes – involve distributional, and eventually productive, distortions. It is obvious that some such distinction is desirable in any theory of group interaction, since – as we saw in chapter 1 (pp. 34–7) – most social and political theorists are agreed that voluntary associations (including those between business leaders and between workers) produce social capital that outweighs their social costs (Piore and Sabel, 1984; Coleman, 1990; Putnam, 1993). Indeed, most democratic theorists would follow de Tocqueville (1835–40) in arguing for the external benefits of group interactions, rather than Hobbes (1651), whose experiences of the English Civil War made him somewhat jaundiced about collusions. Furthermore, the weight of recent theoretical work on democracy and community (Habermas, 1984; Dryzek, 1990; Hirst, 1994) is strongly in favour of associations' beneficial spillovers into the economy, and critical of over-regulatory action (paradoxically including pro-competitive intervention) by the state. North tries to capture this theoretically by insisting that institutions help to solve collective-action problems over co-operation – in both market and non-market interactions – that would otherwise take the form of prisoner's dilemmas (in game theory an interaction such that if one player co-operates, it always pays the other to defect, so each player's best strategy is always to defect). In the end, the gains from trade themselves depend on various informal and formal restraints, like norms of reciprocity, rules against force, theft and fraud, and restrictions on what can and cannot be marketed (human rights, including laws against slavery and trade in children).

However, it is clear that North's move is also intended to block the conclusion from Olson's theory that is so threatening to market-minded policy programmes – that modern large-scale organized collective action of almost all kinds undermines the benefits deriving from competitive markets. If, as North argues, institutions are a 'mixed bag' of efficiency-promoting and efficiency-reducing systems, which are constantly open to marginal modification by collective agents (within the limits set by 'path dependency'), then it makes sense for social scientists to conduct detailed studies to evaluate them in the light of alternative forms of co-ordination – for instance, through international comparisons – rather than assume that all will reflect the weight of past collusions. Hence although North's policy recommendations are not dissimilar to Olson's, he devises these from a comparative review of economic history, rather than an abstract analysis of group interaction.

I shall argue that North's distinction is of little theoretical value and, above all, that it fails to block the most subversive implications of Olson's analysis of collective action in market societies. This is of crucial importance for the theory of poverty and social exclusion, since North's move might suggest that social institutions can and do protect the poor from Olson-like consequences of long-term interactions in exclusive groups. But institutions *enable* rather than block social exclusion.

The distinction between institutions and organizations implies that restraints that take the form of 'rules of the game' (of interaction), whether normative and informal, or regulatory and formal, are qualitatively different from the restraints through which individuals co-ordinate (rent-seeking) collective action. It suggests that institutions provide the structures in terms of which organizations are strategically orientated; the 'teams' (organizations) decide how to deploy their co-ordinated skills by taking account both of the strategies of other teams, and of the opportunities and incentives built into the (institutions of the) game.

But this distinction is purely one of perspective. From the standpoint of an individual member, a football club is an institution, whose rules govern his or her actions within the organized groups (directors, shareholders, management, players, supporters) that go to make up the collective life of the club. From the standpoint of the club as an organization, the federal Football League is an institution that structures its strategic interactions as an organization with other clubs, in turn organized in groupings (premier clubs, lower-league professional clubs, amateur clubs, referees and officials, and so on). From the standpoint of the Football League, the Ministry of Sport is an institution, structuring its strategies as an organization, with those organizations representing other sports. *At each level, a collective body is both an institution that restrains competition among its members through rules and norms, and an organization that mobilizes those members for competition at a higher level, conducted within the rules and norms set by a higher institution.* Hence institutions enable exclusions based on organizations.

So the crucial question remains the one about the nature and purpose of the restraints of competition that constitute groups' collective goods. Institutions fulfil the purpose of achieving internal restraint within organizations, while providing their members with advantages (over non-members, who are disorganized, or excluded altogether from the field) when they are competing with others. In this sense, North's distinction does nothing to soften Olson's dismal message for the poor. If institutions are simply the way that organizations achieve their purposes (of binding members to their mutual obligations over cost-sharing and non-rivalrous interactions over one or more collective goods, and over the exclusion of non-members from their benefits), then institutions cannot offset the effects of organizational collusion against the disorganized poor.

Once this is recognized, we are back again in Olson's vicious circle. Collective action in market environments is always about rent-seeking restraints of competition aimed at privileging one social formation (exclusive groups) at the expense of all others. But actually the situation is worse than before, because this critical analysis of North's theory reveals an unexamined assumption of Olson's analysis. His *The Rise and Decline of Nations* never questions the status and purpose of states as collective actors; without saying as much, he treats sovereign territorial authorities as 'institutions' in North's (misleading) sense, rather than as organizations in competition with other states, in a global institutional structure. Olson's policy prescriptions (more market-orientated rules within states) make sense only if we assume that the purpose of all interactions among members (citizens) is to maximize the advantages occurring to that group of human beings, at the expense of all other groups (the citizens of other states). Indeed, the whole concept of nations 'rising and declining' has this assumption built into it.

This, of course, is very significant for Olson's policy programme – in two important respects. First, he pins his hopes for more efficient and equitable distributions (faster growth and fairer shares) on national governments. Only the pursuit of interests common to the whole citizenry could move national governments to design and legislate such institutional rules. All other influences on them, from lobby groups, distributional coalitions and special-interest organizations of all kinds, tend towards inefficient and inequitable regimes of anti-competitive protectionism – tariffs, subsidies, tax breaks, legal immunities, and so on. The central collective-action dilemma for governments, on this account, is how to mobilize consent for free-market policies amid such anti-competitive pressures.

But this assumes that governments have no agendas of their own, other than to legislate the best institutional framework for efficient and equitable interactions. North's earlier work, and the whole public-choice tradition, rebuts this assumption (North, 1981, 1986; Peacock, 1979; Buchanan, 1978). Governments need to do deals with special-interest groups to maximize their own tax-takes, thus affording their constituent groups – politicians, bureaucrats, public-service professionals – opportunities to expand their budgets or discretionary powers. And governments, above all, have to mobilize populations for economic and military competition with other states. The history of public administration can be understood in terms of freedoms granted to

chartered interest groups (territorially or occupationally organized) in return for payments that enhanced the competitive
(usually military) potential of sovereigns, both monarchical and
republican (Spruyt, 1994). We are back once more with Hobbes.

But there is an even more fundamental problem lurking
beneath Olson's policy conclusions, which follows directly from
the one just outlined. Suppose that governments are able to
overcome this central collective-action dilemma, and impose a
strictly market-orientated regime on recalcitrant interest groups
within their societies, and that the world is made up of states,
each with free internal markets of impeccable rectitude. Would
this lead to free trade between states? The question is far too
complex to allow an answer here, though it is immediately obvious that it may well not, since governments with wider geo-politi-
cal ambitions may face strong incentives to build up their
industrial–military strength behind the barriers of tariffs or non-
convertible currencies (as Germany and the former USSR did in
the 1930s).

But in any conceivable economic circumstances, there is one
current universal barrier to free movement of resources that
would be unlikely to be much relaxed – the restriction on the
movement of *people*. Olson's model assumes that capital will
move to wherever in the world it can get the best return. But it
should also assume that people will move anywhere – in the
world – where they can make gainful exchanges of their energies
and skills for wages. This implies open borders. Without this condition, the optimizing properties of markets vanish. Olson's prescriptions for alleviating poverty and discrimination (broadly,
global free trade) lose their force if the Third World poor and
excluded cannot join the world's most effective collective-action
systems for husbanding wealth and privilege, the rich nation
states of the First World.

Nation states, whether of the social democratic or neo-liberal
institutional variety, are nothing more than clubs – groups that
restrain internal competition through compulsory regimes, but
exclude most non-citizens from the shared benefits thus generated. Passports and border controls are the technological devices
by which non-members are excluded. Taxes and social insurance

contributions are their citizens' membership dues. Like free trade, free movement of people is but one policy option among many to be considered, and one which is even less adopted. Exclusion is the essence of states. The poverty of the citizens of developing countries is therefore, in Olson's theory, explicable in terms of the collective action of governments in the rich countries of the developed world. And such collective action (the gains from co-operation among an exclusive group of citizens, mobilized for competition with the citizens of other states) is intrinsic to, and an inescapable part of, the logic of a world made up of sovereign, territorial states.

SOCIAL EXCLUSION AND THE THEORY OF CLUBS

We have now explored the implications for the most vulnerable members of (world) society of Olson's public-choice analysis of group interactions in market-orientated societies. It is time to return to the original terms of the public-choice perspective, and to its fundamental distinction between private and public goods. In this section I shall review the developments in the theory of groups sparked off by Buchanan's work. Club theory both enormously enlarges the scope of public-choice methods for analysing social interactions, and fundamentally subverts many of its original concepts and assumptions, as well as much of its policy programme.

Club theory is specially relevant for the analysis of poverty and social exclusion, because it explains in detail how groups that form to supply each other with a range of collective goods respond to incentives to include or exclude members. In other words, it shows how individuals with different capabilities, resources, risks and vulnerabilities interact in relation to group formation and exclusion, and explains the circumstances in which the most vulnerable will be included in collective goods, as well as those in which they will be excluded.

Buchanan's original aim was to refine the distinction between private and public goods, by drawing attention to an intermediate category – the collective goods supplied to members of exclu-

sive groups, which he called 'club goods'. Such goods were neither purely private (in the sense that their individual use could
be identified and monitored, and that they were rivalrously consumed, and hence both excludable and efficiently marketable)
nor purely public (impossible or too costly to assign to individual
owners, non-depletable and non-rivalrous in consumption –
hence non-excludable and non-marketable). Clubs constituted a
way of providing goods that made them partially rivalrous (for
example, because members were required to pay the maintenance costs in their supply) and partially depletable (for
instance, because members lost utility with extra use, through
the costs of congestion). His example, as mentioned on p. 8,
was a swimming pool, whose members shared the costs of its
upkeep, but excluded non-members, who did not contribute to
these costs, and might crowd out the benefits of shared enjoy-
ment, by technological means (a fence, membership cards).
Responding to Buchanan's pioneering article, club theory subsequently developed an analysis of the efficient allocation of such
excludable, collective consumption goods as leisure and cultural
facilities – single goods being shared by all club members.

However, in the 1970s and 1980s the scope of its analysis was
extended through several theoretical developments. It was
quickly recognized that the most important feature of the economics of clubs was not the nature of the goods supplied (which
were extremely diverse), but the interactions between the members, and the dynamics of competition between clubs. In this way,
as Olson (1971, p. 38) recognized in a footnote, the development of club theory mirrored his work on collective action and
the theory of groups.

A club is a group of interdependent individuals whose interdependency is not simply market-related (Breuer, Faist and Jordan,
1994). In economic terms, there must be technological, rather
than simply monetary, externalities; hence the need for members to be included, and non-members excluded. Groups form
because economies can be gained by sharing certain costs; 'the
reciprocal externalities arise from the existence of average costs
as a common or public element in everyone's budget-
constrained utility opportunities' (McGuire, 1972, p. 89). But

interdependency leaves individual club members with options for actions of two kinds. The first is exit; they can leave the club and join another. The second is voice; they can participate in decisions about the terms of membership of the club, and especially about who is to be included and who excluded.

Initially, club theorists assumed that all club members were alike, and addressed issues of optimal club size (Wooders, 1978). On this assumption, the aim is to give all club members equal utility, and choose club size to maximize the utility of a representative member (Starrett, 1988, p. 48). Where there is congestion rivalry (crowding), efficient club size is reached where the collective good becomes fully rivalrous at the margin. If a new member's contribution (equivalent to the average cost of the collective good) exceeds the marginal opportunity cost to the group, he or she should be admitted; otherwise not. 'An efficient club must involve equality of the marginal and average cost' (Starrett, 1988, p. 52).

However, if the population from which clubs are formed is heterogeneous, the question arises whether segregated or 'mixed' clubs are more efficient. If there are large enough numbers of each 'type' to take advantage of economies of scale, segregation appears to be optional from an efficiency standpoint. This conclusion reinforces the one made by Olson about homogeneity being optimal for organized groups seeking rents, because of their potential for internal consensus (although the club-theoretic argument rests on economies of scale). Thus even if the poor can afford the club's contribution rate, they may be excluded on other grounds, simply because they are 'different', unless there are economies of scale to be realized.

But where there are complementarities over benefits (e.g. enjoying 'mixed' company, or costs/efficiency gains from 'mixed' productive skills), then 'mixed' clubs may be optimal. For instance, ballroom dancing clubs always contain more or less equal numbers of men and women, and black people find it far easier to gain admission to clubs formed around an activity with which they are stereotypically associated as skilful practitioners (jazz clubs, athletic clubs) than those formed around the elitist activities of privileged white groups (dining clubs, golf clubs).

In club theory, efficient allocation through voluntary association can be achieved if technologies and preferences are such that the number of optimally constituted clubs is large. Individuals are able to combat discrimination by moving to another club, or starting a new one, thus guaranteeing themselves equal benefits for an equal share of the costs. But – as Mueller (1989, p. 153) points out – if the optimal club sizes are large relative to the population, discrimination is possible and stable equilibria may not exist, because of the lack of alternatives. Furthermore, optimal club size for members themselves will not necessarily coincide with what is optimal for the population as a whole, and utilities for members have to be set against disutilities for those excluded.

> With an optimum club size of two-thirds of the population, for example, only one such club can exist. If it forms, those not in it are motivated to lure members away by offering disproportionate shares of the benefits gained from expanding the smaller clubs. But the remaining members of the larger club are motivated to maintain club size, and can attract new members by offering the full benefits of the big club, and so on. (Mueller, 1989, pp. 153–4)

The theory of clubs thus offers a crucial theoretical tool for the analysis of processes of collectivization and fragmentation in welfare states. As I argued in the first chapter (pp. 6–7), de Swaan's theory of collectivization is deficient because he does not address the processes by which, even after collective systems are established, individuals and collective actors still face strong incentives to exclude the most vulnerable members of their societies from compulsory public welfare systems, as well as powerful incentives to form private welfare clubs through exit from state schemes. Indeed, I shall argue that this fragmentation process, consisting of exclusion of the vulnerable from so-called 'universal' benefits and services, and the formation of more new mutualities for those with lowest risks, is characteristic of the development of social relations in the final quarter of the twentieth century.

(In a social policy context, of course, what has to be explained is rather more complex than this. At the same time as the comprehensive and public social insurance schemes and in-kind redistributive services of national welfare states are fragmenting, collective actors (states, international employers' and labour organizations) are moving towards institutions that are transnational, supranational and international, under pressure from such factors as mass migration (Leibfried and Pierson, 1994; de Swaan, 1994). The main focus of this book is fragmentation, though the relationship between this and globalization, including transnational collectivization, will be discussed in the conclusion (chapter 7). My contention here is that, as earnings have risen and dispersed in the advanced industrialized states since the early 1960s, as unemployment has grown and various risks diversified, and as technologies have changed, the relevant opportunities and payoffs for mutuality groups have altered. This in turn has been reinforced by policies for deregulating labour markets, cutting back public expenditure, and encouraging the privatization of risks.)

The process of fragmentation can be (provisionally and somewhat schematically) addressed in relation to social insurance. The mutual provision of insurance against loss of income through retirement, accident, sickness and unemployment can be plausibly represented as the product of an agreement between the citizens of a state. Compulsory mutual insurance solved the various collective-action dilemmas facing individuals and collective actors in the period 1880–1960 (de Swaan, 1988, ch. 6). As systems for the collectivization of social risks, social insurance schemes probably succeeded because of the anticipated positive external effects on political stability, productivity, law and order and the protection of the health and property rights of the better off. Highest-risk groups were among the last to be included. In the liberal Anglo-Saxon countries, immigrants – who are among the poorest – still have few rights.

Conventionally, the benefits of such systems are regarded as public goods, because of the compulsory collective nature of their provision. But from the point of view of the individual member the benefit is a pure private good (Breuer, Faist and Jordan, 1994). Part of this good is the feeling of security that enters the individual's utility function, and this utility is not affected when others feel secure too. Each individual can in principle be excluded from benefit (for example, for deliberately avoiding employment, or intentionally retarding their recovery from illness); hence it is an excludable good. Whether it is rivalrous or not depends on the cost function of provision.

Social insurance can be represented as a club because of the interdependency between members, shown in the cost function (Starrett, 1988, p. 50). Individuals who (ex-ante) cost more than they pay worsen the situation of other club members, because they in turn have to pay higher contributions or reduce their insurance level. In club-theoretical terms, it is only possible to determine the optimal number of club members unambiguously by ordering the members according to their 'net' contribution to the club, and assuming that the highest net contributors have priority access to the club (Breuer, Faist and Jordan, 1994).

Thus the individual social insurance member has incentives to exclude poorer people with higher risks from the club, unless they are needed for realizing economies of scale. From the point of view of society as a whole, citizens as voters may have incentives to enlarge the club to one that is bigger than the size that would be chosen by existing members. For instance, a larger social insurance club might produce the collective goods of lower crime rates and a more convivial social environment. Under such circumstances, there may be a permanent distributional struggle over the rights to decide about the optimal club size and optimal club structure of social insurance (Kirsch, 1993, pp. 166ff). The fact that membership is compulsory for full-time employees need not preclude analysing social insurance as a club (p. 168). Part-time and self-employed workers may be deemed ineligible for certain benefits; young unemployed workers who have not yet contributed may be included or excluded; and existing members may be excluded from benefits by changing eligibility conditions – for example, reducing the period of unemployment covered or tightening up on the definition of what constitutes 'actively seeking work', 'availability for work' or 'incapacity for work'.

Many of those who are excluded from social insurance fall into social assistance. This can be represented as another (overlapping) club – the club of all citizens who pay taxes and benefit from welfare systems. However, here the interdependencies are quite different, because – unlike social insurance – most taxpaying contributors are never beneficiaries (they are excluded by work tests and means tests), and many beneficiaries are never contributors (they remain outside the labour market, and hence pay no direct taxes). Hence there are strong incentives for members (voters) to seek other options for action to the ones open to them through 'voice' as citizens in a democracy. For the rich, these include emigration and tax evasion as forms of 'exit'; for the poor, emigration, benefit fraud (such as working while claiming) and crime are the rough equivalents. They are instances of fragmentation in welfare states – actions through which citizens sort themselves into new social formations, including tax havens and close-knit poor communities at the opposite ends of the spectrum of resources.

There is increasing evidence of an overall tendency within welfare states towards the formation of new and smaller clubs with more homogeneous memberships, and this will be analysed in much more detail in chapters 5 and 6. The exclusion of bad risks and the grouping together of narrower risk-pools in such systems reinforces the residential segregation of rich and poor, achieved through 'voting with the feet' (see pp. 167–76). The 'Americanization' of European welfare states consists mainly of a division into two clubs around earnings and income maintenance, a social-insurance club for those in secure, adequately paid employment, and a social-assistance club for the rest (Skocpol, 1988). The whole debate about the 'underclass' – the idea that the poor have become an identifiable underground collective-action group, with interests, strategies and cultural practices that are different from, and often antagonistic to, those of mainstream society – can be reframed in terms of the economic theory of exclusive groups, by using a club-theoretic analysis (Breuer, Faist and Jordan, 1994).

Thus what started as a theory of goods that are intermediate between private and public goods has become a perspective for the analysis of collective action and social exclusion, which radically subverts many of the assumptions underpinning public-choice policy programmes. If, under present socio-economic conditions in advanced welfare states, such welfare goods as income maintenance provision and health care (see chapter 5) come to be treated as club goods, because the relevant options and interdependencies facing citizens in fragmenting solidarities allow actors to choose as members of exclusive groups, then such strategic action becomes central to the analysis of 'the demand and supply of public goods' (Buchanan, 1968), 'the economics of (social) politics' (Buchanan, 1978), and the future of the welfare state (Buchanan, 1986d). In the next section I shall outline some of the theoretical implications and policy issues raised by this approach that will be explored in this book.

STRATEGIC ACTION, EXCLUSION AND RESISTANCE

The development of club theory provides a perspective and a method that have hitherto been lacking in the analysis of poverty. This allows the economics of group interaction to be studied, thus linking human capabilities, resources and risks to the dynamics of inclusion and exclusion. It makes a coherent general theory of poverty and social exclusion feasible, and provides a potential linkage between the methodologically individualistic study of poverty in the liberal tradition, and the group-orientated study of social exclusion in the Continental tradition.

But above all, it allows vulnerable people to appear in this theory as *actors* rather than victims. Although the poor are distinguishable – and thus excludable – in interactions mainly because of their underdeveloped capacities, their lack of material resources and the higher risks they face, they do still act rationally and strategically within this perspective, both in their individual choices of which alternative clubs to join or form, and in the collective action they take within these.

What distinguishes clubs from other forms of interdependency are the elements of collective action, based on agreement, and the mutual commitment of members over time. We would expect to see many different kinds of agreements over the contributions that give entitlements to the collective goods produced through members' co-operation, reflecting different decision procedures and sizes of group.

At one extreme, welfare states can be characterized as large multi-product clubs (Sandler and Tschirhart, 1993), made up of individuals who in turn form memberships of overlapping internal clubs. Their options within these interactions depend on many factors, including whether they are *citizens* with full civil, political and social rights, or *denizens* who lack political (as in Germany) or social (as in Britain) rights, or *aliens*, who have neither, as in the case of illegal immigrants (Hammar, 1990). From the perspective of welfare states as clubs, non-resident foreigners can be seen as potential 'club servants' – non-citizen labour, as in German *Gastarbeiter* schemes – or as potential elements in crowding and free-riding problems (Breuer, Faist and Jordan, 1994).

But at the other extreme we can also recognize the existence of 'informal clubs' without written constitutions or formal contribution structures. These may come into being because interdependencies arise through everyday interactions, rather than through formal meetings; their agreements may never be recorded, nor their members registered. Yet they do fulfil the criteria for analysis in terms of clubs, because members act together for common purposes, responding in concerted ways over time.

Informal clubs often come into existence because their members' potential interdependencies arise through being excluded from the benefits of membership of formal clubs. In order to produce such benefits, formal club members have externalized some costs, and these costs fall on the excluded. Thus the collective actions of informal clubs can often be understood as strategic forms of resistance against the collective decisions of other clubs, including government decisions. Much of my analysis of current social policy issues concerns the actions of such informally co-ordinated interdependencies, and their collective consequences, including the hidden costs for society that they entail.

In this section I shall sketch some of the dynamics of interactions between these large-scale systems of formal collective action (welfare states and their constituent social service schemes) and small-scale, informal clubs. This will provide the groundwork for my analysis in chapters 4–6, in which the consequences of social exclusion will be explored in terms of the resistance actions of the poor, and the hidden social costs of social division and intergroup conflict.

In order to conceptualize this dynamic, it might be useful to start from an imaginary choice situation facing a young, unskilled, unemployed single man or woman, living in a very deprived outer-city district anywhere in a depressed region of (Western or Eastern) Europe. The options open to such a person might be listed schematically as follows:

(a) wait for a suitable opportunity for training, employment (or marriage to an employed person) to become available;
(b) seek informal opportunities for undeclared work while claiming benefits;
(c) join an informal club for collective action to increase the members' incomes by legal or illegal (a begging group, a criminal gang, a protection racket, a drugs syndicate, or a prostitutes' co-operative) means;
(d) join a revolutionary political group;
(e) migrate to another area;
(f) migrate to another country.

With the exception of option (a), all of these are individual or collective actions, taken in response to structures of opportunities and incentives arising from social exclusions, that imply conflicts over how the benefits and costs of such exclusions should be distributed. By defection, collective action or 'voting with the feet', the person in question would be taking strategic action to resist some of these costs, to create new club goods through informal collective action, or to seek access to another bundle of collective goods elsewhere. Millions of such decisions have important implications for the formal systems constituted through welfare states.

Social polarization and new poverty (see chapter 3) have emerged as features of all advanced industrialized welfare states, but at different rates. In the Anglo-Saxon countries they have been more prominent aspects of social relations, they became apparent earlier, and they were more strongly re-enforced by

government policies, than in the Continental European countries. They can be traced to the politically mediated consequences of economic globalization and the new international
division of labour; within such states individuals have been sorting themselves into more homogeneous groupings around such
collective goods as residential amenities, recreational and cultural facilities, health and social services. Even among groups
facing racial discrimination (such as urban African American
people in the USA), migration to the suburbs by higher-income
households left inner-city concentrations of the 'truly disadvantaged' (W. J. Wilson, 1987). They in turn devised strategies for
individual and collective resistance to exclusion, often involving
the formation of 'informal clubs'.

But at the same time, these countries continued to attract
migration from the less developed world, a process greatly accelerated by the collapse of the Soviet and Eastern European
regimes, and more recently by the political upheavals in North
Africa. The paradox of welfare states in the 1990s is that their
particular structures of opportunities and constraints, together
with the relative payoffs for formal (regular), casual (irregular)
and informal (undocumented or illegal) work, have both excluded marginal resident workers and attracted immigrants from
abroad. On the one hand, as regular formal employment and
social protection came to cost employers more, they had strong
incentives to shed low-skilled labour from their payrolls, and use
more part-time, low-paid, irregular or casual workers, a trend
that led to labour-market dualization (Bowen and Mayhew,
1991). But on the other hand, the greater 'flexibility' of the
labour market and the outcomes of policies to relax minimum
wages and conditions for some categories of work have increased
opportunities and incentives for 'informal', as well as casual,
work. Among the resident population, irregular work (under
'non-standard contracts') has mainly been taken up by married
women and young people; and 'informal work' (including undeclared cash jobs and some kinds of crime) has mainly been taken
up by men claiming benefits as unemployed. Legal immigrants
have chiefly been absorbed into the irregular labour market, in
insecure, low-paid, unprotected work, while illegal immigrants

have been drawn into the 'shadow' economy of informal, un-documented work.

Transnational labour migration has always posed dilemmas for national systems of employment and social protection, over the access of non-citizens to employment and claims to social rights in the receiving country, and also over transferring benefits deriving from rights in the sending country. Despite its long history of developing a politics of immigration and inclusion, the United States is experiencing tensions over illegal migrations from the south and east. The precedent set by the Californian referendum decision to exclude children of illegal immigrants from public education and health care is expected to be followed in other states (see p. 38). In Europe, the EU has developed a supra-national form of membership (European citizenship) that seeks to give similar social rights to citizens, in whichever state they choose to work and live. But rights of mobility and even some social rights are applicable to some extracommunitari from countries such as Turkey, the Maghreb and Central European states. Within the EU, these rights are contested (for instance, between the European Court of Justice and nation states) and the collectivization process is much less developed in relation to Eastern European states (Faist, 1994b). Above all, new transnational policies on migration must overcome central features of the logic of collectivization that informs nation states, and the paradoxes of social polarization that have occurred within them since the 1970s.

Welfare states are conceived as closed systems. Their logic implies boundaries that distinguish members (who are the contributors to, and beneficiaries of, welfare goods) from non-members. Distributive justice requires a moral basis in kinship or fellow-feeling, and a commitment to dividing up and sharing among members (Walzer, 1983, p. 31). The distributive logic of closure is threatened by economic migration, and that of justice by strategic action to maximize welfare allocation by members of the indigenous population. The premises of distribution and solidarity in welfare states are built around an identifiable population of members who share interdependencies and interest concerning past and future generations. However, such closed systems are increasingly exposed to forces stemming from a changing global economy. Economic globalization has facilitated both mobility between states, and strategic action within them.

Welfare states protect themselves against unlimited migration by border controls and quotas, and against all forms of strategic exploitation by limiting eligibility for benefits and services, and various forms of welfare policing (detailed assessments, fraud investigations, prosecutions, etc.). However, welfare states also create opportunities for strategic action, including immigration. As Freeman (1986) points out, the availability to citizens of welfare states of minimum wages and conditions, unemployment benefits and health services allows national workers to refuse certain tasks and terms of employment. In turn, employers can instead recruit foreign workers, including subcontract workers (such as current *Werkvertragsarbeitnehmer* arrangements between Germany and the Central European states) and undocumented immigrants. National workers and their unions often collude with such practices, under which certain unpleasant and badly paid tasks are done for low wages by migrant workers (Faist, 1994b).

These immigrants enter welfare states and find spaces to work within them precisely because they are not eligible for the various forms of employment and social protection available to national workers. They do not enjoy full political or social rights, and are likely to be poor by national standards. If welfare states are seen as multi-product clubs, they do not enter as club members but as club servants. They perform the services that members are unwilling to do for each other (for example, in horticulture, construction and many domestic services). The higher the incomes of club members, the more such clubs can afford to pay their servants, and the more services are likely to be provided by migrants rather than members. The extreme case was pre-invasion oil-rich Kuwait, where virtually all Kuwaitis had the employment conditions and perks of public officials, while almost all productive work and all domestic service was done by migrant labour, especially from Pakistan and Palestine.

In European welfare states, immigration – including undocumented migrant labour – provides a certain 'flexibility' without which such economies might be handicapped in international competition. These economies, with their still-regulated minimum wages and conditions of employment, and their still-generous compensation for those excluded from the labour market, rely on immigrants to do much of their dirty, low-paid work. At the lower levels of society, groups of nationals excluded from the labour market form clubs for various kinds of informal mutual support or opportunistic predation, while groups of immigrants in turn take informal collective action for mutual protection and cultural survival.

In Britain, and in the ghetto areas of the USA, the deregulatory policies of the 1980s have caused a rather different situation, that might be called 'hypercasualization'. For many low-skilled workers, the rewards for formal employment are so low, or the terms of irregular employment so insecure, that their best strategy is usually to claim public assistance (income support) and to do occasional undeclared work for cash (Jordan et al., 1992). For some small enterprises, profit margins are so low, and on-wage employment costs so high, that theirs is to offer work on these terms. Such actors can readily reach agreements outside the formal labour market, but not within it.

Thus the absence of regulatory constraints and collective actors (such as trade unions) facilitates a 'flexibility' that goes beyond 'non-standard contracts' (short-term, part-time or occasional agency work, and various forms of 'self-employment') to include informal exchanges and ad hoc agreements on either side of the boundary of legality. The sheer number of such exchanges makes detection difficult. Neither employer nor employee is likely to belong to an organization whose collective interests lie in enforcing labour-market law on their members. The parties to such informal contracts agree together to share the risks and costs of an 'informal' bargain, but externalize the costs of the worker's subsistence (met by public assistance) and both parties' tax liability (including social security contributions). Of course there are further externalities arising from such interdependencies, including unfair competition and the undermining of respect for the law.

Indeed, there is little conceptual distinction between such

interactions and other types of predation – organized begging, drug dealing, prostitution, mugging or burglary. It is easy to see how, under current institutional conditions, all are rational actions by those for whom the rewards from 'informal' activities of this kind can be expected to exceed those from formal employment, where informal opportunities are more abundant than formal ones, and where the risks of prosecution are low, because the actions are so prevalent.

It seems that all these examples constitute cases of market failure and government failure – informal social interactions that occur outside the rules of the market and the public sector (tax and social security regulations). They might be compared with the activities of those 'families' – in practice, informal predatory groups – in the former Soviet Union and Eastern Europe, who intercepted goods between state factories and state retail outlets, and consumed them collectively. There, because of shortages and the absence of a market, such reallocations 'solved' a distributional problem, though at the expense of other would-be consumers. Hillman (1992) calls such groups 'socialist clubs'. Since the collapse of those regimes, new clubs have emerged in those countries, more orientated towards the transition to a market economy and with a greater affinity to the Sicilian Mafia (Gambetta, 1993). In this case, their prevalence can be explained in terms of problems in the definition of property rights and enforcement of contracts, allowing private protection and enforcement agencies to arise to exclude other predators within a given domain, and supplying an effective local monopoly of violence.

The US and British phenomena described above can be similarly analysed as clubs – collective-action groups for the joint supply or consumption of goods, which cause negative externalities to be borne by other producers, consumers or taxpayers. Though these agreements are often very temporary and opportunistic, taken together they constitute a formidable set of practices that are linked into a kind of institutionalized system in deprived areas, as alternatives to the market and the state.

Seen from one perspective, they represent the resistance practices of the poor. Seen from another, they constitute the unintended consequences of market-orientated government policies. From the government's perspective they are the 'underclass problem', and pose serious social policy dilemmas. The distribution of the costs associated with these practices, and of policy measures to combat them, will be analysed in chapters 4 and 6.

CONCLUSIONS

The aim of this chapter has been to introduce the public-choice perspective, to show how its original conceptions of private and public goods have been radically modified by the development of the theory of collective action in groups, and to demonstrate its relevance for the analysis of poverty and social exclusion.

In the first part of the chapter I outlined Olson's theory of collective action, and showed that it implied that all such action in market situations restrains competition between members and excludes non-members, for the sake of an economic rent. Distributional coalitions of all kinds are thus collusions through which organized interests seek to gain at the expense of unorganized individuals. Vulnerable people are vulnerable precisely because they are in no position to organize under market conditions. Markets provoke collusions that block the potential benefits of competition to the poor. Hence poverty and social exclusion reflect the success of collective action by rent-seeking groups in a competitive economic and political environment. The collective goods at stake in such environments are always won through internalizing the costs of co-operation (restraint of competition), and externalizing the costs of exclusion (enforced, disadvantaged competition).

Despite the efforts of institutional theorists, this logic of collective action was shown to apply in all such interactions, including those constituting citizenship of states, and relationships between states. Both formal and informal institutions are necessary conditions for co-operation, but co-operation is itself the manifestation of successful collective action by one social formation, which mobilizes it for competition with others. While market institutions allow efficiency through gainful exchanges, and hence more rapid economic growth, the interactions through which this is accomplished are necessarily costly for individuals who are marginal to collective-action groups, and to members of those groups that lose in competition. For such individuals, the security they enjoyed as members of comparatively poor collective-action groups (such as communities in developing countries, or trade unions in more developed ones) may have been preferable to their new exposed position as individuals with few enforceable claims on others, adrift in global markets. In a richer world, the poor may still get poorer.

In the second half of the chapter, I outlined developments in club theory, deriving from the work of Buchanan. This method allows the systematic investigation of how the formation of collective-action groups relates to individual capabilities, resources and risks, and how individuals interact in an environment made up of overlapping competing clubs, each supplying one or more collective goods. But the subversive implication of this theory is that the poor, as rational actors, have opportunities for countering the costs of exclusion from such formal clubs by semi-organized, informal collective actions of their own.

This recasts social policy issues, by focusing on the unintended consequences and social costs, both of welfare states themselves and of the reformed structures that have been designed to replace them in the USA and Britain. Strategic action by poor people can subvert the aims of policy makers, and lead to a costly escalation of conflicts, seen as struggles over the distribution of resources for final consumption. Migration and 'informal' economic activity (including crime) were used as examples of such strategies, that help to explain the current social policy dilemmas of advanced industrialized societies, and particularly of the USA and Britain.

Club theory greatly extends the scope of the analysis of group interactions, beyond the formal collective action of cartels and labour unions, lobby groups and professional associations, and into the myriad interdependencies of civil society. It shows that the collective goods at stake in such interactions are very diverse, from cultural and social benefits shared among a group of similar (refined or rough-and-ready) tastes, to the spoils of predation, exploitation or discrimination. It also shows that these collective goods may be distributed among members in many ways; they may be collectively consumed as indivisible and shared, or redistributed as private goods for final consumption.

These concepts and methods have been available to social policy analysts for several years. Why then have they not been previously used to develop a theory of poverty-related social exclusion? This will be the subject of the next chapter.

3

Missing Links

———⇒◆⇐———

This chapter will try to explain the need for a new theory of poverty and social exclusion by analysing existing ones. Why do they not capture the processes that were outlined in the previous chapter? I will argue that this is because they address issues of poverty and social exclusion from perspectives derived either from the liberal tradition, or from the social protectionism of national, compulsory, collective institutions. Thus they miss forms of collective behaviour that may be inclusive or exclusive, but occur outside those particular frameworks. And they also miss the implications of compulsory inclusion in welfare states as exclusive, competing economic units within a globalizing environment.

In other words, the theoretical debate about poverty and social exclusion reflects the struggle between economic individualism (the present-day manifestation of the dominant strand within the liberal tradition) and the version of collectivism that characterized the era of the welfare state. This is understandable, given the configuration of political interests and organizations in Britain and Europe. However it is also unfortunate, since it means that the other collective phenomena to which I have drawn attention come to be discussed in terms of different debates, particularly over social deviance and enforcement, which also miss the dynamic of inclusion and exclusion, and lead to a distorted policy agenda. Above all, there is no framework of analysis to serve either academic or political purposes that takes full account of the social costs and benefits of collective decisions.

Exclusion arises from the need to set boundaries (of family, clan, club, community or nation) around interdependency, and from the technological capacity to partition goods for private ownership and use. The paradox of the present age is that economic globalization – the growth of world trade, international units of production and human mobility – has simultaneously increased interdependency between citizens of different states, and capacities for excluding marginal local individuals from previously shared goods. In a world where each person's welfare is closely related to the behaviour of individuals in distant countries (for instance, over resource depletion, pollution or international migration) it is far easier, through new technological means, to exclude consideration of one's neighbours' actions and opportunities from decisions about one's own. The social consequences of poverty and exclusion often enter comfortable citizens' calculations only (literally) by the back door, in the form of crime.

Given that the basic ingredients of the theoretical framework given in chapter 2 have been available to social scientists since the mid-1960s, why have they not been used to analyse these phenomena? The answer is that they have been deployed for slightly different purposes, mainly to develop theories on the evolution of welfare states (de Swaan, 1988) in the tradition of earlier explanations and categorizations of the collectivization process (Flora and Heidenheimer, 1981; Alber, 1982). But this chapter will argue that the omission can also be traced to the divergence between the Anglo-Saxon study of poverty in the liberal tradition, and the Continental European analysis of social exclusion in the mercantilist tradition. Not only has there been no theory of poverty and social exclusion that explains the economics of collective action in exclusive groups; there has really been no theory of poverty *and* exclusion at all.

In Britain, studies of poverty have long aimed at proving that, below a certain level of resources, individuals were excluded from participation in mainstream social activities (Townsend, 1979; 1993; Mack and Lansley, 1984). The evidence of exclusion was thus that they did not possess, consume or do certain things (with efforts to show that this was because they could not afford them) that many or most others did. As critics have pointed out (Ringen, 1988), these methods bias such studies towards income as a measure of poverty; they also construct social exclusion mainly in terms of participation in market exchange. They make little direct attempt to study the social relations of poverty – how the poor relate to each other, and to members of other economic groups.

The other side of the British social policy tradition is the study of collective income maintenance systems. This addresses poverty in terms of the adequacy of benefits rates, and has tackled the question of what constitutes a moderately decent household budget (Bradshaw, 1993). It looks at social exclusion through the 'social division of welfare' – Titmuss's (1958) distinction between fiscal, occupational and public welfare systems – and particularly at the growth of means-tested schemes, and of groups with no entitlement to state assistance (Lister, 1990).

In recent years, this approach has been widened by use of the concept of 'social citizenship' (Roche, 1992). Economic individualism and the social policies of the 1980s are criticized from the normative standpoint of the attempt through collectivized income maintenance systems to provide a material basis for full membership of a political community. There are links between this approach and the Continental tradition, which also addresses employment rights as part of social citizenship (Coenen and Leisink, 1993), and thus with the policy agendas of the European Union.

Discussion of citizenship allows poverty to be analysed within a framework of institutional relationships for democratic decision-making, interdependency and political membership, and in this sense is an advance on the study of social rights as insulated from other aspects of social relations. However, it focuses on formal political institutions as the expression of the collective life of a community, at the expense of other aspects of collective behaviour. One of the most interesting aspects of present-day social relations is the failure of formal politics to capture the interdependencies that are most relevant for collective action, and the consequent disillusion with government as the means of solving collective-action dilemmas. It also implies that analysis of issues of social exclusion in terms of citizenship will miss many relevant features of the social world.

For instance, citizenship deals in interactions between individuals with formal membership entitlements within a nation state. But it is clear from the prevalence of migration, especially undocumented migration, that many people are choosing to trade off their political rights against economic opportunities. It is one of the ironies of the collapse of the Soviet Union and its satellite states that the victory of freedom and democracy that this heralded has been followed by a massive attempt by those populations to flee to the West; according to *Eurobarometer* (1992), over 30 per cent of citizens of those countries were actively considering emigration. They prefer to vote with their feet, rather than wait for promised economic improvements, with the result that the destruction of the Iron Curtain has required the hasty erection of systems for restricting the influx of immigrants to the EU. Similarly, many citizens of developing countries, often those with relatively good educational and occupational qualifications, are prepared to sacrifice their political rights in their countries of origin to attempt to live and work, either legally or illegally, in an advanced economy. This is by no means a set of purely individual decisions, since communities of immigrants in all cosmopolitan metropoles provide organized informal support for such action and constitute an important feature of the social relations of late twentieth-century urban life.

In Britain, a similar phenomenon is evident among the indigenous as well as the immigrant population. Since the attempt by the British government to impose the poll tax, a large and growing proportion of people with citizenship rights have chosen not to register as electors, and hence have effectively sacrificed their democratic entitlements. The original reason for doing this was to resist a tax that was widely perceived as unfair, often as part of a co-ordinated protest movement, but it now seems that many individuals prefer the autonomy and anonymity of remaining unregistered, as well as the tax saving this involves. The 1991 census is reckoned to have missed some 4 per cent of the population, and up to 30 per cent of young men in some districts (Brown, 1995).

This example illustrates the dynamic of inclusion and exclusion in current economic conditions. The government attempted to include the whole of the population in its tax base; the aim of the poll tax was to impose responsibility for taxation policies, by making even the growing number of claimants of means-tested benefits liable for part of the amount payable by each citizen. Yet the actions of a substantial group of (mainly young, mobile) individuals, many of them linked together in networks for common purposes, both defeated this objective by defection, and created the links out of which other collective resistance movements could be co-ordinated. In 1993–4, the campaign against the Criminal Justice Act brought together a large number of such groups in a series of protest demonstrations that in turn merged into the various actions against the export of live animals at the end of 1994 and the beginning of 1995.

The important thing to notice about these is that they have taken place outside the framework of formal politics – indeed, the official opposition parties did not support these forms of resistance to the poll tax or the Criminal Justice Act. Collective action was directed against the government, but largely by people who had traded in their formal political rights in favour of the freedom to organize in new ways, in part made possible by such technological innovations as computer networks and electronic communications. In other words, the traditional analysis of citizenship could not capture either the purposes or the methods involved in these forms of collective action. Indeed, although many of the most active participants were poor, in terms of the measurements used by social policy analysis, they were not protesting about their poverty, or seeking remedies through the programmes of government agencies. Instead they were challenging the attempt by central government to impose institutional constraints on the lives of citizens, and seeking new forms of collective organization outside the framework of the labour market and the state.

But there is another price to be paid for the analysis of poverty and social exclusion in terms of citizenship, especially within the liberal tradition, and that is the narrow focus of this concept on individual rights and responsibilities, at the expense of interdependency and collective action. Indeed, the whole debate about 'social citizenship' has been largely diverted into this cul-de-sac – the search for a 'balance' between rights and responsibilities conceived as formal reciprocities between individual members of market-orientated political systems (N. Barry, 1990; Plant, 1990). This straitjacket was successfully imposed by such neo-conservative academics as Lawrence Mead (1986), who insisted on the 'social obligations of citizenship' in relation to the relief of poverty, and used these as a justification for restricted entitlement and increased conditionality in welfare administration. Instead of rebutting the premises of this analysis, proponents of social citizenship have imposed upon themselves the task of justifying their programmes in terms of 'duties' to correspond to the 'rights' given by income maintenance systems. This was in large part the framework adopted by the British opposition parties' Commission on Social Justice (Borrie, 1994), and it has also influenced thinking in several European countries (Adriaansens and Dercksen, 1993).

In this chapter I shall argue that the established methods of social policy analysis have become locked into an argument between economic individualism (drawing on the liberal tradition's repertoire of arguments about moral hazard and adverse selection in the benefits system, and asserting the laws of the self-regulating market) and the compulsory collectivism of the welfare state. This leaves little scope for the study of changing social relations, especially new forms of collective action that are highly relevant to the explanation of poverty and social exclusion.

TWO TRADITIONS

Perhaps the simplest way to define the difference between the two traditions of social policy analysis in their post-war form is that Continental scholars study the welfare state as an organizing principle for societies, and Anglo-Saxons study it as a response to the socially undesirable consequences of market interactions (or an interference with the effective operation of markets). What Continental social theorists have in common is a critical analysis of the institutions of state power that combine regulation with public provision. Both German and French schools of social science have been enormously influential upon British and, to a lesser extent, American sociology. But they have been deployed to analyse social relations, including relations of governance, other than those of poverty. In that field, economics and public administration remain the primary theoretical influences.

This is not to say, of course, that German and French social theory has not changed the Anglo-Saxon academic discipline of social policy studies; a glance at any British journal in that discipline would rebut such a claim. What they have done is to enrich and deepen the analysis of the state, and of the workings of governance (for instance, the interpenetration of the public and private spheres through the development of welfare agencies). However, these developments have scarcely touched the analysis of *poverty* within that discipline's tradition, and sociologists have given little attention to it as a topic in the past 20 years. They appear to regard other forms of exclusion as more fertile ground for the study of *social* processes; poverty is seen as a matter of *administrative* inclusion or exclusion.

By contrast, economics has gained ground as an influence on social policy studies, especially in the United States, during this period. The American academic and political agendas have echoed the traditional concerns of liberal political economy that have existed since the late eighteenth century: 'the impact of poor relief . . . on work motivation, labour supply and family life; and the limits of social obligation' (Katz, 1989, p. 4). This helps to explain the easy transition of ideologies and policies (such as those of the New Right) in both directions between the US and Britain, and the close parallelism between research agendas. Consider for example the rediscovery of poverty in the US (Harrington, 1962) and Britain (Townsend and Abel Smith, 1965); the Great Society Antipoverty Programmes and the Community Development Projects (1965–70); the brief interest in negative income tax credits and tax credits (1970–3); the mounting criticisms of the welfare state and the development of a politics of cuts in welfare spending (1979–82); and the influence of Murray's (1984) concepts of underclass demoralization and dependency, and Mead's (1986) of social obligation and workfare.

However, there were also differences between the US and Britain, especially in the influence of research on policy. Haveman (1987) points out that US sociologists and anthropologists were so heavily criticized for their contribution to the 1960s anti-poverty agenda that research leadership passed in the 1970s to economists. Hence, 'the War on Poverty was conceived of as an economic war: the designs, debates, and the evaluations were all conducted in economic terms. Economics was the central discipline in both the notion and the research components of the war' (pp. 51–2). Between 1965 and 1980, annual federal spending on poverty-related research increased from $2.5 to $160 million (the latter equal to 30 per cent of all federal research and development spending). This rise in expenditure altered research priorities in the social sciences. Between 1962 and 1964, five leading economics journals published only three articles on poverty-related research; by 1971–3 the number had increased to 59. For five leading sociology journals, the increase was from 15 to 51 in the same period (Evanson, 1986). Much of this research was directed at questions about how anti-poverty programmes affected work incentives, and was carried out by economists. The Office for Economic Opportunity sponsored the famous Seattle–Denver income maintenance experiments, designed to test the effects of income guarantees on work incentives. Public policy analysis, a new discipline dominated by economists, produced ambiguous findings about these experiments (e.g. Robbins et al., 1980; Pechman and Timpane, 1975). These were interpreted to support the neo-classical and neo-conservative discourses of welfare that were developed in the 1980s.

In Britain, there was no such increase in government spending on poverty research, and no such interest by economists or sociologists. Sampling of the main British economics and sociology journals of the early 1970s shows a tiny number of articles on poverty in both disciplines. Poverty research remained the province of social policy researchers, working in the Fabian traditions of Titmuss and Townsend. New methods, involving the construction of large data sets from government surveys, and eventually in large initiatives to gather new data (such as the British Household Panel Study), were adapted from work done in the USA by econometricians, rather than forged out of British poverty studies. As the stars of neo-classical economics and neo-conservative politics waxed in Britain, and then in the USA, the Institute for Fiscal Studies and the Institute for Economic Affairs rose to prominence in the 1970s, and gained a larger share of influence for economic thought in policy studies. On both sides of the Atlantic, a fertile intellectual environment for the renaissance of these discourses of poverty was created, and transatlantic traffic in ideology and research findings increased. While the British opposition parties looked first to Scandinavia, then to Germany, and finally (in some desperation) to Japan (Coates, 1993, pp. 13–14) for social policy inspiration, governments in both countries looked back to the nineteenth-century origins of political economy for its principles.

Even among those in Britain who were most committed to defending the welfare state, the analysis of poverty was still framed in terms derived from the liberal rather than the Continental tradition – for instance, in P. Townsend's (1979) notion of the poverty line as level of resources required by individuals and households for participation in the customs, activities and pleasures generally available in a (market) society. The two traditions, seemingly intertwined and interdependent during the hegemony of welfare states and social democratic politics, had again diverged. The Continental European countries remained institutionally conservative, even though corporatist economic management proved less effective, and evidence of poverty grew. They saw post-war social institutions as necessary features of social integration, and directed research and policy towards combating social exclusion (Room, 1990). In Britain and the USA bold measures of institutional redesign were focused on welfare systems aimed at eliminating moral hazard, curbing bureaucratic expansionism, cutting state expenditure, increasing work incentives, and restoring market mechanisms – the classic preoccupations of the liberal tradition.

In the liberal tradition, even in the reluctant collectivism of Keynes and Beveridge, social legislation and redistribution must always be accountable to the laws of the market, to show that economic management and welfare provision do not attempt to overthrow their inexorable logic. In this sense, redistributive institutions and measures for inclusion always have a *provisional* character; their functioning is conditional on market factors. Social policies – even those that command massive popular support, such as the American New Deal, or the Labour government's post-war programme – are seen as responses to particular economic circumstances (unemployment, post-war reconstruction) rather than institutional means for securing societal goals. It is a remarkably irony that the German electorate clings so tenaciously to the social institutions that were imposed upon it in defeat by occupying forces, while the British under Margaret Thatcher have radically redesigned all those that were democratically adopted at that same time, and reverted to a pre-war tradition of budgetary constraint and obedience to the laws of the market.

Within the logic of liberalism, poverty is not seen as a form of social exclusion but as the impersonal and inescapable operation of economic forces at the microlevel. To interfere with such processes is to distort and dislocate nature's way of allocating resources and ensuring productive effort. Joseph Townsend was the first and crudest evangelist of this creed, claiming that

> hunger is not only peaceable, silent, unremitting pressure, but, as the most natural motive to industry and labour, it calls forth the most powerful exertions; and, when satisfied by the free bounty of another, lays lasting and sure foundations for good will and gratitude . . . The free man should be left to his own judgement, and discretion; should be protected in the full enjoyment of his own, be it much or little; and punished when he invades his neighbour's property. (1786, p. 57).

This passage illustrates the close connection in liberalism (since Locke) between exclusive private property and the natural law of poverty. Private property, made possible by the invention of money and the enclosure of 'improved' land, is both justifiable because higher productivity trickles down to the poorest, and necessary because it enables freedom of choice within the protected circle of the individual's rights to non-interference. Compulsory measures for redistribution represent unjustifiable claims against private property, and unsustainable attempts to increase individuals' incomes without industry or improvement. Hence the apparent exclusion that is involved in private estates and the dismantling of shared resources for common use is in reality the means to greater prosperity for all, so long as the poor are not protected from the natural consequences of their actions by laws promising them unearned subsistence.

The Poor Law Report of 1834 expressed the same view in slightly less abrasive terms, in its condemnation of the Speenhamland system:

> It appears to the pauper that the Government has undertaken to repeal, in his favour, the ordinary laws of nature; to enact that the children shall not suffer for the misconduct of their parents, the wife for that of the husband, or the husband for that of the wife; that no-one shall lose the means of comfortable subsistence, whatever be his indolence, prodigality or vice: in short, that the penalty which, after all, must be paid by some one for idleness and improvidence, is to fall, not on the guilty person or on his family, but on the proprietors of the lands and houses encumbered by his settlement. Can we wonder if the uneducated are seduced into approving a system which aims its allurements at all the weakest parts of our nature – which offers marriage to the young, security to the anxious, ease to the lazy, and impunity to the profligate? (Checkland and Checkland, 1974, p. 135)

In such passages, the rhetoric of Charles Murray and Lawrence Mead, Margaret Thatcher and Newt Gingrich, is instantly recognizable. The irony, of course, is that the system that the Commissioners were condemning was not so much the classic public assistance (welfare) of the 1970s, but the mishmash of selective and conditional poor relief and welfare-to-work schemes that is evolving in the US and Britain in the 1990s. It is liberalism's obsession with 'compulsory inclusion' – the imposition of work obligations through official systems of wage subsidization and forced labour – that leads it cyclically into a morass of conditionality, surveillance, selection and enforcement which, in turn, drives up the social costs of public provision.

Even the most human face of liberalism bears the stamp of these antecedents. John Stuart Mill, a very fair-minded critic of Continental social theory and socialist political programmes, still insisted that the laws of production and population should govern the resources available to be distributed. As far as the principles for such distribution were concerned, 'That is a matter for human institution solely. Things once there, mankind, individually or collectively, can do with them as they like.' However, the *consequences* of distribution 'are as little arbitrary, and have as much the character of physical laws, as the laws of production' (Mill, 1848, bk. II, ch. i, sec. 1). He feared that under communist or socialist systems, guaranteed subsistence would weaken or eliminate 'prudential restraint on the multiplication of mankind' (II, i, 3). Hence he favoured the protection of private property, the 'less eligibility' principle in poor relief, and *laissez-faire* in public policy and administration:

> To give profusely to the people, whether under the name of charity or of employment, without placing them under such influences that prudential motives shall act powerfully upon them, is to lavish the means of benefiting mankind, without attaining the object. (II, xii, 2)

Keynes and Beveridge seemed to have found a way of employing these means without removing that disciplinary influence. Keynes insisted that economic management focused on *aggregates*, not individuals, and did not require an institutional shift into state socialism (1936, p. 378). Beveridge argued that social insurance and full employment were consistent 'with the proviso that all essential citizen liberties are preserved' (1944, p. 29). But their very willingness to make themselves accountable to 'natural' economic laws indicated that they worked within this tradition. The institutions that they inspired were always vulnerable to a demonstration that they interfered with the self-regulation of markets and the self-discipline of citizens – precisely the attack mounted by the New Right in the 1970s and 1980s.

In the Continental tradition all this is beside the point. It is not the individual's level of resources that matters, nor his or her independence, autonomy, prudence or competence. It is the poor person's relationship to the family, the community and the state that is of primary importance. Membership is the key concept: 'Just as the family . . . finds in the community its universal substance and subsistence, conversely the community finds in the family the formal element in its own realization' (Hegel, 1807, p. 478). 'When men are thus dependent on one another and reciprocally related to one another in their work and the satisfaction of their needs, subjective self-seeking turns into a contribution to the needs of everybody else' (Hegel, 1821, p. 129). 'Since the state is mind objectified, it is only as one of its members that the individual himself has objectivity, genuine individuality, and an ethical life' (p. 156).

Hence social provision was primarily concerned with *inclusion* rather than redistribution, and with membership rather than individual rights. For example, Bismarck's social insurance schemes, copied in most Continental European countries before a modified insurance principle was adopted in the Anglo-Saxon ones, were an *alternative* to full political and civil rights, and a measure to check both liberalism and socialism:

> His central political consideration was not the creation of new rights, consistent with a new interpretation of the rights of citizenship, but the preservation of the traditional relationship of the individual to the state. In a sense, social rights were granted to prevent having to grant political rights . . . The whole thrust of his measures was to preserve the traditional system of political inequality. (Rimlinger, 1971, p. 112)

Within this tradition, the normative role of the state is to give significance, cohesiveness and purpose to the activities carried out by individuals in civil society. Corporatism is an institutionalized way of representing individuals in decision-making pressures; the welfare state was designed to include individuals as producer groups through their membership of hierarchically ordered corporate bodies. Poverty becomes a social problem when citizens, through their economic circumstances, lose membership, representation and hence integration in the corporate life of the community, and in the state.

THE DEFINITION AND MEASUREMENT OF POVERTY

Poverty was 'rediscovered' in the United States (Harrington, 1962), in Britain (Townsend and Abel Smith, 1965) and somewhat later in Europe (Engberson and Van der Veen, 1987; Leibfried and Tennstedt, 1985), after a period when it was widely assumed to have been banished by the welfare state. This section will not attempt to review the copious literature of the debate that followed. It will instead argue that the terms of this were set by the agendas of the liberal tradition, by focusing on poverty lines, social minima and relative deprivation rather than social interaction. The literature of the liberal tradition was mainly concerned with the definition and measurement of poverty, and explaining its persistence in welfare states as a failure of social security systems.

In Britain this whole debate was dominated by Peter Townsend's major study of *Poverty in the United Kingdom* (1979), based on research that started in the late 1960s. He aimed to break out of the liberal tradition by arguing that poverty should be defined in terms of *relative* deprivation: that is, the lack of resources for playing the roles, participating in the relationships and following the customs expected of members of that society. The hypothesis that he investigated, and claimed to confirm in his study, was that a certain modest level of resources (above the social assistance rate but within range of possible upratings of universal benefits) would give an income sufficient for this kind of participation, but that below this threshold of income, 'withdrawal or exclusion from active membership of society becomes disproportionately accentuated' (Townsend, 1993, p. 36). The idea that modest universal benefits could prevent exclusion well reflected the Beveridge model of the welfare state (Esping-Andersen, 1990), and provided the intellectual basis for various 'New Beveridge' programmes among British opposition groups.

Townsend's definition was aimed at displacing the older sub-sistence and basic needs concepts, used in earlier British research (Rowntree, 1901; 1918) and many international com-parisons (Brandt Report, 1980). Thus the *relativism* of his con-cept of deprivation lay in the social construction of what constituted adequate shelter, warmth, privacy, space, diet, hygiene and so on; but he insisted that basic human needs had some core *objectivity*, which could be identified and measured by social scientists:

> Perceptions which are filtered through, or fostered by, the value or belief systems of sectional groups, the style or the whole com-munity can never be regarded as sufficiently representative of 'reality out there'. There have to be forms of 'objective' observa-tion, investigation and comparison against which they may be checked (even if these standards remain necessarily incomplete as well as necessarily creatures of socially produced modes of scien-tific thought). (Townsend, 1972, p. 48)

Since the publication of his 1979 study, there have been a vari-ety of criticisms of his attempt to define and measure poverty in these ways, all of which have drawn attention to the apparent con-tradiction between a definition in terms of social activities and relationships, and a method of measurement in terms of material resources. Piachaud (1987) pointed out that Townsend's research consisted of a survey of households' 'styles of living', followed by the construction of a 'deprivation index' – an apparently arbitrary list of items (consumption goods, amenities and activities) with no obvious rationale for their selection or links with poverty – and a demonstration of the point, at around 150 per cent of the social assistance benefit standard, where 'deprivation' (thus measured) seemed to increase rapidly. Piachaud argued that this did not resolve the problem of cultural variations and preferences, or demonstrate convincingly the existence of a poverty threshold. Since the aim of anti-poverty policies was always to increase opportunity and choice, and thus presumably *diversity* in 'styles of living', it was perverse to try to measure it as if there could be a single index of items indicating poverty.

Sen (1983), addressing poverty in countries with very different standards of living, argued that there was an irreducible element of absolute need in any viable conception of poverty. He suggested that Townsend had confused the lack of certain commodities in households with their *capabilities* to meet social conventions, participate in social activities, and retain self-respect. The latter were absolute requirements for full membership of a society, as implied in Townsend's definition, whereas what he was measuring was relative standards (inequalities) in resources and incomes. This point was echoed by Ringen (1988), who, in a wider critique of international estimates of poverty, criticized their reliance on income as an 'indirect' measure of poverty, even though the definition was in quite other terms.

These criticisms prompted Mack and Lansley (1984) to seek another definition of the poverty line, and another way of measuring deprivation. They surveyed the general population to seek a consensual view of the 'necessities of life' in current British society, and then measured whether a sample of low-income families could afford them. Poverty was thus defined as 'an enforced lack of socially perceived necessities', and they too discovered that there was a level of income (just above the rate of social assistance) at which this appeared to increase sharply. Another way of showing how far many households' incomes fell short of such standards was to research the needs and costs of families of different sizes and compositions, living in different regions, to discover a 'modest but adequate' family budget standard. In 1985 Bradshaw, Atkinson and Parker initiated the Family Budget Unit, following American research precedents, to discover what was needed to 'satisfy prevailing standards . . . for health, efficiency, the nurture of children and for participation in community activities', based on expert normative judgements (for example, by nutritionists) and empirical analysis of actual expenditure patterns (Family Budget Unit, 1990).

All these attempts to link a particular level of income with a form of social exclusion reflect a strong requirement in the liberal tradition: to establish *poverty* as a condition for redistribution. In the effort to overthrow the most restrictive version of this tradition (the legacy of Malthus, Chadwick and Spencer, manifested in present-day authors such as Murray), researchers feel impelled to prove that the poor constitute an identifiable category within the population, distinguishable by their wants, and handicapped by these in their attempts to live as full and competent members of the community. This community, in turn, is assumed to be one in which economic relations, if not specifically market ones, predominate. The welfare state was justified (by Beveridge) primarily in terms of the evidence of poverty in the interwar years; hence poverty had to be 'rediscovered' to justify further measures of redistribution, and fresh evidence (of its persistence and growth) adduced to sustain arguments for such a programme, through the work of a Poverty Lobby (McCarthy, 1986; Whiteley and Winyard, 1987).

The irony of this is that it plays into the hands of the very opponents against whom it is directed. Although researchers and the Poverty Lobby in Britain are always careful to present the case for raising the rates of universal, flat-rate benefits, and especially child benefit, it is too easy for governments to argue that any increase in redistributive measures should be 'targeted' on the poor. This happened in the late 1960s, when the 'rediscovery' of poverty and the foundation of the Child Poverty Action Group was immediately followed by the introduction of the first housing benefits for which those in low-paid employment were eligible (rent and rate rebates) under the then Labour government, and soon afterwards by that of Family Income Supplement (a benefit for low-paid full-time employees with children) under the Conservative administration. In the 1980s the Thatcher government shifted income maintenance provision very substantially towards such means-tested provision, arguing that it was the most effective way to reach those most in need.

In the United States, it was these public assistance programmes that proved most politically vulnerable in the 1980s. While social insurance was largely insulated from the drive to cut public expenditure during the Reagan presidencies, the attack on 'welfare' was directed against means-tested programmes, and especially Aid to Families with Dependent Children. As will be argued later in this chapter, the neo-liberal and neo-conservative critiques of these forms of income maintenance stood the Poverty Lobby's evidence on its head, by accepting that the poor *are* a distinguishable category, and that what distinguishes them is their dependent and deviant behaviour, promoted by the conditions under which they receive welfare payments.

In the Continental European tradition, of course, there is far less emphasis on poverty as the justification for social security systems. To a large extent, social insurance redistributes *within* social status groupings over the stages of the life-cycle; rates of benefits are related to earnings, and thus there are wide differentiations, and the overall pattern of distribution is not egalitarian. Such systems emphasize the inclusive nature of social security institutions as aspects of corporatist social regulation.

More recently, research on poverty has been influenced by work in the US, as numbers claiming social assistance have risen rapidly. In the Netherlands, studies of claimants' strategies (Engberson, Schuyt and Timmer, 1993) responded to the work of W. J. Wilson (1987) and J. C. Scott (1990). In Germany, Leibfried et al. (1995) conducted longitudinal studies of social assistance claimants, to show that a large proportion moved in and out of poverty, thus confirming work by Duncan (1984) and Bane and Ellwood (1986).

Theory and research on poverty in the United States and Britain thus face a difficult dilemma. They are trapped in a tradition where discourses of poverty are double-edged. Without a demonstration that there is a category of people whose lack of resources damages their capacity to participate in a market environment, research evidence is unlikely to win widespread support for redistributive policies. But this same evidence can be used to justify selective assistance, which in turn is the most vulnerable to ideological assault and, hence, to political pressure.

INEQUALITY AND SOCIAL SECURITY

Yet the Continental European countries have not been insulated from concerns about poverty, or from the arguments and analyses developed in the United States and Britain. In all these advanced capitalist economies, inequalities in incomes have tended to increase since the early 1990s, and more individuals and households have fallen through the various systems of social security designed to protect them, and into social assistance. In Europe this phenomenon is referred to as 'new poverty' (Room, 1990). Despite more generous benefits and systems of employment protection (or perhaps, as neo-liberal critics would argue, because of them), some European countries have also had higher levels of unemployment than the United States and Britain since the early 1980s, and this in turn has caused political concern, and a reassessment of social security systems.

Whereas it is extremely difficult to prove that poverty is an identifiable condition characterized by specific forms of exclusion, it is rather easier to demonstrate that inequality of incomes has grown. Townsend uses official statistics from the United States and Britain to show that the share of total disposable income of the richest 20 per cent of the population rose by 3.1 and 8 per cent respectively between 1979 and 1989, while that of the poorest fell by 0.8 and 1 per cent. In the same period, the average annual disposable income *per person* of the richest 20 per cent rose by 20.4 and 40.3 per cent respectively, while that of the poorest fell by 2.1 per cent in the US, and in the UK stayed constant, while that of the poorest 10 per cent fell by 5.7 per cent (Townsend, 1993, table 1.2, p. 15).

Since this kind of evidence is readily available, and has often been used by international organizations such as the EC, the OECD, the ILO and the World Bank, economists in Britain (Desai and Shah, 1988; Lewis and Ulph, 1988) and the Netherlands in particular (Hagenaars, 1985; de Vos and Hagenaars, 1988; Van Praag and Teekens, 1992) have used various methods that take income as a proxy for poverty. Although these methods have been criticized (Stark, 1988; Atkinson, 1989), they are more likely to gain acceptance outside the liberal tradition, with its inbuilt scepticism over arguments for redistribution derived from inequality alone.

Furthermore, econometric studies pioneered in the United States have subsequently been applied to the comparative analysis of income data (Smeeding et al., 1990). These methods have influenced the European Commission, which accepts estimates that poverty grew from 30 million to 44 million inhabitants of its members states between 1981 and 1987 (O'Higgins and Jenkins,

1987), and has launched a series of anti-poverty programmes. The Commission has also, through Eurostat, sought to improve its statistical indicators of poverty, and has funded studies to test the utility of different poverty lines in seven EC countries (Deleeck, 1991; 1992).

However, of greatest concern to theorists and researchers in Continental European countries has been the growing evidence of 'dualization' in income maintenance provision – the split between the earnings-related social insurance coverage enjoyed by regular workers, and the means-tested social assistance schemes on which those who are marginal to the labour market are forced to depend. This division, which has become institutionalized in the United States (Skocpol, 1988), is increasingly evident, even in the Scandinavian countries (Marklund 1988; 1992), and in the Netherlands, where it is linked with the growth in long-term unemployment and single-parent households (Netherland Scientific Council, 1985). If it occurs in these countries, which spend the highest proportion of their national incomes on social protection, this phenomenon is clearly evidence that the welfare state project faces a serious challenge.

Significantly, Continental European scholars are more likely to perceive this challenge in terms of social exclusion than poverty alone, and to relate it to developments in the labour market. In Germany, for example, Negt (1985) estimated that official unemployment at around 8 per cent accounted for less than half of all those of working age dependent on public transfers; another 15 per cent were outside the labour market for six months or more of each year, including early retirement schemes, invalidity benefits, job creation schemes and social assistance. He argued that much the same proportions held in other European countries. Møller (1989) demonstrated that these proportions held in Denmark from 1984 to 1990. Reviewing these findings, Abrahamson concludes:

> Chances are that new cultures of poverty develop, especially within the cities of the old industrial metropolises. If the creation of cultures of poverty spread, so does the chances of social disintegration, social unrest, etc., which, in turn, may be a threat to the social order. (1992, p. 24)

In Britain, a great proportion of research resources during the same period has been devoted to analysing the operation of the income maintenance system, criticizing the government's changes in it, and monitoring new arrangements. While a number of studies have reviewed the workings of the whole system (Berthoud, 1984; Hill, 1990), a larger number have been concerned with the operation of particular benefits, such as family credit (Corden and Craig, 1991) or the social fund (Berthoud, 1990; Stewart and Stewart, 1989). Monitoring of 'winners and losers' is carried on through prestigious bodies such as the Institute for Fiscal Studies, and a host of local authority, voluntary agency and higher educational units (G. Craig, 1992). Another important theme has been low take-up of means-tested benefits (P. Craig, 1991), one of the main arguments with which those who advocate modest universalism can rebut the dominant policy themes of selectivity and conditionality.

British research is thus characteristically more concerned with the success or failure of social security systems in delivering income to claimants, and usually less with the social relations that are constructed through these systems. The exception to this is the growing volume of research on gender and poverty, focusing on inequalities of resources within households, and between households headed by men and those headed by women. Until the later 1980s, social policy studies neglected these issues, partly because they tended to use households as their units of account, and made the uncritical assumption that incomes were pooled and resources shared (or that it was methodologically impossible to determine the extent to which pooling and sharing occurred). These assumptions were undermined by research on households allocations (J. Pahl, 1988; Graham, 1987; Brannen and Wilson, 1987), and the recognition that men tended to earn, control and consume more than women, and women to manage aspects of household expenditure, often denying themselves a share of consumption. The study of women's poverty is now a well-established topic in social policy (Glendinning and Millar, 1992), and the analysis of this phenomenon seeks explanations in labour-market, kinship and household relations. However, as Jenkins (1991) points out, the insights from these developments are not always incorporated into other methods and topics.

It would be absurd to try to summarize the great variety of methods, topics and traditions encompassed by theory and research on income inequality and income maintenance systems. As a broad generalization, however, it seems that Continental European scholars are becoming more concerned about poverty as it grows apparent that the institutions of the regulated labour market and social insurance do not include the whole population within their compass, and hence that a new status of exclusion, with new risks of alienation and social disintegration, is developing. Evidence of poverty, provided through statistics on income inequality and through numbers claiming social assistance, is part of this disturbing picture. In Britain and the United States, by contrast, the institutional divisions between fiscal, occupational social insurance and public assistance systems are so deeply entrenched that social policy is seldom seen as a primary means of social integration. The 'social division of welfare' (Titmuss, 1958) is not so much a research topic as an assumption in the liberal tradition (Esping-Andersen, 1990).

CITIZENSHIP AND SOCIAL INTEGRATION

This may help to explain why – particularly in Britain – citizenship emerged as an important theme in social policy studies during the latter 1980s, and why, in the wake of the anxieties about social integration in Continental Europe, this theme has been taken up there. The reference point for this renewed interest was T. H. Marshall's (1950) analysis of the establishment of social rights through welfare states. But the central issue about his historical account of the broadening of citizenship as membership was the dynamic between social and civil and political rights. In his very Anglo-Saxon, liberal version of this development, civil and political rights provide the framework of liberty and democracy which is then complemented by social rights, granting 'equality of status, though not of income' (p. 56). A Continental European account, using the German case for instance, would be far more likely to emphasize the inclusive, integrative and regulatory function of social provision (only much later balanced by the individual freedoms of full civil rights), and the collective self-rule of democratic politics (Rimlinger, 1971).

Once welfare states were established, these historical differences could for the time being be ignored; democratic citizenship with social rights seemed to provide a largely similar basis for membership in all the advanced capitalist countries, and few social policy studies made use of the concept. But when the United States and British governments responded to the global economic changes of the final quarter of this century by limiting social rights and welfare expenditures, opposition to these policies required a broader normative framework within which to criticize them. The notion of citizenship provided such a framework, and a supply of evaluative concepts (notably *justice*) with which to analyse these developments. The advantage of these was that they derived from the liberal tradition of political thought, but had been refined in the era of welfare states to take account of those social institutions. A notable example was John Rawls's *Theory of Justice* (1970), which seemed to provide many arguments with which to criticize the Thatcher and Reagan reforms.

The interesting point about this theoretical turn was that it reorientated the social policy debate towards issues of *social integration*, but by a route that was the characteristic liberal one. In this tradition, the notion of citizenship implied that political integration (democratic membership and participation in the collective self-rule of free individuals) was the primary means of social integration. Hence the analysis of social relations is conducted in terms of a moral and political order, mediated by abstract nouns rather than social institutions: it is more philosophical than sociological. This can be recognized especially in the work of Plant (1988; 1990; 1994), Dahrendorf (1988; 1990) and Marquand (1988; 1991). It contrasts with Continental European concern about institutional systems of social regulation (Luhmann, 1977), and with integration through the labour market and social insurance as the basis of citizenship (Coenen and Leisink, 1993).

The theory of citizenship starts from the search for universal principles of justice, accepted as morally binding by all members of the polity, and offsetting the fragmentation implicit in both globalization and social polarization. Since the working class – the focus for the collective action that led to social democratic institutions – can no longer provide the basis for redistributive policies or social order, some other general principles are needed to supply this (Plant, 1991). Modern liberal theory argues that social citizenship constitutes a set of principles that everyone in a society has reason to accept (J. Rawls, 1989; 1993). Questions of political justice can be discussed on the same basis by all citizens, whatever their social position, or more particular aims and interest, or their religious, philosophical or moral view (J. Rawls, 1987, p. 6). So in place of the embryonic individuals, still ignorant of their future endowments and life chances, who made a self-interested 'contract' to guarantee each other's liberties and a degree of mutual protection in Rawls's earlier theory, these *citizens*, whatever their divergent beliefs and practices, are able to agree about the principles of justice, and thus agree on a framework of political institutions, because of an 'overlapping consensus'.

This implies that individuals have good reasons to give priority to political membership as a principle of social organization over all other principles and interests. But it does not give a convincing account of what these reasons are, or why they should override commitments to mutually antagonistic groupings (around issues of faith, ethnicity or any other principles), and thus to fundamental conflicts. It also implies that citizens will be motivated to use their democratic rights to address collective-action problems, and that public policy is the most suitable instrument for overcoming the unintended (and unjust) consequences of individual strategies within market or informal interactions. Yet – as we saw in the last chapter – the associations and interdependencies that constitute much of the cultural life of advanced capitalist societies are explicable in terms of a dynamic of inclusion and exclusion that transcends citizenship. Mass migration and the social organization of legal and illegal immigrants in cosmopolitan cities provide the strongest evidence that political membership is not the principle to which the highest priority is given.

The largely orderly nature of most interactions within such immigrant communities, and between members of these and indigenous groups, suggests that political membership is not the most important element in social integration either. Indeed, issues of citizenship are the focus of conflict in such a cosmopolitan environment. Citizenship is a concept that serves to define members and exclude non-members, or at least to differentiate the population into full members, denizens (those with residence and some other rights, but not political rights), and aliens. Where there is scarcity and competition, nationality (often as a cloak for racism) becomes an organizing principle for conflict-orientated action. The vote in 1994, to exclude the children of illegal immigrants from Californian schools and health care (see p. 38), was an example of this. In 1995, the British Home Secretary announced that staff in social security, housing and the National Health Service would be trained to report to immigration authorities anyone suspected of being a 'temporary or illegal' immigrant and claiming these benefits (House of Commons, 1995, cols 1027–8).

This indicates that the social citizenship of welfare states – essentially institutional systems for defending the employment security and living standards of national citizens against international competition – now cuts across the populations of advanced capitalist societies in complex ways. The strongest arguments against free mobility and equal rights within an internationalized political environment are mobilized in terms of social citizenship (Bauböck, 1991). Yet post-war structures for employment and social protection do not effectively include the indigenous population; they defend the much reduced working classes of rich states against the claims of the poor, at home and abroad. Despite restrictive definitions of citizenship and considerable organized antagonism, immigrants forgo political rights (and, in the case of illegal immigrants, social rights also) to come and 'claim their foreign aid for themselves'.

But interest in citizenship as an organizing principle is not confined to those who seek justifications for social democratic institutions. It has also been taken up in two quite different ways by the political Right. First, in Britain particularly, a minimalist version has been developed, to try to capture the mutual obligations of individuals and public servants – the Citizen's Charter (D. Taylor, 1992). Here the ideal is not political consensus and social integration but pluralism, diversity and the pursuit of choice, the decentralization of decisions and insulation of individual agents achieved by markets. Hence the structure of public agencies should allow citizens as 'customers' to express their preferences, and gain reliable access to a bundle of goods, supplied through quasi-market mechanisms. This implies that social services have no specific function in relation to social order; they are simply ways of overcoming market failure.

In the early 1980s, the theorists of this relationship between citizens and the state sought a new medium (such as vouchers) through which as 'consumers' they could signal their preferences for such goods as education, health and community care. When this radical approach was rejected by the government, individuals' scope for 'choice' was narrowed to strategic action. Given that government reforms led to much greater variation in local standards of provision, and higher visibility of such variations, people could move to areas where their preferred bundles of public goods were available. This 'voting with the feet' (Tiebout, 1956) accentuated social polarization, as better-off households left the inner city for the suburbs, or concentrated in 'gentrified' city districts (see chapter 5). Meanwhile, those denied this option, who relied on the state for income and services, developed strategies for maximizing claims and minimizing contributions.

In the USA, where these tendencies had been evident for longer (Miller, 1981; W. J. Wilson, 1987), theory of citizenship was developed by conservatives, seeking a normative basis for policies to counteract the latter strategies. In this way the liberal analysis of social citizenship rights is stood on its head: the obligations of membership must be reasserted, to 'balance' the entitlements given by the welfare state (Mead, 1986, p. 246). In the American debate, this view is now part of a 'new consensus' (Novak et al., 1987) on family, work and welfare – that the very existence of social rights for the poor entails responsibilities, and that the obligations of citizenship should be enforced by welfare agencies, as part of a programme for social integration.

This view goes beyond C. Murray's (1984) account of the moral hazard and perverse incentives (to lone parenthood, large family size and work avoidance) in welfare systems. It argues that unconditional benefits or weak enforcement are the cause of cultural detachment of the poor, and that welfare policy and practice must insist on parental duties (Novak, 1987) such as child support, and work obligations, including training and work schemes as conditions for benefits (workfare). Thus citizenship provides a normative basis for policies aimed at social integration, but through the compulsory imposition of duties, not the implementation of rights.

This conservative interpretation has now come to dominate the political scene in the United States, strongly influencing President Clinton's legislative programme for the second half of his term. It is based on the perception of welfare dependence as strategic: 'joblessness reflects choice more than necessity' (Mead, 1988a, p. 265). But the analysis of this strategic element goes beyond a critique of the incentive structures of benefit systems. Mead points out that: 'Millions of immigrants, legal and illegal, have flooded in to the country, to do jobs for which, apparently, citizens are unavailable' (1989, p. 158). The strategy of welfare dependence, which has become part of a 'culture of poverty', relies for its persuasiveness on the ease with which the poor can get payments, in comparison with the effort required to stay in work. But Mead insists that it is a self-defeating strategy, and that it is not in the medium- or long-term interests of the poor to avoid work obligations in this way. Hence policies for stricter enforcement not only serve the purposes of society, by achieving social integration, but also the interests of the poor themselves, by increasing their income and self-esteem (Mead, 1988b, 1989).

AN ALTERNATIVE PERSPECTIVE

Both the view of social citizenship developed by opposition theorists in Britain, and the conservative analysis that is fashionable in the United States, see it as a means of social integration. But the former suggests this is achieved through rights, and especially those given through compulsory collective welfare systems, whereas the latter insists that it is through duties, the detailed enforcement of family and work obligations. Only the view implicit in the British government's Citizen's Charter regards citizenship as concerned with contracts for specific goods between government and individual members, and hence about preference and choice, not social integration.

In this section, I shall argue that the poverty and exclusion of a large group of inhabitants of advanced capitalist countries cannot usefully be analysed in terms of the rights or duties of citizenship. This is partly because, as was demonstrated in the last section, many immigrants from outside these countries are prepared to trade off their political and (in the case of undocumented migrants) social rights for the sake of economic opportunities, and to live without full citizenship as members of these societies. But it is also because the institutional structures of the United States and Britain in particular, but increasingly also of the European countries, provide opportunities, incentives and social supports for action outside the framework of social citizenship rights and duties, so that policies framed in these ways are increasingly irrelevant for certain groups.

This is most obviously the case with many young people. Social citizenship assumes that problems of social integration arise because they are not easily absorbed into the labour market and the social institutions that derive from it; hence policies should either seek to enable those forms of inclusion (by increasing employment opportunities and benefits) or to require them (by compulsory training and socialization). But what if young people have adapted to their exclusion from labour markets and benefits by seeking other sources of satisfaction, stimulation, meaning and security? What if they see formal employment as, at best, an instrumental means of pursuing these other goals, and at worst an irksome irrelevance? And what if the same applies to conventional family structures, and particularly to patterns of long-term financial dependence by women on men?

For these questions to be very critical for current theory and policy analysis it is not necessary to maintain that any one preoccupation or lifestyle has drawn a huge proportion of young people away from formal employment and family life. It is enough to show that a number of different sources of satisfaction – travelling, autonomy, drugs, mysticism – and a number of means (including crime) of pursuing them have allowed new forms of social organization to develop, especially among those with the least promising prospects within formal institutional structures (Beckett, 1995). The important point about this development is that those who organize their lives in these new ways do not all see it necessary to protest (for instance, by political demonstrations) against formal systems, unless these impinge directly on their values and lifestyles, but instead get on with seeking their own satisfactions strategically, using those parts of the formal institutional structure (of work and welfare) that are advantageous, and finding ways around the rules and regulations that limit them.

In Britain, the most obvious manifestations of the latter trend, among young people in particular, is the high rate of non-registration for elections – a device by which citizens hope to evade local taxes (originally the poll tax), particularly if their lifestyle involves frequent moves from place to place. But the increased mobility of a significant proportion of the younger population also manifests itself in other diverse phenomena – the New Age Traveller movement, begging, and homelessness. Whereas the former is usually constructed as a conscious rejection of mainstream lifestyles and goals, and the latter two as evidence of growing poverty and exclusion (or victimization), research evidence suggests that this distinction is spurious. Interviews by Bishopp, Canter and Stockley (1992) with 'homeless' young people showed that they were more likely to define themselves as 'on the move', and to value the autonomy and choice that this allowed them.

This evidence does not emerge from official statistics or large-scale surveys for quantitative analysis. It comes from qualitative research on the practices of young people, and from the numbers *missing* from official enumerations such as censuses, school rolls, and even benefit offices, as increasing numbers do not even bother to register for employment. The latter phenomenon is beginning to be recognized by policy-makers; in the north-east of England, the employment service is using unattached 'outreach' workers with a training in youth work to try to make contact with young people in deprived areas who no longer seek work through the public agency that is supposed to link them to the labour market.

Yet these important phenomena have not clarified the academic analysis of poverty and social exclusion, or the political debate, because both are locked into an unproductive and unilluminating conflict over the concept of the 'underclass'. The idea of a significant category of poor people who were distinguishable from the mainstream of society either by their behaviour (Mead, 1986; Gilder, 1986; C. Murray, 1989) or by their structural situation (W. J. Wilson, 1987; 1989) featured strongly in the American debate from the publication of Auletta's (1983) study of diverse groups who appeared not to 'assimilate to society'. The usefulness of this category has always been disputed by those who point to its dubious historical pedigree and links with racist and Social Darwinist thought (Piven and Cloward, 1977; MacNicol, 1990; Mann, 1991; Bagguley and Mann, 1992; Morris, 1994). Nevertheless, it has been widely used by both sides in the debate about citizenship – to draw attention to the erosion of social citizenship (Dahrendorf, 1988, 1990; Marquand, 1991; Jordan, 1989), and to denounce the poor's disdain for their obligations.

Thus the concept of an underclass is defined (or rejected) in terms of the liberal discourses of poverty, and disputed by reference to whether or not the poorest have identifiably distinctive attitudes (or structurally determined interests) towards the family and the labour market. This argument seems to imply that the social integration of the majority is achieved through these two institutions, and that there is an identifiable set of mainstream attitudes and orientations towards them from which the underclass deviates in measurable ways. It diverts attention from the detailed study of the diverse actions and strategies of many groups within society, both in relation to these and other institutional structures, and in relation to each other (Jordan and Redley, 1994). The idea of an underclass is useful in analysing one dimension of social exclusion, but this limited value certainly does not justify the amount of attention it has been given in the literature, or the attempt to explain all poor people's actions in terms of this structural factor, or their dependence on welfare benefits. Research attention could more usefully be directed at the economic rationality of their strategies (Jordan and Redley, 1994).

Focus on the concept of the underclass has distorted the investigation of poverty and social exclusion. For example, the evidence of attitude surveys has been used to claim that they do not have distinctive beliefs and cultural characteristics. Indeed, Heath (1991) points out that data from the British Social Attitudes Survey (1989) indicated that 'underclass' respondents were more positively orientated to work than others, and the British Election Survey revealed no distinctive political attitudes or behaviours. Yet there is often little correlation between what is said by respondents in such surveys and their everyday actions. Mead recognizes this in arguing that research evidence suggests poor people have ideals and intentions that belie their actual choices. 'Parents want their children to avoid trouble but lose control of them to a street life of hustling and crime. Children want to succeed but lack the discipline to get through school. Girls want to marry and escape poverty but succumb to pregnancy and welfare' (1988b, p. 65); they '*want* to work but feel they *cannot*' (p. 66). Mead uses this as evidence that the poor need the discipline and training provided by enforcement of conditions for welfare benefits.

This is sociologically naive. Any interview research, whether by means of survey, questionnaire or less structured in format, invites the respondents to display cultural competence within the public domain of that society. It calls on them to account for their situation in terms of the formal structure of institutions that regulate the sphere in question (A. W. Rawls, 1987; 1989), to demonstrate their knowledge about what is expected of someone like themselves, and explain their circumstances using cultural resources (meaningful repertoires of action). It should be no surprise that poor people justify their circumstances by reference to their efforts to find work and provide for their families; what is more interesting is how they go on to describe the ways they decide what to do, and how they are influenced by the particular opportunities and constraints that confront them (Jordan et al., 1992). Such accounts can therefore be compared with those of other groups, facing different institutional structures of incentives and costs, and pursuing different strategies (Jordan et al., 1994; Jordan and Redley, 1994).

Because the underclass debate has spawned a moralistic literature that constructs the poor as threatening, burdensome and a source of social contagion, many liberal researchers have avoided the investigation of poor people's actions, as likely to be used to add fuel to that view. Thus there has been very little research in Britain that captures the everyday lives of poor people in any dimension except their lack of material resources (Bradshaw and Holmes, 1989). Alternatively, researchers who do qualitative studies address a particular claim of the conservative camp – such as the 'dependency culture' (Dean and Taylor Gooby, 1992) – and seek to rebut it by showing that the aspirations and attitudes of welfare beneficiaries are much the same as those of other citizens. In the next chapter I shall use what evidence there is to argue that poor people have developed distinctive forms of social organization, and that these should be understood within a dynamic of inclusion and exclusion.

CONCLUSIONS

This chapter has consisted of a somewhat concentrated review of a vast literature on poverty and social exclusion. The focus has been on how all this rhetoric and research seems to miss certain aspects of social interaction that are more likely to be visible through journalism or personal observation than in formal discussions of the topic.

The Anglo-Saxon debate about poverty directs attention to the characteristics of individuals and households in a market environment, and to whether their lack of access to material resources precludes full and competent participation in society. The Continental debate about social exclusion deals mainly in the labour market and social insurance as compulsory, collective measures for social integration and regulation. The limitations of both these frameworks have encouraged the emergence of a newer one, about the rights and duties of citizenship. Here the contest is between those who draw on normative political theory to argue for more inclusive forms of social citizenship rights, and those who seek evidence from the study of marginal individuals that social welfare institutions are failing in their tasks of discipline and enforcement of the duties of citizenship.

All this leaves largely uninvestigated the fields of study that were opened up in the first two chapters. It seems strange that such methods as public-choice theory and qualitative sociological research should have been so little used in these domains. The explanation advanced in this chapter is that social policy studies, especially in the United States and Britain, have become locked into longstanding political traditions. Increasing inequalities in incomes have been used on one side to argue for more resources to be devoted to compulsory collective systems, and on the other to insist that these alone will not achieve the goals of government policy. A degree of consensus has emerged, particularly in the United States, around the need for stronger measures of enforcement in the welfare state, in order to achieve more effective social integration.

This implicitly acknowledges a problem over how the poor respond to formal institutional structures, whether these are new, deregulated labour markets or streamlined welfare systems. It indirectly recognizes that they have neither been adequately protected by existing social services, nor adequately rewarded by free-market initiatives. But it does not provide a convincing analysis for either of these phenomena, or encourage a deeper investigation of them. In the next two chapters I shall attempt to remedy these omissions.

4

Globalization and the Fragmentation of Welfare States

In this chapter I shall return to the task defined in chapter 2 – to explain the fragmentation of welfare states, and the decline in incomes of the poorest members of such societies, in terms of the dynamics of collective action within the global economic system. Using the theoretical framework developed in that chapter, national welfare states can be seen as collective actors in a world environment of competition between sovereign territorial polities, and also as institutional structures for co-ordinating the economies of such polities, and mobilizing their populations for such competition. The task is to show how interactions between individuals inside and outside welfare states (citizens and foreigners) transformed these institutional structures, and led to the impoverishment and exclusion of certain vulnerable people. It is also to reveal the hidden costs and unintended consequences of the policy programmes through which national governments and international regimes tried to steer or regulate these processes.

To make this task more manageable, in this chapter I shall focus mainly on interactions *within* the advanced industrialized welfare states, and draw most of my examples from just one of these, the United Kingdom. However, it is important to understand the processes that will be analysed here within the wider context of a changing global economic environment, so the chapter will start by setting the relevant interactions in their historical and comparative context – the collectivization of welfare provision in advanced industrialized economies, and its fragmentation within the past two decades.

Welfare states addressed the collective-action dilemmas of the interwar period – poverty, unemployment, the stalemate between capital and organized labour, the rise of communism and fascism, nationalism and militarism – in terms of new social institutions for managed economic growth and welfare distributions. Theoretically, they can be modelled as co-ordination games between the encompassing organizations for employers and employees and the state, through which the many prisoner's dilemmas of the 1930s were overcome. Yet their success rested in good measure on the somewhat autarkic nature of the national economies in the post-Second World War situation. Later, as world trade expanded and new technologies for international exchanges of all kinds were developed, these institutional systems were transformed by the action of external forces, which was mediated through interaction between their citizens. The fate of the poor depended on the totality of these interactions, the ways that rules and systems were changed, and the collective actions of groups inside and outside these rules.

The political transformations of the final quarter of this century, including the collapse of the Soviet and East European regimes, imply that when capital broke free of the constraints of national welfare-state games through new capacities for international mobility (some time between 1965 and 1975), this simultaneously transformed the strategic options open to individuals. It opened up the possibility of changes in the institutional structures of societies through which exchanges between individuals, rather than negotiations between collective actors, could become the most relevant determinants of outcomes. In an enormous variety of ways, some dramatic (as under the Thatcher governments in Britain) and some small and cumulative, all developed countries carried out such institutional changes. The last attempt to manage a fully integrated welfare state by processes well modelled in the post-war game collapsed with the Swedish Social Democratic government in 1992.

A microcosmic case study in this paradigm shift is provided by New Zealand. Until the mid-1970s, its economy was managed by corporatist methods, and its industries protected from overseas competition because of bilateral trade agreements with Britain. When Britain joined the European Community, New Zealand farmers had to compete in world markets; they could no longer afford to subsidize both industries and the welfare state. As consumers and voters, New Zealand citizens had to choose between continuing to rely on expensive and poor-quality home-produced manufactures, or the dislocations of opening up their economy to global forces. In the early 1980s, a Labour government chose the latter course. During the second half of that decade, the index of income inequality rose faster in New Zealand (at 1 per cent per year) than in any other OECD country, including Britain (0.75 per cent) in the Thatcher years (Barclay, 1995). The price of houses doubled in real terms in the 1980s; poor ghetto areas appeared; unemployment among Maoris rose to 25 per cent; prison populations soared.

The central point here is that the shift from relatively closed, managed or planned economies to comparatively open ones, once accomplished, increased the scope for individual exchange, and reduced the scope for government action. In the case of New Zealand, the shift was clearly made under a kind of duress, as its economy was faring badly and it was difficult to demonstrate the success of the old institutional structure. But in giving individuals more choices, the changes also made the links between interactions more opaque. The outcomes listed above were all (unintended) consequences of decisions by New Zealand citizens in voluntary exchanges – investing in Hong Kong, buying Japanese cars, taking holidays in Sri Lanka, and so on. Why should any one individual feel responsible for redundancies among fellow workers, or cuts in state benefits, when these can plausibly be represented as inevitable consequences of foreign competition?

When Margaret Thatcher proclaimed that 'there is no such thing as society, there are only individuals and families', she was appealing to a new sense of autonomy within such arrangements, and also to a new capacity to disown responsibility for poverty and unemployment. The New Right in the USA and Britain advocated policies to accelerate the shift, and give further scope for individual freedom, through policies of deregulation, privatization and benefits cuts.

The public-choice perspective was in the vanguard of the shift in theoretical analysis from a focus on interactions between collective actors over economic aggregates to one on exchanges between individuals (Buchanan, 1986b, pp. 20–3). It made heroic assumptions about the nature of agents – that they are rational and self-interested, seeking to maximize their utility subject to the constraints they face – and about interactions – that they can be explained in terms of voluntary agreements between such agents. This did not eliminate the need to study power, or to analyse the sources of economic power (implicit in the notion of *rents*). But it did provide a distinctive and appealing view of interaction in a number of alternative settings, that both helped to discredit the old paradigm, and provided arguments for these institutional transformations.

Social science has reflected this paradigm shift in many other ways. For example, in the 1980s, Marxist analysis moved towards methodological individualism in its explorations of class relations (Elster, 1985; Roemer, 1982). Sociologists identified 'late modern' or 'post-modern' tendencies in society that included the cultivation of choice (Bauman, 1992), the management of risk (Beck, 1992) and the pursuit of lifestyle politics at the expense of the 'emancipatory politics' of mass political movements (Giddens, 1991). Theory on social polarization recognized that this related to decisions at the level of informal household relations as well as in the economy (Gershuny, 1983; R. E. Pahl, 1984).

The present theoretical challenge is to find ways of capturing the new collective-action dilemmas that are posed by outcomes of millions of interactions between autonomous individuals. Social policy analysis has been particularly slow in moving in this direction. It has been largely locked within the old paradigm, still addressing government policies and welfare state institutions, and doing little to clarify how interactions produce new exclusions and interdependencies, or the social costs of new forms of individual and collective action.

What makes the required task especially difficult is that each of the institutional structures must be investigated to see how interactions within them can best be explained. It is only by looking in some detail at these structures and interactions that it is possible to make convincing links between the decisions of some (comfortably-off) citizens and the outcomes for other (poor) ones, or to measure the costs of social exclusion.

Furthermore, the analysis must introduce another theoretical element into the explanation of such interactions. Throughout the development of my theory of poverty and social exclusion so far, I have emphasized the dual character of social formations, as *institutions* for restraining competition among their members, and as *organizations* for mobilizing them in competition with others. In this chapter I shall focus on the forms and outcomes of such competition.

Within collective-action groups, individuals interact as members, whose mutual obligations can be understood in terms of the costs and benefits they share (ch. 2, pp. 48–62). In interactions with members of other groups, they respond in ways that exploit or conserve the gains associated with their membership of the relevant collective-action formation. So, for instance, individual trade unionists and employers interact strategically, in line with the incentives and constraints given by the wider interactions within and between their unions on the one side, and employer federations and cartels on the other.

Such interactions, between individuals and between groups, can be modelled as *games*, in which each party tries to maximize his or her *payoffs*, by taking account of the actions of the others (Binmore, 1992; Lyons, 1992). It is not necessary here to expand upon the theory of games, because the examples given in this chapter are extremely simple. The relevant point is that individuals and collective actors choose *strategically*, taking account of the strategies of their competitors. In this chapter, I shall attempt to model a number of policy issues as games, showing how the structure of the payoffs to the relevant actors shapes their strategies, and how this in turn explains the outcomes. The assumption behind both one-off and iterated (repeated) games is that they have an *equilibrium solution*, which represents the outcome when each player adopts his or her *best reply* to the others, taking account of their moves and strategies (in other words, no player can improve his or her payoff by adopting another strategy).

I shall also analyse post-war welfare states as games between capital, organized labour and the state, but show how these were transformed from co-ordination games about economic growth into noncooperative games about the distribution of incomes. I shall then show how the slowing of economic growth in advanced industrialized societies and the intensification of distributional conflicts led to institutional changes that in turn rewarded individuals for adopting new strategies in new collective-action units. Above all, these changes encouraged individuals in the mainstream of society to prioritize the household as the relevant social unit for interactions with others. I shall show how this affected economic and political relations, and how the poor in turn responded to these changes.

THE TRANSFORMATION OF WELFARE STATES

The examples chosen in this chapter come from education, the labour market and the benefits system, and the detailed analysis is all based mainly on British studies with some comparisons with the German case. In the education example, a club-theoretical explanation of the dynamic of interaction between parents within the systems established in the late 1980s seems most appropriate. In the labour-market example, what is to be explained is the polarized outcomes in the distribution of jobs between households (both between men and women on the one hand, and between job-rich and job-poor households). Here a game-theoretical analysis, involving strategic bargaining games between 'insiders' and 'outsiders', and between household partners, is adopted. Finally, the benefits example is modelled as a prisoner's dilemma game between claimants and the authorities over transaction costs.

The aim is to explain important features of social organization in terms of the actions and strategies of individual agents. There is ample evidence from every country of the decline of class and class-based organizations as the dominant forms of membership through which individuals define their identities and pursue their interests. However, alternative forms of association and collective action that have been claimed to replace class as organizing principles (notably 'new social movements') clearly do not provide the basis for an explanation of the phenomena of poverty and social exclusion.

One outstanding feature of social relations in these countries in the final quarter of the twentieth century has, to all appearances, been the priority given to the household unit (predominantly the nuclear family) over other forms of interdependency, such as wider kinship, community, trade union or political party. It is not that individuals have ceased to belong to these (though active membership of class-based formal organizations in particular has fallen); it is more that choices seem to have become more strongly orientated towards the interdependency requirements of that unit, and less to those of others. Research suggests that, as actors within the public sphere and as citizens, individuals are conscious of this, and justify 'putting the family first' (Jordan, Redley and James, 1994).

There is clearly a link to be made between this phenomenon and the division of these societies into a comfortable majority and an impoverished minority that has been the other universal feature (Dahrendorf, 1988; Galbraith, 1992). But there is no obvious organizational means by which individuals giving higher priority to household interdependencies have translated this into collective action to exclude the poor. It is true that in some countries, notably Britain and the United States, the defection of blue-collar workers (who were often trade unionists and traditional supporters of the Labour party and the Democratic party) to Margaret Thatcher and Ronald Reagan was a crucial factor in the institutional changes through which polarization was accelerated. But in other countries, such as New Zealand and Australia, similar changes were made by Labour parties; while in others still, such as most of the Continental European countries, much more institutionally conservative regimes prevailed, but similar social phenomena emerged, albeit less dramatically.

Therefore we must seek the explanation in some less visible forms of interaction, through which individuals all acting to protect one form of interdependency (households) engaged together. Both club theory and the theory of collective action in exclusive groups will be used in this chapter to develop this analysis. Game theory is introduced to explain how collective-action groups, including 'welfare clubs' and 'informal clubs' as well as households, interact to produce a particular configuration of outcomes.

I shall argue that a crucial factor in the changes in economic relations that occurred in the 1960s and 1970s was the availability of new sources of labour power (notably in the newly industrializing countries) at lower wage rates than those commanded by labour in the advanced economies. This implied that the rents enjoyed by organized labour in the advanced industrialized economies (in the form of higher wages and benefits) could now be competed away, through the strategic action of international companies. In the first instance, this applied mainly to unskilled industrial workers, but with technological advances affecting both production processes and communications it gradually applied to more skilled manual workers, and then also to technicians and workers in service occupations, and finally even to professional and managerial staff.

Labour-market relations in the advanced economies in the last quarter of the century can therefore be understood as strategic struggles over two kinds of rents. In the first place, individual employees and trade unions acted to protect their job rents as best they could, in the face of employers' strategies for eroding them (through diversification and internationalization of production). In the Continental European countries, trade union movements continued to be relatively successful in strategies for inclusive representation of employees, and for concerted action to sustain the regulations governing labour-market conditions. In the United States and Britain, trade union movements were crucially divided, and governments committed to labour-market deregulation were elected and re-elected in the 1980s. The consequence has been that the rents of a broad section of workers have been competed away. In the United States by 1995, real incomes of college graduates were falling as rapidly as those of high school graduates; between 1989 and 1993, median family incomes fell, by $2737 per annum in real terms (Elliott, 1995a).

On the other hand, the new conditions in the labour market, especially where deregulation went furthest, allowed employers to seek rents through establishing monopolistic power to exploit certain forms of labour. Whereas many unprotected workers were simply forced to accept below-subsistence wages that reflected their marginal product as unskilled labour in capital-extensive production processes, others (such as people living in isolated, deprived communities, or immigrants, or home workers) could be exploited for these rents. A crude example – which led to a strike by French seamen – was when a cross-channel ferry company based in Britain employed Polish crews in February 1995. The average salary of the French seamen was 10,000 francs per month (£1250); Polish seamen were paid 2500 francs (£310), worked much longer shifts, and had no social security cover (*Guardian*, 24 February 1995).

The purpose of this chapter is to analyse social interactions concerning these two forms of rent. I shall argue that these extended far beyond the labour market itself, and shaped the other forms of social organization that characterize these societies in the 1990s. Above all I shall argue that, especially in those countries where labour-market deregulation went furthest, it is more plausible to model labour-market interactions in terms of bargaining games between 'insiders' and 'outsiders' (Solow, 1990), and between men and women in households (Jordan, Redley and James, 1994), than between trade unions and employers. After all, by 1995 trade-union membership in the United States stood at barely one-eighth of the workforce, and in Britain at 45 per cent.

This is because, as labour-market structures changed (even in the Continental European countries), the opportunities for part-time employment grew almost as rapidly as full-time regular jobs declined. Whereas this weakened the position of trade unions in their collective defence of job rents, it opened up strategic options for households, in terms of their combinations of male and female labour supply. My analysis will seek to show how patterns of employment in mainstream households reflect strategies for protecting the rents enjoyed by men with insiders' jobs (careers with promotion, perks and pensions) against competition from outsiders.

In prioritizing household strategies over other forms of collective action to protect job rents, these decisions allowed mainstream households to enjoy improving living standards throughout the 1980s. But they left other households more vulnerable to the new forms of exploitation that became available to employers in that decade. Therefore they were forced to rely on rather different strategic defences against such exploitation, best modelled as bargaining games between them and the tax and benefits authorities. All these interactions gave rise to forms of social organization that differentiated mainstream households from marginal ones, and that polarized strategic behaviour as well as incomes (Jordan and Redley, 1994). Some of the consequences of that development will be analysed in the next chapter. For the purposes of this one, the aim is to capture the main features of the dynamic of inclusion and exclusion in these interactions.

WELFARE STATES AND THE POST-WAR ORDER

The perspectives developed in chapter 2 allow us to see welfare states as forms of collective action from two standpoints. From the point of view of their own citizens' collective interests, they created institutions that overcame the inefficiencies, inequities and downright perversities of the interwar period. But from the point of view of the world economic system, they were rather successful distributional coalitions, which captured the rents associated with advanced industrial production for their capitalists and workers, to the long-term disadvantage of their counterparts in developing countries. They allowed those nation states to achieve rapid economic growth between 1950 and the mid-1970s, and to develop international regimes of all kinds that reflected their overall dominance in world exchanges. At best, the Soviet bloc represented a set of countervailing principles and collective-action systems, reacting to or resisting these advances in a global context.

Welfare states restrained the destructive pre-war conflicts between capital and organized labour by transforming prisoner's dilemmas in interactions between particular employers and workers into co-operative games between collective actors representing all employers and the whole organized labour force, in each national polity. This transformation was institutionalized in Continental European welfare states, where 'corporatist' systems of interest-group representation allowed the 'encompassing organizations' for capital and labour to negotiate agreements through the good offices of a growth-orientated state (Cawson, 1982; Schmitter, 1989; Crouch, 1983). In this way, the collective-action problems of interaction between large groups of rational actors were transformed into small-group encounters, with all the greater possibilities for negotiated agreement identified by Olson (1965), and all the higher probabilities of reflecting the general interests of all citizens associated with such representation described in his later book (1982, pp. 51–73). These systems were most elaborately developed, and lasted longest, in the Scandinavian countries, and especially in Sweden (Esping-Andersen, 1990).

In the liberal Anglo-Saxon polities, neither encompassing organizations nor corporatist institutions were successfully sustained, but Keynesian economics, dealing in statistical aggregates allocated through processes of negotiation between collective actors, encouraged quite lengthy experiments in such collective action, and allowed governments scope for extensive economic interventions and steering (Mishra, 1984). Above all, the very concept of managed economic growth, pursued in the common interests of both employers and employees, enabled competition within and between industrial interests to be restrained, and a degree of co-ordination to be achieved, albeit haltingly.

For 25 years, the interests of individual company directors, workers and pensioners could plausibly be represented as best served by agreements over aggregate national levels of investment, profits, employment, wages and social insurance benefits that reflected their interdependence in a national economy, where shareholders' dividends arose from expanding purchases by national employees and pensioners out of past and present earnings. Individuals could be shown to have good reasons for keeping the rules of their own collective-action groups (employers' organizations, trade unions), and the agreements reached between them – if investment targets, pay freezes and tax increases could be linked together – and represented as the best available solutions within the opportunities and constraints of the national welfare state game (Castles, 1986).

The advanced industrialized countries dominated world trade in manufactures in this period. The big economies each enjoyed a sphere or region of near monopoly – Central and South America for the USA, the Commonwealth for Britain, North Africa for France, and so on. The producer rents gained from this trade with the developing world were shared between the domestic interest groups through the social institutions of welfare states. Such distributions restrained inequalities and reduced social tensions. They discouraged both the totalitarian excesses of Continental Europe in the interwar period, and the narrow individualism of the liberal Anglo-Saxon tradition.

However, after 1965, distributional struggles within welfare states intensified (Brittan, 1975; Gough, 1979). As supplies of labour became scarcer, the share of wages in these economies grew, and profits fell (Kindleberger, 1967). In Olson's terms, this reflected the more successful mobilization of internal collective-action groups as 'distributional coalitions' under conditions of institutional stability. From this period onwards, capital in the advanced industrialized economies looked for more profitable investment opportunities in the developing world. These became available, both through new technologies, better communications, new organizational systems, and the relaxation of restraints on international transactions. The main beneficiaries of these new strategies were the newly industrializing countries, and especially those of South-East Asia.

It is quite instructive to compare the institutional systems of the 'four tigers' of South-East Asia with the welfare states of the advanced industrialized First World. Hong Kong, Singapore, Taiwan and South Korea have achieved rapid growth, especially in their manufacturing sectors, without redistributing a large proportion of their GNP in social services. South Korea and Taiwan in particular have adopted a 'Japanese model' of economic management, reflecting the success of that country in the immediate post-war period. This includes state control of the financial sector, the allocation of investments in line with national objectives, managed trade and international capital flows, supervision of the transfer of technology from abroad, and policies for ensuring that the most important sectors of the economy remain in the hands of national firms. In this way their governments have protected compromises between capital and labour, and national economic management from global market forces (Bienefeld, 1991). They have quite subtly but obdurately resisted pressures to deregulate their economies and make their foreign trade more open. Above all, they have – as limited democracies or overt autocracies – prevented the development of internal distributional coalitions, and hence of pressures for redistribution through social services.

The growth of national income per head in these countries suggests that they have been more successful in capturing the rents available in new, rapidly expanding global markets than their competitors from the First World. This evidence is complemented by the signs of slower growth in the advanced industrialized economies, and especially of the relative decline of some of the most generous and egalitarian welfare states, notably Sweden, which has led to the present crisis of the much-vaunted 'Scandinavian model'. Finland, of course, with its present unemployment rate of 18 per cent, is a special case, related to the collapse in Eastern Europe. But so too is the more optimistic situation of Norway, almost autonomous because of its oil bonanza, and thus able to resist pressures from global economic forces, and continue its idiosyncratic patterns of redistribution. Sweden, by contrast, is trying urgently to remodel its economic and social institutions, and reverse the trends through which the tax-financed proportion of its population (supported through benefits or public sector employment) grew from 1.1 to 4.1 million between 1960 and 1980, while the market-financed fell from 4.1 to 2.1 million. During this same period, Sweden fell from 3rd to 13th place in the league table of GNP *per head*, by far the most spectacular decline among the rich countries (Lindbeck, 1995).

These developments suggest that the success of welfare states depended on particular conditions of the kind that prevailed after the collapse of the gold standard and the withering of international trade in the 1930s, and the dislocations of the Second World War. Welfare states were institutional systems for restraining economic competition and avoiding costly political conflict between the major collective actors in advanced industrialized societies. But they mobilized populations within nation states, taking for granted their capacities for autonomous policy-making within a global system of interactions between sovereign territorial polities. The engine of their growth was expanding world trade, in which they enjoyed great competitive advantages over developing economies; the rents they earned through trade in manufactures grew steadily as these new structures were built up in the post-war period. But this very growth in trade increased the strategic options open to capital within the advanced industrialized states and, combined with intensified internal competition between capital and labour in the late 1960s through the more cohesive organization of distributional coalitions, produced a situation in which these rents were vulnerable to action by competitors in the developing world.

Thus it became more obvious that the expansionist economic policies of the post-war era depended on post-war trade and payment controls that at the time seemed incidental or even damaging, and that the progressive liberalization of commodity and capital markets which had increased economic interdependence between the advanced industrialized countries in the 1970s had also weakened their capacities to manage their economies autonomously (Bienefeld, 1991; Held and McGrew, 1994). The coming of fully convertible currencies, the removal of capital controls, the deregulation of capital markets, and the return to levels of world trade that prevailed before the First World War, all threatened the effectiveness of welfare states as systems of national economic management. They set in motion a logic of global economic exchange, flexibility and the removal of restraints and barriers, in which the national interest could be defined (by the New Right) as synonymous with well-functioning markets, maximizing efficiency and welfare in a world context.

The main beneficiaries of the great liberalization of economic institutions in the 1980s were the newly industrializing countries of South-East Asia, and the international financial institutions who operated in global capital and currency markets. These same developments produced international credit regimes whose policies reinforced the liberalization programme, and which were able to enforce it upon economically weaker states. In all this the irony was that those industrializing countries able to use the 'Japanese model' relied on institutional systems and economic policies similar to those that succeeded in post-war Europe, before the redistributive phase of the welfare state developed; yet the IMF and World Bank imposed quite different, liberal, open regimes on more vulnerable, indebted developing countries.

But as well as transforming both the environment in which exchanges took place, and the balance of advantage between advanced industrialized countries and newly industrializing ones, this greater interdependency between the leading economies, and this weakening of national economic management capabilities, also transformed the structure of opportunities and incentives for individuals *within* welfare states. It weakened the institutional constraints that bound them to the particular collective-action systems of such states – trade unions, social insurance systems, local government services – and orientated them towards global markets and the accumulation of new property rights in private welfare systems. This will be the subject of the next section.

THE TRANSFORMATION OF THE LABOUR MARKET

The first manifestations of the shift described in the last section were the relative decline of industrial employment in the 1970s, and the emergence of mass unemployment in the second half of that decade. In all the advanced industrialized countries except the USA and Japan, male industrial employment declined *absolutely* in the 20 years following the first 'oil shock', with the largest decreases occurring in countries such as Belgium and the UK, which previously had the highest proportions of such employment. Unemployment rates stabilized in the late 1980s in most of these states, but have risen more rapidly in the 1990s in those countries (for example, the Scandinavian nations) that were most successful in continuing to manage their economies through social democratic institutions in the previous two decades. My aim in this section is to sketch how new patterns emerged during the past 20 years, as a background to my analysis of current interactions.

It is by now well accepted in the literature that what triggered these changes was the new capability of international companies, who took advantage of new technologies of communication and production to locate many of their labour-intensive operations in newly industrializing countries with lower wage rates and fewer environmental controls, thus concentrating high-technology, capital-intensive production in the advanced economies (Scharpf, 1985). This greater flexibility in the division of labour within such companies allowed them to reduce costs, both by increasing the productivity of labour in their high-tech production units, and by reducing their numbers of unskilled staff within the advanced economies, in favour of lower-paid workers in the developing ones. This in turn meant that these international companies could compete very successfully with smaller, national firms, which were consequently forced to seek greater flexibility in their use of labour power by some other means.

Many such companies, particularly in traditional heavy industries such as shipbuilding, textiles and steel production, simply closed, causing mass redundancies; others greatly reduced their staff; others still recruited more short-term, part-time and subcontract workers. Similar trends were later evident in services, and in the public sector as well as the private, as employers recognized ways of cutting labour costs, and governments tried to reduce public expenditure during a period of slower economic growth (Myles et al., 1988).

As new opportunities for more cost-effective use of labour power within the new international division of labour were developed, the payoffs for firms from collective action within the institutional frameworks of welfare states declined, and those for alternative strategies, using overseas production sites and more 'flexible' deployments of their workforces, gave better returns. Conversely, for organized labour from the early 1970s onwards, the payoffs for maximizing their memberships and co-operating in governments' 'full employment' strategies fell, and those for co-operating with employers in workforce reductions rose. Faced with threats to the security of their employment and the level of their wages and salaries, individual employees in turn sought new strategies that relied less on their membership of trade unions and professional associations, and more on a maximization of the benefits of co-operation in a household work strategy. In other words, the most relevant collective-action unit became the household rather than the union.

From the perspective of the world economy, such strategies can be seen as actions to protect rents, originally gained through the success of welfare states. With the new international division of labour, many workers in the advanced industrialized countries were being paid more for their services than the wage or salary needed to keep them in their jobs; in microeconomic terms they were receiving an income higher than that arising from the marginal cost of their labour power, and the excess represented a 'job rent' (Mueller, 1989, p. 230). Whereas these job rents were largely won through collective action in welfare states, they came to be defended by strategic interaction in households.

The total effects of these changes on national labour-force patterns have been complex. The most universal results have been the overall decline in male, industrial, manual and full-time permanent employment, and the growth in female, service, white-collar and irregular (especially part-time) work since the mid-1970s. But there have also been important variations between countries. As Esping-Andersen (1990) has shown, the fall in regular, well-paid jobs for men has been much slower and smaller in successful industrial economies such as those of Germany and Japan, but the growth in 'post-industrial' employment – in professional, managerial and technical occupations – has been faster in more service-orientated economies, such as that of the United States.

Using the analysis developed in the last section, we can see how this reflected different responses by collective actors to the new opportunities and constraints facing them. In Germany, for example, there was one kind of equilibrium solution to a bargaining game between the 'social partners' in which a comparatively high proportion of the job rents of the remaining full-time workforce was protected, while industrial employers focused production on high-specification, 'quality-orientated' products for the home and overseas markets, and the necessary reductions in the workforce were managed mainly through the social insurance system, in the form of early-retirement schemes (Crouch, 1992). But there was comparatively little growth of employment in the service sector, or among women, and a group of 'new poor', claiming social assistance, became more evident in the 1980s. With the collapse of the regimes in Central and Eastern Europe, and the unification with the former GDR, this equilibrium solution was threatened, particularly by the opportunities for relocation of production to lower-wage economies such as the Czech Republic, and by high unemployment in the *Neuen Länder*.

The German solution was sustainable in the late 1980s mainly because of Germany's success in exports of manufactured goods. This was achieved through high levels of industrial investment, which in turn depended on successful co-operation between the financial and manufacturing sectors. In Britain, attempts to reach a similar equilibrium solution under the new rules and payoffs in this game in the 1960s and 1970s failed. The financial sector (the City) was strongly orientated towards the global market, and could not be drawn into reliable co-operation over industrial investment (Hutton, 1994). The trade union movement could unite and act together only in resistance to any form of government-imposed pay restraint. Employers increasingly sought the rents available through the use of unprotected labour.

As a result, by the end of the 1970s the social democratic game had been transformed into a prisoner's dilemma, with each player's best strategy one of defection. The Conservatives were elected in 1979 on a promise to dismantle the whole game between collective actors, and substitute one involving individuals in markets. But of course, as many commentators have since pointed out, the rules of the new game institutionalized the default solution to the old game. They left the financial sector free to develop quite successful strategies for gaining high short-term returns through international transactions. They condemned the trade union movement to further fragmentation and exclusion from collective decision-making. And they actively enabled the strategic pursuit of monopoly-based rents in a new deregulated labour market.

The result has been characterized (Hutton, 1994) as a kind of low-level equilibrium, in which the British government attempts to attract overseas investment, the manufacturing sector concentrates on standardized products for mass markets, and trade unions conduct a rearguard defence of shrinking numbers of protected workers. The government's policies depend for their success on Britain's strategic position as an offshore, low-wage assembly site for international corporations, based mainly in the US and Japan, seeking access to European Union markets. British-based firms, denied the resources and rewards for pursuing a high-productivity, high value-added strategy, resort instead to opportunistic exploitation of the rents available to them through the weakening of trade unions and the loss of social protection.

Such analyses capture important aspects of the differences between the German and the British economies, but they cannot fully explain the whole configuration of labour-market outcomes in the two countries, let alone the closely related patterns of social organization through which the poor are excluded from other aspects of collective life. Furthermore, they cannot encompass an analysis of developments in the United States, a far larger and more diverse economy, whose dynamic could never adequately have been modelled in terms of the social democratic game. There, some sectors of economic activity in some regions (such as information technology in California) seem to have established the kind of high-level dynamic, or virtuous circle, that characterized the German economy, but without the institutional systems that are seen as crucial to that success in Germany. Much of the rest of the American economy exhibits a low-level equilibrium like Britain's, with falling wages and a prevalence of exploitative employment conditions. In the US in 1988, 2 per cent of the workforce became unemployed in any month, compared with 0.4 per cent in Europe (Hutton, 1994, p. 19).

What has to be explained is thus the survival of a substantial segment of well-paid, protected jobs (and its growth in some sectors, notably financial, professional and business services in the US and Britain), alongside the rapid expansion of 'non-standard' contracts of all kinds, from part-time to marginal and self-employment. Labour economists started to observe and analyse 'dual labour markets' in the early 1980s (Berger and Piore, 1980; Wilkinson, 1981; Atkinson, 1984; Atkinson and Meager, 1986). The last noted some similarities between emerging patterns in Britain and the USA and the Japanese labour market, with its high-tech sector of large firms offering protected lifetime employment, and its larger and lower-paid sector of smaller enterprises and subcontract workers. Further research, particularly in Italy, showed that labour-market segmentation (Standing, 1986) could in part be explained by the strategies of companies pursuing 'decentralization' through dispersing work among a network of satellite firms and outworkers (Murray, 1983; McNabb and Ryan, 1989). This analysis was echoed in research on the segregation and segmentation of women's employment (Dex, 1985; 1988) and on homeworking (Hakim, 1980; 1984; 1988), showing that in their search for flexibility (and presumably also rents), employers' strategies focused on women.

In the US and British contexts, this dualism does not reflect a division of *employers* into 'primary' and 'secondary', with radically different strategies. Large industrial companies typically adopt an approach that involves the recruitment and retention of a core of permanent staff with opportunities for promotion, training, pensions and fringe benefits, and a contrasting engagement with a periphery of temporary, casual or subcontract workers, which can be built up or run down in response to short-term changes in demand for their products (Handy, 1989). They invest in the former, offer them security and efficiency wages, and aim to increase their productivity during their working lives (through retraining). The latter are paid lower wages and used as a reserve labour force. The same patterns are to be found in agencies providing routine public services (Gallie et al., 1993).

To compete with larger firms using this strategy, smaller ones are likely to recruit large proportions of part-time employees, thus saving on some on-wage costs. This alternative is also prevalent in retailing, catering and leisure, in public-sector health and community services, all of which employ large numbers of women. In Gallie et al.'s British study, enterprises with more than 75 per cent part-time employees were small and concentrated in marketed routine services. Hence employers' use of non-standard contracts varies both by size of firm and by industry, and such work is not associated with a single strategy, but with several different ways of combining the retention of core staff with flexibility in the use of peripheral workers. Furthermore, the periphery is made up of a very diverse mixture of part-time, fixed-term and subcontract workers, whose terms and conditions, prospects and satisfactions cover almost as wide a range as those within the core. Among these, however, there is an identifiable group of irregular, low-paid, marginal workers, with neither reliable nor adequate earnings.

The size of this group in Continental European countries is generally smaller, though of course there are certain workers (such as the *Werkbetragsarbeitnehmer* subcontract labour from Poland, the Czech Republic and Slovakia, who come for three months to Germany, mainly for construction work) who are open to exploitation (Faist, 1994a). This is because statutory labour-market regulation (minimum wages and conditions and employment protection) have remained in place for the most part, and workforce reductions have been managed through social insurance benefits. In Denmark, for example, in 1990 there were almost twice as many claimants of various kinds of early retirement pensions (350,000) as there were individuals receiving unemployment benefit for more than five months a year (190,000) (Abrahamson, 1992, p. 24). In the Netherlands, disability benefits have been the main means of achieving the same end. Firms have thus been able to avail themselves of state schemes for income protection in pursuit of policies of 'rationalization'. They have also been able to recruit some low-cost labour power through government schemes for subsidizing the employment of long-term claimants.

But all these strategies must be explained as 'best replies' to equivalent ones by individuals who constitute the supply side of the labour market. Although the rules and payoffs of the games are very different in the US and Britain on the one hand, or Continental European countries on the other, all such individuals must be assumed to respond strategically (in terms of investments in education and training before entering the labour market, decisions about what work to take, for what hours, and at what pay and conditions, when to seek promotion or retirement, and so on) to the strategies of employers. Furthermore, these 'best replies' from the supply side are not made by isolated individuals, totally insulated from each other's decisions. They are made, above all, by individuals organizing themselves into households, and co-ordinating their choices in relation to each other's. Potentially also they are made by individuals who can act collectively through trade unions, and who can vote for measures to change the institutional structure of the game.

We are therefore looking for games through which to model the interaction between the strategies of employers over 'flexibility', and the strategic decisions of employees within these social relations. These should then explain those features of the organization of social life through which the poor are excluded in the advanced capitalist countries, and the social benefits and costs associated with these.

STRATEGIC GAMES OVER EDUCATION: SCHOOLS AS CLUBS

The first supply side issue to be addressed here is education and training. Faced with the strategic options open to employers under current economic conditions, how do individuals try to pursue their interests through decisions about these issues, both within households and collectively? In what sort of games can these strategies be seen as 'best replies' to those of employers in search of 'flexibility' and (ultimately) of rents through exploitation?

In the German context, such questions are not particularly meaningful, because little has changed since the post-war educational structure established twin-track secondary education (*Grundschule* and *Gymnasium*) for less and more academic pupils, followed by virtually universal coverage of vocational education and training (through *Hochschule* and apprenticeships) and higher education. There has been no political pressure to change this structure, and though there are ways in which parents can influence their children's chances within this system, its hierarchical yet inclusive structure is designed (like other German social institutions) to produce comprehensive social integration which is stratified rather than egalitarian. Of course, these forms of education and training do not guarantee employment, and groups such as immigrants find it difficult to gain places in apprenticeships that lead to reliable jobs (Faist, 1995); however, access to labour markets is certainly more collectivized, institutionalized, and thus inclusive, in Germany than in the Anglo-Saxon countries.

In trying to explain the strategies of parents and young people in the latter countries, we should see education and training as being (from their point of view) an *investment* with a view to future returns, in the form of higher pay and other private benefits, but with some current opportunity costs. But from the community's point of view, as well as improving the productivity and earning power of those individuals it also contributes to the productivity of others, improves citizenship competencies (such as political and cultural skills), lowers crime rates, and increases the yield to the community through taxes. These should be regarded as the social benefits of education and training (Barr, 1994). They explain why electorates (even anti-collectivist liberal ones like those of the USA) have historically given political support to educational systems financed out of public expenditures.

Researchers have attempted to estimate the private and social returns on various levels of education and training, and to make international comparisons, by calculating the excess earnings (over a lifetime) of those with qualifications on one level over those with qualifications at the next (lower) level (Psacharopoulos, 1992; Blaug, 1987). Figures for the period between the 1950s and the early 1980s show private returns in most advanced capitalist countries rather higher (at around 12 per cent) than social benefits (10 per cent) (Psacharopoulos and Woodhall, 1985). Higher education is by far the most expensive of the stages, and government funding schemes make an attempt to balance how social and private benefits are earned by leaving the appropriate proportion for parents and young people to fund through their own payments.

Therefore we might plausibly represent the choices facing parents at the start of their children's school careers as investment decisions, with the maintenance grant and loan schemes and state subsidies for college fees as compensation for the spillovers onto the community, in the form of social benefits, for this element of their private costs. Their subsequent actions thus reflect predictions of the expected long-term future returns, given current trends in labour markets. They must therefore try to take account of the strategies of other parents, and of employers, as well as of the institutional structure of government subsidies to education and training.

In Britain and the USA, unlike Germany, the opportunities for training for employment are very limited. There is no collectivized structure of apprenticeships, and employers have not supplied such access systems in significant quantities, or of decent quality. Young people, even those who stay on for sixth-form or high-school education, must seek a pathway to core 'good jobs' (those still offering security, intra-firm training and promotion) through peripheral 'entry jobs' that are irregular and badly paid. A study by Gregg (1995) showed that the real wages of such entry jobs have not risen since 1979. Given the polarization between 'good jobs' and 'bad jobs' in Britain and the United States, there are strong incentives for parents to seek schools that will enable their children to do well enough to go on to higher education. Good schools, in the private or public sectors, provide such a benefit.

Since the Education Act of 1988, the British state educational system has been restructured to require institutional actors (administrators and teachers) to be more accountable for their decisions; and to enable lay actors (parents) to exercise more choice – both collectively, through voting, and individually – about management and policy issues. In particular, because school budgets have been devolved to head teachers and governors, parents can be elected to governing bodies to make such decisions; they can also vote for schools to leave the orbit of their local authority and thus, through 'opting out', achieve considerable autonomy (over the selection of pupils and the focus and goals of the educational programme).

The new institutional structure of education in Britain thus provides a chance to study how individuals act in pursuit of their interests – the strategies they deploy, both as parents of their particular children, and as electors with opportunities to influence the strategies adopted by their children's schools in relation to other schools' strategies. The most promising way of analysing these choices is to see schools within these new rules as *clubs*. Within these, parents have the above powers to influence collective decisions (voice); but they can also choose to live in an area where the local school provides what they seek for their child ('voting with the feet'); or, if their child can pass the relevant exams and interviews, between selective and non-selective schools (exit); or even to shift their children right out of the state system and into private education (self-exclusion).

As club managers, head teachers and governors seek to attract a roll of pupils whose contributions (in terms of the state funding they attract) are at least equal to the resources expended on educating them. Whether this is best achieved by an inclusive intake of children from their local district will depend partly on its demographic characteristics (the available mix of high-yield/low-cost achievers and low-yield/high-cost 'problem' children). But it will also depend on the strategies of other schools. If one or more of these opts out of local authority control and relies upon drawing away many of the former group, then it will become increasingly difficult for others to sustain this inclusive strategy.

Research shows that parents try, in choosing children's schools, to balance a number of factors. While almost all better-off parents seek access to examination passes that will give good university places, many trade off a school's high place in such 'league tables' against the preparation for wider social life available through a good state comprehensive school, with its heterogeneous intake (Jordan, Redley and James, 1994, ch. 8). If large numbers of ambitious parents prefer private schools, or selective opted-out schools, no comprehensive school in that district is likely to offer a high enough rate of examination passes to attract that group of parents. Their best strategy, particularly if their children do not pass screening devices for selective schools, is probably to move house in search of a successful comprehensive school elsewhere. Recent reports give examples of parents willing to pay £8000 to do this (BBC Radio 4, *Today* programme, 15 February 1995).

It is easy to see how the actions of parents within this new structure have both polarized educational opportunities and driven up the costs of schooling. As opted-out schools have sought to cream off high-yield/low-cost children, they have forced other schools to adopt similar strategies, and made it far harder for those with no such strategic option to achieve success, either in terms of examination results, or in establishing a satisfactory mix of pupils. Where the latter get a reputation as 'sink schools', staff and pupil morale suffers, and social problems escalate, increasing costs to the schools themselves and to the wider community (through truancy, delinquency and so on). Such schools have strong incentives to exclude their most difficult pupils – in England and Wales 10,000 were thus excluded in 1994 (BBC Radio 4, *Today* programme, 2 June 1995). At the same time parents in these catchment areas are more strongly motivated to choose private education, or to bear the costs of moving to another area. These options are not open to poor parents. Children attending the least successful state schools are denied realistic opportunities to escape their situation through educational attainment, because the actions of better-off parents condemn their schools to tasks of managing deprivation and disillusion.

This dynamic is cumulative. There is evidence that children in such schools adopt behavioural strategies to engineer their own exclusion, calculating that their current satisfactions and long-term life chances will be improved by admission to 'special units' for disruptive pupils (Garner, 1994). Others turn to crime or drug use as ways into the informal economy, which represents an attractive alternative to marginal employment. This in turn contributes to better-off parents' anxieties to avoid the risks of 'bad' association in unsuccessful schools, and raises the price that they are willing to pay (in travelling or moving costs, or for private education) in order to escape such 'contamination' (Jordan, Redley and James, 1994).

Even though these choices increase the private costs borne by better-off parents, they can be seen as part of a rational investment strategy so long as the returns on higher education are sufficient to justify these allocations of resources. In Britain there was evidence to suggest that returns to higher education were rising in the 1980s, as part of the dispersion of earnings between secure, well-paid jobs and marginal employment. But evidence from the United States shows that these rises cannot be assumed within new-style labour markets. Estimates of returns to college graduates in the US pointed to a fall in the late 1980s (Woodhall, 1992), and this has continued right up to the mid-1990s (Elliott, 1995a). Real salaries of college graduates are falling as fast as those of blue-collar workers (Barker, 1995; Elliott, 1995b).

There are two possible contributory factors to such a fall. The first is that the deregulation of labour markets has resulted in the erosion of the rents of an ever-larger proportion of the workforce. In the early 1980s, the fall in real wages was confined to unskilled occupations, but now a much larger segment is exposed to overseas competition, as a great number of technical tasks in a wider range of industries and services can be relocated more profitably, in lower-wage economies, and the costs of such relocation are reduced by improved communications.

But this also implies that, just as membership of trade unions has declined, and collective action has failed to stop the fall in real wages, so too individual strategies for conserving the job rents of the better-off are beginning to founder. In this case, it begins to look as if the strategic actions of parents over access to higher education, which have reinforced the disadvantage and exclusion of children from poor families, are turning out to be collectively self-defeating.

As Hirsch (1977) pointed out, the returns to higher education are 'positional', in the sense that they derive from its superiority in relation to other forms of education, and the access it gives to similarly superior jobs. But positional goods are vulnerable to congestion; the advantageous view gained by standing on one's toes in a crowd is lost if all others do the same, and the result is that the effort expended is wasted. Thus positional competition can pose a collective-action problem.

The way in which returns to higher education might decline can be captured in an 'overqualification game' between parents and employers. Parents aim to make a cost-effective investment in higher education, and employers to gain the best possible recruits for positional (core) jobs. Suppose that competition among parents for positional advantage is intensified, so that they are willing to bear higher costs, in school fees and other outgoings, in longer dependence, and in maintenance and fees for higher degrees and postgraduate training courses. But the employers will respond to this by more intensified screening of job candidates, such as to go on raising the level of qualifications required of applicants. Respondents in a qualitative study of such decisions pointed out that their own offspring would need degrees to get jobs that they themselves required only 'O' levels to obtain (Jordan, Redley and James, 1994, ch. 8).

The overqualification game can be modelled as a prisoner's dilemma because, even though it costs parents much more to gain extra educational credentials, and firms slightly more to introduce elaborate screening processes, individual parents can never risk giving advantage to their competitors in the search for good jobs, and individual firms can never allow their rivals advantage in recruiting the best applicants. The collective good at stake for parents is universal availability of individually cost-effective higher education (Van der Veen, 1994). The players are Ego and Others, and the choices are unrestrained competition or restrained competition. But if any individual chooses restrained competition he or she receives the 'sucker's outcome' of relative disadvantage, so all must compete without restraint, and bear the higher costs of overqualification.

Of course, parents could overcome this problem by voting for a political party that promised to collectivize access to the labour market by something like the German model. But British research suggests that voters were unconvinced that any such solution was available. Although many saw a conflict between their current competitive strategies and their political principles (for example, the value of 'fairness'), they did not see a collective action to that end as open to them – hence they chose to 'put the family first' (Jordan, Redley and James, 1994, ch. 8). This applied even to those describing themselves as 'socialists' – and even, as subsequent news suggests, to the leader of the British Labour party himself.

The costs associated with this collective-action problem can be illustrated from a British example. Until recently, the relevant qualifications for the solicitors' profession were gained through secondment by firms of articled employees to study for professional exams. Recently new postgraduate degrees in legal practice, costing around £5000, have been set up in such numbers that it is estimated that only half those who complete them successfully will gain articles. It is not difficult to imagine parents, themselves solicitors, postponing their planned retirement to pay for their offspring to do such courses (with a 50 per cent chance that this investment will bear fruit), and in doing so blocking access for the new generation to the lucrative partnerships to which their investment is targeted. An individually rational strategy is thus collectively mutually frustrating.

HOUSEHOLDS, JOB RENTS, AND THE DIVISION OF LABOUR

The second set of decisions to be analysed in relation to employers' strategies for flexibility concerns the division of labour between partners in households. Given that the majority of households containing people of working age comprise heterosexual couples with children, and the next largest group consists of such couples without children, it is important to consider the rationale behind the configurations of labour supplied by such households. In this section I shall analyse them as strategic replies to employers' decisions, and as the outcomes of bargaining games between partners within households (Ott, 1992).

In what follows it is therefore assumed that each individual is seeking to maximize his or her utility, taking account of the actions of others, and that the issues at stake include such choices as where and with whom to live; when to have children, and how many; allocations of unpaid domestic work and child care; as well as what hours to offer in the formal labour market, on what terms, and in which roles. But the institutional structures for, and hence the outcomes of, labour-market interactions are also assumed to be related to the political choices of individuals who could, at least hypothetically, combine in various coalitions to take collective action, through trade unions or political parties for example.

Given that the supply of labour power for the formal market reflects interactions over these other vital decisions between men and women, and that patterns in births, cohabitations, marriages and divorces, and the division of unpaid household labour, have all changed equally strikingly in the past two decades, the rise in the number of married women entering the labour market in the advanced economies, and the fall in the age of their children when they have chosen to do so, have been outstanding features. However, as is frequently pointed out in critical analyses of this development, women who rejoin the labour market after having children do not do so on the same terms as men who develop uninterrupted careers within it, or indeed as women who do not have children. Even in countries such as Sweden, with longstanding traditions of high participation rates among married women, good child-care facilities and high proportions of female membership in trade unions, women tend to be concentrated in certain occupations, and disproportionately in part-time posts and subordinate roles. With the partial exception of the USA, where they have made measurable progress in recent years (Esping-

Andersen, 1990), women are under-represented in managerial and other senior organizational positions; indeed, they are often overqualified for the work they do.

There is an ever-growing literature that understands these phenomena in terms of social exclusion. It is certainly true that women face forms of discrimination in the labour market, both because of power-laden prejudice by men, and because the institutional structures surrounding paid work rely on their unpaid domestic and child-care roles, and do not enable their full potential in the labour market to be realized. In all these ways they do indeed suffer from forms of exclusion that relate to non-economic factors, and that therefore discriminate against them because of characteristics that are not relevant to their employment capabilities. Furthermore, gender segregation, which first developed in British labour markets in the eighteenth century (Berg, 1988; Witz, 1992), tends to push them into, and hold them in, health and social care work, routine marketed services (such as retailing and catering) and specific sections of productive industry.

But the analysis adopted here assumes that women, who constitute a small majority in all these countries, are choosing to pursue their interests through individual bargains in partnerships with men, and through these in household labour-market strategies, in preference to seeking collective-action solutions through trade unions or the political process. Such choices clearly reflect collective-action dilemmas and particular constraints affecting women in present-day interactions, but they need to be analysed within the same assumptions that are used throughout this chapter, if a coherent action theory of inclusion and exclusion is to be developed. What has to be explained, after all, is why women have disproportionately supported political parties that uphold their traditional roles, as well as how men subordinate them in public and private social relations.

The sociologist R. E. Pahl (1984) proposed the concept of a 'household work strategy' to try to capture his research observations of the work and gender relations in a small community in the south-east of England. The majority of the households in his survey combined formal labour-market activity and informal 'self provisioning' (including home improvements) in a purposeful way, involving complex, interlocking divisions of labour. A minority had restricted access to formal and informal work, often lacking the skills demanded for the former, and the material resources required for the latter. Pahl argued that social polarization could be traced to the divergence between the life chances of 'work rich' and 'work poor' households.

But this does not explain the dominant division of formal labour in mainstream British households – men with incremental careers, through which they seek promotion, pensions and fringe benefits, and women returning to labour-market roles that lack these advantages. Given that women now leave education with much the same qualifications as men in these countries, the question must be why so few of them enjoy the job rents that are still available in the labour market. In principle, they might be able to get their share of these either by bargaining with their partners to develop their own careers through more equal allocations of unpaid household tasks, *or* by collective action to legislate and enforce more effective anti-discrimination measures in the public sphere.

The first possibility can be modelled in the form of a so-called 'Battle of the Sexes' game between the partners in each household in the mainstream population. Assuming that both start with equal career-relevant credentials and abilities, at every point where a labour-market decision is to be made concerning each one of them there could be considerations (such as the need to travel further, or the demands of longer hours) that affect the other, for instance by requiring them to do more unpaid work in the home. Therefore each such choice involves two possible solutions, both giving the same overall (household) utility, but one favouring the man's career, and the other the woman's. Figure 1 represents such a decision (over whether to accept a promotion) diagrammatically, the man's payoff being shown first in each quadrant. The top left corner implies that neither accepts (both give up the opportunity); the bottom right that both do, and hence the unpaid work remains undone (or done by paid labour at prohibitive cost).

WOMAN

MAN		change	don't change
	change	−1, −1	3, 0
	don't change	0, 3	0, 0

Fig. 1

In such a game, there are two possible Nash-equilibria, in which it does not pay either of the players to change his or her strategy, given the strategy of the other. The question is therefore how to determine which of these will be chosen, given that one would represent a stable solution to the game giving rise to a male career, and the other to a female career. But in an iterated 'supergame' (repeated plays, representing a succession of such decisions) it should be possible to establish a reliable pattern of 'taking turns' between the solution favouring the man's career and that favouring the woman's. However, while this game may adequately model a partnership in which there are no children, and the couple live in an area with good career opportunities for both, these payoffs are unlikely to apply if either of these conditions does not hold. Because child care is so time-consuming, whichever partner assumes responsibility for this is required to make a career *sacrifice*, rather than simply to stand still (their payoff becomes negative, not zero), and it is of the nature of incremental careers that backward steps are very damaging. Because of discrimination against women, and the break that accompanies childbearing itself, the great majority of couples choose the birth of the first or second child as the point to invest solely in the man's career. This is reinforced where a promotion requires a move away from the area where the woman was employed, further disadvantaging her in any attempt to sustain her career.

The shift to a single career strategy, with the man accumulating job-related assets, and the woman in a 'supportive' role, taking responsibility for the organization of the household and child care, can still be represented in terms of a Battle of the

Sexes supergame. However, the notion of 'taking turns' no longer applies to particular career decisions, but to stages in the life-cycle. During the children's dependency she can do interesting combinations of paid and unpaid work, consistent with being 'supportive' of his career. Later she has the option of developing these into a second career, with the man taking the supportive role (if he takes early retirement, for instance, or his career founders). In the qualitative research study referred to above, couples also indicated that the woman's choice of where to live on retirement would be adopted (Jordan et al., 1994, ch. 7). Furthermore, because the woman is likely to outlive the man, she stands to gain more benefit from his pension rights in the last phase of the life-cycle.

But the other question still remains: why do women not seek a more reliable share of men's job rents through collective action? After all, the strategy of investing in a partner's career only succeeds if marriages survive, and one in three in Britain at present ends in divorce. Would it not be a better reply both to men's strategies as partners, and to employers' strategies in the labour market, to act collectively to achieve equal opportunities – for instance, by campaigning for state-funded child-care provision?

The difficulty with this that constitutes the relevant collective-action problem is that – without a household bargain with their partners over sharing the private benefits from job rents within the household – women would be required to compete with men for their share. In this competition, they would start as 'outsiders' in the present situation, because it is predominantly men who now enjoy the efficiency wages, training opportunities, promotion prospects, fringe benefits and occupational pension rights that constitute these 'insiders'' rents. But if all the qualified women entered the market for full-time core jobs of this kind, they would represent a major alternative source of labour power, and offer employers a whole new strategic option. In competing for their share of rents, they would risk competing them away altogether.

This is the essence of Robert Solow's (1990) model of the labour market as a game between insiders and outsiders. The outsiders know that if they make their labour power available at anything below the going rates of pay (reflecting the rents of insiders), employers may simply offer a reservation wage, just sufficient to clear the market, thus eliminating rents completely. Outsiders therefore opt to restrain competition, and accept low rewards (unemployment benefit or marginal work) so as not to destroy the rents of insiders. In Solow's game, they wait in the hope that such jobs will eventually become available to them.

But Solow's version is not entirely convincing, because it assumes that outsiders are aware of a collective good (a sustainable stock of insiders' job rents), and restrain competition for a possible future stake in this. But it does not specify the collective-action group, or the selective incentives or sanctions, through which such restraint is accomplished (Olson, 1965). Indeed, outsiders constitute precisely the kind of unorganized category of individuals that Olson treats as incapable of taking collective action for the sake of the benefits of restrained competition. To carry conviction, the model needs to identify something in the game that gives actors compelling or persuasive reasons not to compete for rents, in terms of private payoffs in the current situation, or group interactions.

This something can be explained in terms of women's situation. As individuals they would be only slightly better off in terms of personal earnings if they competed away men's job rents; and as *partners* in households where the man had such a rent they would be much worse off if their actions destroyed these rents. In other words, the relevant collective-action unit to restrain competition is the *household*, where the woman has a stake in her partner's job rent. Women have strong incentives not to compete, and strong sanctions against such competition, within their partnerships. Seen from this perspective, unrestrained competition threatens their partner's career and job assets. Thus their best strategy is to accept the status quo, be supportive, and take a part-time job, for the sake of their stake in the benefits of their partner's insider status and its benefits (Jordan, 1989).

It is this that most satisfactorily explains the present configuration of household labour supply as the 'best reply' to employers' strategies for flexibility, with men pursuing job rents through careers, and women taking part-time work, usually with small career prospects. Not all these are low paid, even though these well-qualified women could probably earn much more. Furthermore, as surveys repeatedly reveal, levels of job satisfaction for women in part-time employment are high. As with choices over education, it is the household that is given priority over other forms of social organization, and here again the strategy seemed successful in Britain in the 1980s, where the household incomes of couples with at least one member in regular full-time employment rose at quite a steady rate. However, once more the auguries from the USA are not encouraging; with median household incomes falling in the 1990s, it is evident that the job rents of a larger segment of such employees are vulnerable in a deregulated labour market (Elliott, 1995a, b). The price of this strategy, hitherto paid by the poor, is now being met by a broader range of households. The reasons for this will be considered in the next section.

COLLECTIVE ACTION AND THE POOR

In this section I shall analyse the lower end of labour markets in the advanced economies – the choices facing individuals and households who are unemployed or in irregular, marginal work. These are people without job rents, some of whom are being exploited by employers who have gained a monopoly position to extract a rent from their labour. The aim of this analysis is to explain their actions as 'best replies' to the strategies of employers, government agencies and each other in this situation.

Implicit in the model of mainstream households developed in the previous section is the claim that their strategies are aimed at excluding such people from access to job rents, and from a share of the benefits from such rents. Because it gives priority to the interdependency between household members, and is aimed at protecting this social formation by conserving those rents still available to employees, the mainstream strategy necessarily excludes those others from its benefits. It relies on electoral support for policy measures for restraining competition from such outsiders that would threaten to compete away job rents in the way set out in the last section. As a collective-action unit, the mainstream household both institutionalizes the sharing of benefits and costs of men's career development, and restrains women from competition in the labour market that might erode men's job rents. But I shall argue that it also blocks the formation of a distributional coalition (political pressure group) in favour of redistribution from insiders to outsiders.

In principle there is a third (collective) strategy open to women as an interest group, in addition to the two modelled in the previous section. This is to lead a grand coalition of outsiders in a bargaining game with insiders that aims to offer restrained competition for their rents, in exchange for a universal share in those rents. A coalition between women and the poor would have a clear electoral majority, and the institutional mechanism through which this could be achieved would be something like a basic income scheme. This would give all citizens an unconditional income as an individual entitlement, unrelated to their labour-market or household roles (Walter, 1988; Parker, 1989; Van Parijs, 1992). As a rough approximation, insiders as holders of job rents could be expected to be net contributors to such a scheme, and outsiders net beneficiaries. The basic income would provide outsiders with a reliable form of income security, and would give them incentives to participate in labour markets on their current terms, rather than seeking to undercut insiders' rents; their interests would therefore be best served by keeping the bargain, and thus a self-enforcing 'social contract' could be reached.

Many social and political theorists have argued that, under present labour-market conditions, basic income represents the only feasible *inclusive* institutional structure for balancing the market-oriented interests of the better-off with the protection of the poor, and thus linking efficiency with social justice (Dahrendorf, 1989; Jordan, 1989; Van Parijs, 1992; Barry, 1994; Van Parijs, 1995). Some feminist theorists have argued that it is also the measure that is most in line with women's collective interests (Pateman, 1995). However, although it is now taken more seriously in policy debates (Borrie, 1994; Purdy, 1995; Aitken, 1994; Brittan, 1995; Young and Halsey, 1995;

A. B. Atkinson, 1995; Duncan and Hobson, 1995), it is useful at this point to analyse why no such strategy has ever been widely canvassed, why no major political party has ever used it to mobilize electoral support, and why the poor have not organized themselves around it. I shall also analyse how the poor have responded to the strategies of employers and mainstream households.

In the Continental European countries, it was until recently quite plausible to maintain that the institutional structures of the post-war era still provided the best available protection against the dislocations of global market forces, together with the best available opportunities for growth in the incomes of mainstream households. This was because, as has already been argued, the rationalizations of their labour forces by employers, in the face of intensified international competition since the early 1970s, have been accomplished through the social insurance systems, making extensive use of relatively generous early retirement pensions and disability benefits in particular. Even where a large group of long-term unemployed claimants have run out of social insurance benefits, and fallen into social assistance (as in the Netherlands, Belgium and Denmark), the somewhat 'softer' welfare state allows them to survive for longer periods without too much pressure to accept low-paid work. Hence the existing structure could claim to manage the changed overall situation by easing the passage of its least productive workers, with the political support of those still enjoying insider status. The latter get income protection through benefits, the former through labour-market regulation. Even where the decline in industrial employment has been largest, and the costs (in terms of government borrowing and interest repayments) highest, as in Belgium, this system has allowed a comparatively successful management of the dislocations associated with globalization. Belgium's relative position among the rich countries, in terms of GDP per head, has scarcely declined (Pacolet and Debrabander, 1995).

However, the strains in that system have recently begun to show, and are manifested in concerns about the high rates of youth unemployment in many countries, and the high costs of social insurance schemes. The latter has been a particular worry in Germany, with fears that firms would start to withdraw industrial investment and look to lower-cost sites abroad, because of high on-wage contributions. Hence there is a growing debate about the basic income proposal, especially in France (Duboin, 1985), the Netherlands (WRR, 1985; Hoogenboom and Roebroek, 1990; Centraalplanbureau, 1993), Belgium (Van Trier, 1994) and Denmark (Loftager, 1994; Christensen, 1994). On the other side, the 'passivity' and 'dependence' of claimant populations have come to be perceived as a problem by those who see the need for measures to persuade or require them to participate in economic roles (Adriaansens and Dercksen, 1993). Such analyses draw on the writings of American authors to argue the case for more conditions and more enforcement in the benefits systems. They also put forward the case for special employment measures, combined with schemes to 'insert' the long-term unemployed into labour markets, as in France. For governments, this strategy complements the compensatory measures taken during the first waves of industrial restructuring and mass unemployment in the late 1970s and early 1980s.

In the US and Britain, the deregulation of labour markets and the growth of low-paid marginal employment and self employment have accompanied the downsizing of the full-time labour force and the growth of unemployment. British research (White, 1991) shows how, with each wave of redundancies through a downturn in the business cycle, the proportion of core, decently paid, secure jobs contracts and the periphery of low-paid marginal work expands. Hence the number of people in households with no member in employment, and households with one or more marginal members, continues to grow, with a good deal of movement between these two groups.

The defining characteristic of poor households is that the mainstream strategy outlined in the previous section is not open to them. Without access to a career and its attendant possibilities of security and job rents, they must orientate themselves towards the opportunities and incentives of the market for marginal work, the availability and rewards of informal work, and the structure and rules of benefits systems. Their choices of how to combine these reflect their strategic replies to employers in search of 'flexibility', to the benefits authorities, and to each other.

Unlike the mainstream, where one lifetime strategy seems to emerge as the dominant equilibrium solution to such bargaining games, the labour-supply behaviour of poor households seems far more variable. As seen through the official statistics, there are large pools of long-term unemployment, a large flow between unemployment and marginal work, and a large segment of households with one member in regular, long-term, low-paid work and others in part-time or irregular employment. It looks as if there exist three groups who have adopted quite different strategies in relation to the same institutional structures of opportunities and constraints, the 'dependent', the 'risky' and the 'steady' households.

However, British research in deprived communities suggests that this is rather misleading. There are indeed at least three different ways of trying to gain an income that is sufficient to cover household outgoings, but all of these combine elements from the labour market, the benefits system, the informal economy and communal systems of mutual support, and households move between strategies over time. There is no one reliable way of securing such an income in the conditions of uncertainty that prevail where the labour market has undergone deregulation, resulting in hypercasualization (see chapter 2), and where the benefits system, lumbering in the wake of work choices, makes detailed assessments of eligibility in constantly changing situations, and thus provides no reliable, regular payments (see chapter 5). Poor people's strategies must therefore themselves be flexible enough to orientate themselves to all these sources of income and support, and combine them in different ways, depending on current circumstances (Jordan et al., 1992).

The choice between these three different strategies depends upon what is the primary source of household income at any time – the benefits system, marginal irregular work by the main household earner (usually the man), or low-paid regular work by this main earner. One reason why the man is usually the main earner among poor households in Britain is that part-time employment in the labour-market segment largely reserved for women (cleaning, catering, social care) is widely available, and hence the woman can usually supplement the man's earnings when he is in work of either kind, and then withdraw when he is unemployed, because of the reduction in benefits he would get if she continued (Kell and Wright, 1990; Harris and Morris, 1986). But all three strategies are orientated towards the benefits system, and towards each other. Workers who take low-paid regular jobs calculate that they will do better in these (supplemented by family credit and housing benefits) than through the much more variable earnings available in marginal employment, in competition with others currently using that strategy. Irregular workers assess these risks before accepting such offers, and the long-term unemployed assess the wage that would be necessary to make it worthwhile for them to sacrifice the continuity of their claims (Jordan et al., 1992, ch. 4).

All three strategies also include an orientation towards informal work opportunities (cash jobs that are not declared to the tax or benefit authorities). In our research study, two-thirds of the households interviewed indicated that they had done small amounts of such informal work at times, and that it was a culturally accepted practice (within reasonable limits) in their community (Jordan et al., 1992, ch. 6). It gave them room for manoeuvre in budgeting for large bills and 'extras', and for handling periods when benefits were delayed or suspended (see below).

Finally, all three strategies are also orientated towards networks of support, through kin and friends. There is some evidence from research in one working-class district that these networks tend to segregate employed from unemployed households; for the former they are vital for job-finding. However, the same study found greater density of mutual support among the long-term unemployed, mainly involving kinship links, and with considerable financial support (Morris, 1992; Morris and Irwin, 1992). Similarly, the large-scale study conducted by Gallie et al. (1993) found that unemployed people sustained their leisure activities and social contacts, but tended to focus on other people in the same situation. In our study of a deprived community, there were complex kinship and friendship networks in which men gave information about informal work opportunities and assistance with home improvements, and women gave support over child care and other practical assistance. They also provided a medium for informal markets, for instance those involving animals, birds and fish, stocks of which were built up during periods of employment, and run down during unemployment (Jordan et al., 1992, ch. 7). Similar evidence from Canada is given by Felt and Sinclair (1992).

In order to sustain the flexibility to use any one of these strategies, depending on current opportunities, partners in poor households must bargain with each other over labour-market choices, pursued in contrasting markets, which contain more marginal, irregular work for men, and more regular, part-time work for women. Each such choice can be modelled as a Battle of the Sexes game, as in the figure in the previous section, especially over how child-care hours are to be shared between them. Because of the unpredictability of work opportunities for men, there is no stable equilibrium outcome for this game, and in our research negotiations over the priority given to men's overtime or women's regular (but lower paid) work commitments were frequently required (Jordan et al., ch. 6).

The potentially irreconcilable conflicts in such decisions could be solved if the woman had access to child-care support from kin or friends; this was why such networks played a crucial role in sustaining partnerships and their strategies for gaining adequate incomes. Contributions to the reciprocal support given in communal networks therefore represented an investment decision; they could later be the basis for claims for assistance in a crisis, or with a change of circumstances. For men too, investments in male networks, involving exchanges of labour and information about informal work, gave flexibility and room for manoeuvre in overcoming the income crises that were unavoidable in a hyper-casualized labour market.

Policy debate has focused narrowly on two issues: benefits dependency and undeclared work by claimants. Hence policy in Britain, as in the USA, has been aimed at limiting the availability of income maintenance for the poor, while steering them towards the formal labour market. In Britain, the government's programme since the early 1980s has been one of 'targeting' assistance on 'those in greatest need', both by limiting eligibility for national insurance unemployment benefit (to be recast in 1996 as a 'job seeker's allowance' lasting only six months), and by imposing stricter tests of availability and active work search. Benefits administration increasingly involves detailed investigation of claimants' resources and requirements, as government policy and the growth of long-term unemployment shift the balance from insurance-based to 'targeted' assistance.

These assessments are aimed at reducing public expenditure, both by screening out claimants with adequate means, and by excluding those who are not 'involuntarily unemployed'. But they also drive up *transaction costs* for each claim, since the individual investigations required consume large amounts of staff time. One way of counteracting this is to force claimants to bear part of these costs. It has become standard administrative practice to suspend payments of benefits in all cases requiring investigation of eligibility. Stricter testing and more complex assessments also involve delays in processing even standard claims (McLaughlin et al., 1989). During such periods, it is the claimant who absorbs the costs; the household must survive without assistance, and can get into serious debt, or even become homeless.

In so far as many potential applicants consider the claiming process too costly (P. Craig, 1991), these procedures are successful in terms of reducing expenditure, though not in terms of equity. However, experienced claimants develop counter-strategies to resist the effects of official administrative practices. From the claimants' point of view, stricter tests, administrative delays and benefits suspensions all change the relative payoffs of declared and undeclared work, making the latter more attractive. Given that most of the work available in the formal labour market is low paid and short-term or irregular, they reason that the risk of debt or destitution when they are forced to claim again is not worth taking, and prefer to take what is available on an informal (undeclared) basis. In our research on low-income couples with children, two-thirds of the respondents indicated that they had done occasional small 'cash jobs', and most irregular workers justified this in terms of the transaction costs associated with claiming (Jordan et al., 1992, chs 4 and 6). They told stories of how they had been unfairly disqualified, or had their payments suspended or delayed, to show that it was incumbent on them as responsible parents to do occasional undeclared work.

These interactions can be modelled as a prisoner's dilemma game between claimants and staff, with transaction costs represented as negative payoffs. In each case, the staff have to choose between suspending payment for full investigation, or paying after the minimum delay. From the claimant's viewpoint, suspension means that the staff have defected and he or she must bear a high cost; quick payment represents co-operation. The claimant must choose between keeping the rules (from the staff's perspective this represents co-operation) or bending them by doing undeclared work (defection). The payoffs are such that the staff do best (save most costs) if they suspend benefits and the claimant keeps the rules; the claimant does best by bending the rules, but getting quick payment from the staff. If both defect, the costs are high for both (extra investigation for staff, loss of benefits for claimants); if both co-operate, the costs are lower for both. However, the equilibrium solution to the game is mutual defection, because if either co-operates it is to the advantage of the other to defect. Figure 2 shows this diagrammatically, with the negative payoffs (representing costs) for the claimant shown first in each square, and for the staff second (Jordan, 1995).

STAFF

		Co-operate	Defect
CLAIMANT	Co-operate	−2, −2	−7, 0
	Defect	0, −7	−5, −5

Fig. 2

There are several important points about the costs associated with interactions that take this form. It might be argued that, since most claimants are *long-term* beneficiaries, a one-shot prisoner's dilemma game misrepresents what is a series of interactions. Axelrod's work (1984) on iterated prisoner's dilemma games suggests that the cycle of mutual defections can be broken by players 'signalling' willingness to co-operate by adopting a strategy of minimal retaliation (start with a co-operative move and only defect once in response to another player's defection). But the British government has signalled just the opposite of this with its well-publicized 'clampdowns' on fraud and introduction of new restrictions. The point is that policies for changing the payoffs – for example, by increasing the costs to claimants by lengthening suspensions or benefits cuts, or increasing prosecutions and penalties for detected offences – do not change the equilibrium solution to the game, because as soon as one side co-operates, it still pays the other to defect. Yet there is a strong impetus within the game for policy-makers to try to increase enforcement, and in so doing to raise enforcement costs also, thus increasing both public expenditure and the impoverishment of poor people.

The second point is that claimants' resistance to such policies and administrative practices is unlikely to take the form of isolated, individual action. In deprived communities informal activity, including undeclared work, becomes co-ordinated in club-like ways (see chapter 2). The existence of networks of information and contacts also reduces the risk of detection, because a culture of resistance develops among the membership, with its own norms of conduct and everyday practices of opposition to the official system of enforcement. Such forms of resistance rely on the 'hidden transcripts' of underground communications and covert actions, under the cloak of compliance (Scott, 1985; 1990). They are much more difficult to suppress through enforcement measures, because risks are dispersed through anonymity and collusion.

These strategies allow the poor to compensate themselves to some extent for their exclusion from the benefits of the mainstream community, and particularly from job rents. They repre-

sent an alternative to political action, though they are not incon-
sistent with it. The poor can always use other forms of collective
action, such as riots, if the opportunities and incentives make this
attractive. The relative success of resistance strategies, including
undeclared work and crime, is reflected in the discrepancy
between income measures of the living standards of the poorest
households, and *expenditure* measures (IFS, 1995). By income
measures, the worst-off have suffered an absolute impoverishment
in real terms since 1979; by expenditure measures they have not.

The full implications of these developments have only gradually penetrated the policy debate and the social scientific
research agenda (Jordan and Redley, 1994; Evason and Wood,
1995). There is now growing recognition of the issues, with a
government report estimating an annual £1.4 billion in false
claims (BBC Radio 4, *Today* programme, 10 July 1995). Yet this
has increased rather than diminished pressure for costly enforcement measures. The government is now introducing bar-codes
on benefit payment books in order to combat fraud (*Today* programme, 9 August 1995). Local authorities are trying to introduce systems to prevent fraudulent claims for student grants
(*Today* programme, 18 July 1995). The Labour party leadership
has expressed support for councils such as Reading's Labour-
controlled administration, whose benefit fraud squad is inviting
residents to inform on fraudulent claimants of housing benefits
(*Today* programme, 9 August 1995).

While the poor are able to take these self-compensatory
actions, and while political parties (including the Labour party)
are able to mobilize political support in mainstream households
to suppress them, no coalition for redistributing job rents is feasible, and the basic income proposal will not be put on the political agenda. The future possibilities for this policy development
will be further discussed in chapter 7.

CONCLUSIONS

This long chapter has sought to explain the shift, particularly in
the Anglo-Saxon countries, from collective strategies in games

involving interactions between capital and labour, to individual and household strategies that prioritize the nuclear family over other forms of social organization. It has argued that these can be seen as 'best replies' to employers' strategies in labour markets, where there were collective-action problems over universally available forms of social protection. Hence individuals and couples in Britain and the US could be shown to act in defence of their stake in remaining job rents, but in so doing to exclude the poor from any share of these, and thus from any reliable form of collective protection against exploitation.

This explains why the poor have developed distinctive forms of social organization that are different from those of mainstream society. It also explains why they have come to rely on their own actions and strategies, in households, networks and communities, rather than on trade unions or political action; in the US and Britain alike these last two have virtually ceased to play a role in industrial relations or the political process.

But my analysis has also raised doubts about whether these strategies can be sustained, either by mainstream households or by poor people. Evidence from the United States suggests that interactions similar to those in Britain have been unsuccessful in defending job rents. In a deregulated labour market, median household incomes have declined markedly in the 1990s, a factor that has brought insecurity to a far wider band of families. Furthermore, declining rates of return to investments in higher education, reflected in falling earnings of college graduates, cast doubts on the viability of mainstream strategies for conserving the advantages earned by parents and passing them to the next generation (the classic goal of middle-class household strategies).

Poor people's strategies can likewise be seen as individually rational but collectively mutually frustrating. They serve to help them, in households and in communities, to resist exploitation by employers and deprivation by the benefits authorities. But in so far as these can both be traced to the deregulation of labour markets, they do nothing to address this original evil; instead, by opportunistically combining low-paid, marginal and informal (undeclared cash) work, they actually contribute to the casualization of employment, and hence to their lack of collective formal protection.

Furthermore, the divergent strategies of mainstream and marginal households, that for the past two decades have resulted in poverty and social exclusion, are now beginning to produce costly social conflicts. As mainstream households grow poorer and more insecure, they look for others to blame. In the United States, right-wing politicians have found ready scapegoats among the poor, and especially among African American welfare mothers. A 'politics of enforcement' has come into being, focusing on the culture of resistance among poor African Americans, and aiming to use coercion against it. This will be further analysed in chapter 6.

5

Community, Polarization and Social Exclusion

The previous chapter, though lengthy, was certainly not an exhaustive account of social interactions in advanced industrialized states. Many of these cannot be captured in its analysis of games around the rents available in labour markets. Its central theses – that interdependency in households is being given increasing priority over other forms of mutuality, especially in the Anglo-Saxon countries, that welfare agencies operate increasingly as exclusive clubs, and that poor people co-ordinate resistance to exclusion through 'informal' (and often illegal) economic activities – would be open to contradiction if it could be shown that these other interactions offset the consequences of household priority, club formation and informal resistance. Above all, they would be contradicted if some principle according to which the poor are *included,* and their vulnerabilities shielded, could be identified. One important candidate for this role of countervailing principle is the concept of *community.*

Indeed, the possibility that some spontaneous, inclusive, co-operative and redistributive principle is at work in many social interactions now fuels the hopes and energies of socialist oppositions to the market Utopianism of the New Right in the advanced industrialized countries, and also informs the policies of beleaguered centrist governments in most of these states. It is increasingly difficult to negotiate self-enforcing agreements between capital and labour that will provide *either* 'full employment' (in the postwar sense), or adequate income protection (through social insurance) through the good corporatist offices of the state. Hence the main thrust of inclusive collectivism shifts to other interactions, outside the realm of older, statist institutions. Socialists must now reluctantly accept, as those on the right and in the centre now confidently proclaim, the fact that citizens are moved by individual self-interest and value the scope for autonomy and choice provided by the economic conditions and institutional structures of the 1990s. But this still leaves open the possibility that they will recognize that they have good (self-interested) reasons for supporting certain universal, collectivist schemes for health care and other welfare provision (suitably adapted to ensure productive efficiency), and for the regulation of a safe, sustainable and convivial environment. Perhaps these systems can supply the social institutions within which citizens may interact co-operatively and inclusively, to the benefit of all, including the poor.

If so, the hopes for this rest substantially on the idea that *community* can supply individuals with ways of harmonizing interests and softening divisions and conflicts, especially in relation to poverty and social exclusion. If the basis for new forms of integration and inclusion is unlikely to be a corporatist contract between the 'social partners' in the next century, then it must lie in the recognition and institutionalization of other forms of interdependency within whole populations. The notion of community preoccupied political theorists in the 1980s (Mulhall and Swift, 1992), and although communitarians seemed to lose the theoretical argument with their liberal opponents, they have emerged as the new influential voices counselling governments. They seem to offer the prospect of systems of moral obligation, providing a low-price 'cement of society', and thus an affordable way of binding together various divergent elements. In particular, they suggest new possibilities for offsetting, counteracting or even correcting the unintended consequences of 1980s individualism – crime, drug abuse, single parenthood, 'welfare dependency', and so on. This explains the otherwise surprising guru status of purveyors of somewhat folksy, homespun and backward-looking civic moralities of responsibility and voluntary public-spiritedness (Etzioni, 1993).

In this chapter I shall investigate the claims of community as an organizing principle, and the evidence about how voluntary non-market exchanges affect configurations of poverty and exclusion in present-day society. I shall argue that despite the hostility of communitarian theorists to the public-choice perspective (Etzioni, 1988; Wolfe, 1989), its central theses can be captured in the conceptual framework of that analysis, in terms of interdependencies over collective goods, and the sharing of certain costs and benefits among group members. When restated in these terms, it becomes clear that the idea of community raises all the same issues of social exclusion of vulnerable people as are found in other groups and organizations – how collective-action units are formed, which collective goods are at stake, how co-operation and restraint among members are sustained, and who is included and who excluded.

However, the concept of community does provide a useful point of entry to the analysis of social polarization in advanced industrialized societies. In this chapter I shall particularly address the consequences of choices over where to live in present-day societies, with their high rates of mobility and good communications. Within the public-choice perspective, these choices can be seen as 'voting with the feet' (Tiebout, 1956) over bundles of collective goods, available in different combinations of quality and quantity, and at different prices, in each district. Evidence on social polarization can thus be analysed in terms of the consequences of individual decisions, and I go on to examine the implications of more homogeneous local communities (in terms of incomes of residents) for poverty and social exclusion.

The overall aim of the chapter is to show how individual decisions over collective goods produce configurations of 'communities of choice' (among mainstream households), and 'communities of fate' among the poor and excluded (Hirst, 1994). It is also to analyse the social costs of these developments, and the problems of policies directed at reducing these costs. I shall argue that the phenomena connoted by the concept of community (mutuality, the sharing of costs and benefits, redistribution among members) can, in societies that are divided along the lines of the present-day US and UK, become part of the problem of social polarization and exclusion, rather than part of the solution. In other words, community can serve to integrate membership groups with antagonistic interests, and to mobilize them for conflict, and in conditions of polarization and exclusion it will tend to do just this, rather than sustain political programmes of harmonization and inclusion.

COMMUNITIES AND COLLECTIVE GOODS

From the perspective of public-choice theory, the analysis of social interaction starts by identifying the collective goods that are at stake when groups organize to pursue their interests. Collective action is explained in terms of common interests in maximizing the joint supply of such goods, and minimizing the costs of producing them. Individuals form and join groups according to their preferences for such goods; they are included or excluded according to their potential contributions and costs, and according to how members can maximize their joint benefits.

Theory of community usually starts from a rejection of this perspective. Communitarians insist that social formations – families, networks, associations, societies – are logically prior to individuals, and are not based on individual calculations of utility (Etzioni, 1988, ch. 12). All interactions take place in the context of norms, practices and institutions that steer, stabilize and regulate them. They are guided by a 'logic of appropriateness' (March and Olsen, 1989), through roles and rules that give individual actions their social meaning, and provide routine, predictability and order in informal as well as formal encounters. Through morality and systems of social obligation, individuals are socialized into patterns of behaviour that make other kinds of social institutions – such as markets and polities – possible. Community is thus seen as a necessary condition for modern societies.

As we saw in chapter 1 (pp. 22–7), human interdependency is

traced to certain fundamental features of all social interactions that are presupposed in the very idea of individuals pursuing interests rationally or strategically. These include *reciprocity* (the notion that meaningful communication and economic exchange require respect for the social value of each member, and willingness to obey very basic principles, such as taking turns and queuing, rather than grabbing or jostling); *sharing* as a potential benefit of interaction, usually involving the conservation of common-pool resources; and *redistribution* as the basis of all property rights, since the requirements of final consumption of basic goods by individuals demand collective guarantees from the group on the availability of regular food and shelter. In this view, public-choice theory is not an explanation of social behaviour, but a mistaken prescription for how individuals should act in a society committed to economic efficiency above all other goals. A proper understanding of interdependence and mutual moral obligations requires an analysis of how human groups construct meaning and order for themselves through their social practices (Wolfe, 1989; 1991).

The difficulty for communitarians in offering moral obligation as an alternative to economic self-interest as the fundamental principle for social organization is how to explain specific choices in a complex social environment. For instance, Alan Wolfe, one of the most intelligent critics of the economic perspective on social choice, acknowledges that society no longer supplies individuals with reliable rules for everyday conduct or long-term planning:

> What makes us modern, in short, is that we are capable of acting as our own moral agents . . . Instead, moral obligation ought to be viewed as a socially-constructed practice, as something we learn through the actual experience of trying to live together with other people . . . We need civil society – families, communities, friendship networks, solidaritic ties developed at the workplace, voluntarism, spontaneous groups and movements – not to reject, but to complete the project of modernity. (1991, pp. 46–7)

In other words, modern people have to work hard at finding their own rules of behaviour, and forming their own groups and communities in which to act out their responsibilities to others.

From the public-choice perspective, all this can be gathered up and explained within the rubric of cost-sharing and the restraint of competition. Norms of reciprocity and self-restraint, like laws of property, are demonstrably in the interests of all members of a group when they can all benefit from orderly exchanges; Adam Smith and David Hume recognized that it was this ability to make binding moral agreements that distinguished human beings from instinctual animals and capricious gods (Levy, 1992). The breakdown of such restraints is extremely costly (Hobbes, 1651, ch. 13), because both grabbing (animal-style) and omnipotent opportunism (in the manner of Greek gods or German professors) destroy the potential gains from trade. Thus theory of community, while irrefutable, tells us nothing about the specifics of social interaction: it cannot predict the outcome of any particular encounter. The interesting questions are always about how the relevant collective-action groups are formed, around which collective goods, who is included, and who excluded. These questions can only be addressed in any systematic way through considering individuals' preferences, the costs associated with supplying collective goods, and hence the contribution rates required for effective collective action.

This is especially obvious in late-modern societies, where rapid mobility both within and between states reflects choices about collective goods – group formation, entry to and exit from clubs, and 'voting with the feet'. The task of this chapter is to show how collective goods that have conventionally been treated as being supplied on a national basis by the state (health and old-age care, infrastructural services, education, the physical and social environment) are in practice constructed through such decisions, and how the economics of individual choices is reflected in variations between the quantity and quality of such services at the local level. In other words, I aim to explain such phenomena as social polarization and the emergence of concentrations of poverty in terms of the economic theory of social inclusion and exclusion. This in turn will cast doubt on community as a panacea for social divisions and conflicts; community (in the sense of membership of groups organized around identifiable, specific collective goods) becomes part of the problem, rather than part of the solution.

To understand these phenomena, we need to see decisions about where to live and which social services to use as analogous to 'voting with the feet' and joining exclusive clubs in public-choice theory. As argued in chapter 1 (pp. 25–33), residential districts can be analysed as sites that have been developed by an owner (a private landlord or the local council) to provide a bundle of environmental and social services, in exchange for a ground rent, or the return on a building plot that is sold (Heath, 1957; McCallum, 1970; Foldvary, 1994). The rent or sale value will reflect the extent to which the site's value has been added to by the provision of such goods as transport links, shops and recreational facilities, water, sewerage and fuel supplies, fire service, street lighting, schools and hospitals, libraries, sports fields and cultural facilities, and so on. It will also reflect other factors, such as the local crime rate (and hence insurance costs), proximity to work opportunities and areas of natural beauty.

Each private developer invests in building a new residential community with the economics of such factors in mind; each local council tries to develop its locality as a balance of micro-communities that reflects the optimum mix of such collective goods, from the point of view of revenue generation over a long period. The aim is to attract residents (as in the interactive computer game 'SIM-city') who will in turn invest their private energies and resources in their communities, thus further increasing the value of the site. If a residential development generates a lively set of interactions, such that new businesses, voluntary associations and cultural facilities are produced through mutually gainful exchanges, this benefits a landowner who has other nearby sites for development, and the council, whose revenues are increased through all these improvements.

In supplying social and environmental services, local councils also provide some employment, thus stabilizing the local economy. In Britain particularly, post-war councils built and administered large-scale housing schemes, subsidizing the rents of working-class families as a way of maintaining a loyal electorate, and sustaining a stable and rather harmonious indigenous community. Thus local authorities were able to pursue a degree of economic planning and social engineering through their networks of public services. This contrasts with the situation in the US, where social provision was more minimal, and social housing a residual category. The institutional reforms of the 1980s in Britain, especially in the housing sector – where a large proportion of council houses were sold, and others transferred to non-profit housing associations who mainly provided for special needs – shifts the British situation close to that of the US. In Continental Europe, the relative scarcity of council housing is counterbalanced by a far higher investment in infrastructural, recreational and cultural resources, in both urban and rural areas.

As mobility, both within and between states, has increased in the post-war period, and kinship and friendship ties have become less important as a source of welfare provision among mainstream citizens of advanced industrialized states, so districts have tended to become more homogeneous in their populations (Miller, 1981). Older concentrated (or congested) areas have been broken up, both by local authority demolition and reconstruction, and by the development of residential districts in the suburbs. Better-off households have moved from older, inner-city districts into outer, dispersed communities, with their more attractive physical amenities, their better schools and clinics, and their more convenient or commodious houses and gardens. Others have moved right out of cities into villages, free-riding on strong local bonds of social obligation and low crime rates, while contributing little to networks of mutual aid. The consequence has been self-selecting communities of people with similar incomes and preferences for bundles of collective goods; but it has also been the creation of bleak out-of-town housing estates, consisting either of social or private developments, with very few facilities and little mutual support, to which residents of the former congested inner-city districts have moved or been moved; and a residue of inner-city ghetto districts, with run-down or derelict housing, and the worst standards of public provision of all kinds.

This kind of social polarization produces a different sort of social exclusion from the ones analysed in chapter 4. It means that households with the highest incomes cluster around the most desirable sites, and enjoy the best collective goods of all kinds, including social services. They can combine the advantages of being able to pay for the most improved sites, the benefits of consuming the goods supplied by the most successful local authorities, and the gains to be made by associating with others in exclusive local clubs, thus enabling them to internalize certain costs, and protect their lifestyles from the disutilities of congestion. These clubs include private education and whatever health care, welfare services and cultural goods they prefer to supply for themselves in this way, rather than from the public authority.

At the other end of the scale, residents of bleak outer-city estates or inner-city ghettoes have little choice over which bundles of collective goods (and bads) to consume. They rely disproportionately on public services of all kinds, and on networks for mutual support and resistance activity. Their informal clubs and collective-action groups will be far more fully analysed in the next chapter. Finally there are still more transient or marginal groups, such as migrant communities, travellers and homeless people, whose groups and networks are dispersed through districts with other mobile or transitional residents, and who may not rely (for instance, in the case of illegal immigrants) on any public benefits and services.

This chapter aims to clarify these processes of social exclusion through community formation and 'voting with the feet', and to analyse the costs associated with them, drawing mainly on examples from Britain, the US and Germany. It focuses on how the choices of better-off individuals affect the life-chances of the poor, in relation to such services as health care, social welfare, the social and physical environment. It also addresses the issue of how these same interactions affect the roles of women in households and communities, and how social polarization and exclusion contribute to the emergence of 'race' as a factor in the conflicts of interest between financially comfortable and poor communities.

RESIDENTIAL POLARIZATION

In social policy studies, polarization has been analysed mainly as an outcome (intended or unintended) of national programmes for income maintenance, health care, education and social welfare provision, or as an outcome of local housing policies. For example, in Britain there have been a huge number of studies on income inequalities, demonstrating that these widened in the 1980s (Stitt, 1993; Kumar, 1993; Bradshaw, 1990; Oppenheim, 1990; Johnson and Webb, 1990); on health inequalities, showing that the poor have shorter life expectancy (Townsend et al., 1994; Phillimore and Morris, 1991; Goldblatt, 1990), worse access to health care (Haynes, 1991; Payne, 1991), and more vulnerability to chronic long-term diseases that cause their quality of life to deteriorate (Abbott and Sapsford, 1994; Victor, 1991; Bartley, 1992; 1994); and on inequalities in educational achievement (Brown and Riddell, 1992; Tizard et al., 1988; Garner, 1994; Benabon, 1994); and access to social welfare provision (Hardey and Glover, 1991; Morris, 1992).

In terms of housing policies, the sale of council housing, the drastic cut in public housing construction and subsidization, and the shift towards means-tested housing benefits, have all been shown to contribute to polarization in the quality of housing amenities, and the incomes of residents in particular estates (Forrest and Murie, 1988a and b; James et al., 1991; Williams et al., 1986).

However, such analyses construct individual welfare as the product of official policies, rather than the outcome of social interaction. The perspective adopted here sees actors as seeking the best available payoffs from formal and informal activity within the changing structures of opportunities and constraints they have faced in recent years. In the previous chapter it was argued that these changes encouraged individuals to give priority to household strategies over membership of mass solidarities, such as trade unions. An important opportunity for pursuing such household strategies in Britain until the late 1980s has been a 'housing career' – the purchase of increasingly larger, often older, properties, improved over time by a mixture of paid and household labour (R. E. Pahl, 1984). Because of quite generous tax relief on mortgage interest payments and capital gains, and because house prices rose faster than the general price index, better-off households were able to get a substantial asset virtually costlessly by this means in the period between 1963 and 1988. Such strategies provide an example of what this section will analyse – actions that involve geographical mobility, taking advantage of tax breaks, subsidies or benefits, but are aimed at maximizing utility and minimizing costs, with particular reference to the collective goods that constitute 'community'.

Strategic mobility involves costs of many kinds, which will be analysed in the next section. In Britain, these include the large volume of 'negative equity' which accrued when households rushed to acquire credit for house purchases during the late 1980s boom, which in turn led to borrowing exceeding the value of their houses when the market collapsed. Although this was partly a result of the government's policies on financial deregulation (Hutton, 1994, ch. 3) and owner occupation (such as tax incentives), it was mainly a consequence of household strategies. Choices to seek positional advantage in the housing market, though rational for each particular household, when summed together produced socially wasteful outcomes. Household strategies proved mutually frustrating, as house prices first rocketed upwards and then gradually fell, leaving families with heavy interest payments, and little prospect of recouping their losses. In mid-1995, there were estimated to be 1.5 million households with negative equity, and 1000 repossessions by building societies each week. A further 130,000 home owners had serious arrears of repayments, with no prospects of clearing these (BBC Radio 4, *Today* programme, 15 August 1995).

In Britain and Ireland (O'Connell, 1994), as in the US, the owner-occupied sector is larger (at more than two-thirds of all dwellings) than in the Continental European or South-East Asian countries. The rented sector is mainly used by single people, couples waiting for council or community association housing, and elderly people. Young couples entering the owner-occupied market in Britain have two options, because of the nature of the housing stock. They can either buy a small newish property in a

geos of poverty

rural, suburban or an outer-city residential area, or an older (former working-class terrace house, for example) in an urban setting. The latter option is well suited for energetic, practical couples who intend to devote time and money to improving the building, with a view to moving on to something larger and more expensive. When many such couples choose older houses in a particular former working-class district, the consequent 'gentrification' of the area improves property values, and has positive spillovers into community facilities, such as schools and voluntary associations. Local councils are able to encourage such strategies by selective grants for home improvements, and by environmental regeneration, in certain urban districts. Conversely, where councils undertake demolition, or plan road schemes or car parks, or impose planning restrictions, whole districts can become blighted, young couples tend to move out, property prices decline, and the community's material facilities deteriorate, along with the social infrastructure. Household strategies thus reinforce public policy, and polarization consists as much in the collective outcome of household decisions as in the environmental decisions of local authorities.

These changes in the 1980s are reflected in British research studies. Parkinson's (1994) data on Liverpool show that, in an economically depressed city that experienced an 8 per cent fall in its population between 1981 and 1991, and whose unemployment rate stood at 22 per cent in 1994, deprivation was concentrated in specific districts. A 1989 survey suggested that 41 per cent of the city's households lived in poverty, and 16 per cent in intense poverty, but several parts of the city had far lower rates, and unemployment that was well below the national average. The most deprived inner-city wards had unemployment rates of over 40 per cent; and that of the ward with the highest concentration of black and Asian residents stood at 41.6 per cent. More generally, the British government's own deprivation index (Department of the Environment, 1994) showed that the position of many northern areas improved in the period 1981 to 1991 *relative* to those in the south, but that deprivation was more widespread in Britain as a whole. But within the large conurbations, even those which (like Manchester) improved in relation

to the nation as a whole deteriorated in relation to their surrounding districts, while the same was true for those that suffered *relative* deterioration (such as Newcastle and Birmingham).
The set of places at the top of the rankings of deprivation
appears to have remained relatively constant between 1981 and
1991. This suggests that those places which were most deprived
at the start of the decade remained deprived at its close and,
indeed, many of the very worst areas, such as the inner cores of
conurbations, showed a continuing decline relative to the
peripheral parts of the areas (Robson et al., 1994, p. 8).

Similar phenomena were evident in cities with more successful
local economic strategies, within more prosperous national
economies. In Rotterdam:

> social exclusion is not confined to particular groups but is con-
> centrated in particular areas. In particular the most disadvantaged
> have been increasingly concentrated in areas immediately adja-
> cent to the city centre . . . They are also the areas where ethnic
> minorities have been concentrated . . . In the mid-1990s, despite
> the economic renaissance of Rotterdam after 1985 and the physi-
> cal renewal of the city centre and social housing stock, a picture
> emerges of a large group of unemployed people, single mothers,
> disabled and ethnic-minority households living on minimum
> income concentrated in a limited number of problem neighbour-
> hoods . . . Economic growth has gone hand-in-hand with social
> exclusion. (Parkinson, 1994, pp. 7–8)

In the same period Frankfurt, another economic success story,
has seen a 50 per cent increase in its numbers of social assistance
recipients, of whom half are now of working age. Some of this
related to inward migration, especially from Eastern Europe;
by 1993, the city had the highest proportion of non-national
residents (at 28.5 per cent) of all German cities, and these were
concentrated in specific districts, with 60–80 per cent non-
national residents in one district near the city centre, where
there was serious overcrowding and lack of social services and
amenities (Parkinson, 1994, p. 9). The price of land doubled
during the 1980s and again in the 1990s; the average flat can be
afforded only by a household with an income three times the
average salary for the city, yet the rate of housing construction

is half the national average. Parkinson comments that

> the city policy of restricting housing growth for environmental reasons and . . . the process of gentrification where higher income groups displace lower income groups has caused growing disparities in the housing provision enjoyed by different income groups . . . Economic success has again been the cause, not the solution, to growing social exclusion in the city. (pp. 9–10)

All these are examples of a milder form of the residential polarization that has been occurring in the large cities of the USA during the period since the 1960s, and of the racialization of concentrated deprivation. Although – as W. J. Wilson (1987) has convincingly shown in his studies of American cities – an African American middle class has emerged through improved access to higher education and job opportunities, its constituent households have quickly adopted the same strategy as their white counterparts and fled the inner-city ghetto for the leafy suburbs, leaving concentrations of poor, unskilled, unfit and unemployed people. The decline of employment opportunities in these districts has caused further deterioration of the local economy, and contributed to a rise in crime, drug use, and hustling as ways of life; high rates of imprisonment of young African American men have contributed to the prevalence of lone-parent families, claiming public assistance. This in turn has reinforced the stereotype of the deprived district as a disintegrated, lawless, deviant and destructive social system, and accelerated the exit of more prosperous African American families.

However, these 'communities of fate', made up of the residual category of residents after Darwinian processes of economic selection, are by no means passive, anomic or resigned. They have generated strong resistance cultures, which have expressed themselves mainly in informal collective action outside the political mainstream, and have consisted both in solidaristic and mutually supportive association, and opportunistic, predatory action against the residents of 'communities of choice'. For instance, in southside Chicago the slogan 'Bomb the Suburbs' (the title of a counter-cultural treatise by the dissident William 'Upski' Wimsatt) is prominently emblazoned in graffiti in the

poorest African American districts (Bhabha, 1995). This represents a retaliatory call to arms against the increasingly vociferous
campaign, now orchestrated by Newt Gingrich and his colleagues, for suburban values of family responsibility and the work
ethic to be enforced upon the black ghettoes, in the name of
'renewing American civilization'.

Explicit antagonistic mobilizations of this kind are rarer in
European cities, despite the best efforts of neo-fascist and neo-
Nazi political groups, and the rise of a politics of race and resentment. However, British politicians were shaken in June 1994 by
the uprising of Asian youths in Bradford, in an unprecedented
display of disaffection; previous rioting (for instance, in 1981 and
on several subsequent occasions) had mainly involved Afro-
Caribbean youths in districts such as Brixton in London or St
Paul's in Bristol. Together with similar disturbances among
mainly white youths in Luton and Leeds, these events reminded
the authorities that anger and revenge among the poor in inner
and outer city deprived districts can manifest themselves in spontaneous and costly collective action. The whole issue of inter-
community conflict will be analysed in detail in chapter 6.

One factor that may tend to mitigate polarization along racial
lines on both sides of the Atlantic is the continued inflow of
immigrants from other parts of the globe – in the US from
South-East Asia and Central and Latin America, in Western
Europe from North Africa and the former Soviet bloc countries.
These immigrants mainly move into districts that are intermediate between the suburbs and the residual long-term ghettoes –
districts with much private rented property, bed-sits and cheaper
flats, and with a population constantly in transition. Such complex, multi-cultural and rapidly changing communities absorb
much of the stress associated with rapid mobility (as in the example of Frankfurt above); they do so in part through many small
networks of informal assistance and support, specific to new
immigrant communities. In this way they provide a safety valve,
without which the relentless trend towards polarization among
the long-term resident white and black populations might produce more entrenched conflict. However, they also provide a
focus for resentment and resistance, because the evident conges-

tion and environmental stress in such districts becomes a symbol for fears about the rising social costs of the polarization process.

THE SOCIAL COSTS OF POLARIZATION

According to the theoretical analysis of residential polarization developed in the first two sections of this chapter, local councils should be strategically aware of these tendencies, and should take action to maximize the benefits of 'voting with the feet' by mobile households, and minimize the costs of resistance by residual, deprived households. They should plan the overall built environment with such factors in mind, taking account of the advantages of improving certain residential sites to their full potential value (that is, the one that produces the maximum rent, and hence local taxation contribution), while sustaining sufficient heterogeneity of income groupings, cultural practices and household types in other districts as to minimize the generation of costly criminal subcultures or other forms of resistance-orientated collective action. It is in their interests, for the sake of revenue maximization as much as social harmonization, to do so.

However, many factors make it difficult for local authorities (even of the size of large-scale city governments) to sustain such policies. Some of these relate to the present-day economics of the development of the built environment itself. With the growth in the numbers of car owners, there has been immense pressure on the land outside the old city boundaries, in terms of demand for residential development. The dispersed city, composed of concentric rings of satellite estates and suburbs, was pioneered in the USA and Australia (Los Angeles and Brisbane being the extreme cases in terms of low population density). This in turn makes it difficult for city authorities to sustain a viable public transport network. It gives rise to a vicious circle: dispersed cities increase car ownership and the use of cars, which increases pressure for such facilities as out-of-town stores, and other car-orientated facilities. In Britain the percentage of new retail stores constructed on the edge of town was 13 per cent in 1980 and 69 per cent in 1993; the percentage of shopping journeys made by car grew from 45 to 66 per cent (Beaumont et al., 1995). Cars were also increasingly used for other routine journeys in dispersed cities. In 1971, 80 per cent of seven- and eight-year-old children made their own way to school; by 1990 it was only 9 per cent (Hillman et al., 1991).

As public transport systems decline and cars choke the inner city, through increased commuting from the satellite districts, new road systems are required. Inner by-passes and circular road schemes further carve up the central environment, thus isolating some old residential districts, and destroying the potential for a compact, integrated living, working and leisure area which should be the hallmark of urban civilization. As Rogers (1995) puts it, cars and commuting promote 'single-minded spaces' (housing estates, shopping centres, business parks, industrial estates, office blocks) that are dispersed and divided from each other by arterial roads, at the expense of spaces in which a diversity of citizens can interact for many different purposes, in a compact and convivial environment that includes squares, parks, restaurants and cultural facilities. Furthermore, developers can maximize their rents, under present planning laws and tax regulations, by improving their sites with these 'single-minded' purposes in view, rather than by developing complex, concentrated, multi-purpose communities that mix together residential, business and leisure uses.

These tendencies have been reinforced by changes in the forms and distributions of productive industries and services, and by competition between cities for the location of production sites. As manual employment in mass production has declined, to be replaced by high-tech industry, financial services, professional and knowledge-based employment on the one hand, and low-paid retailing, leisure, personal and social services on the other, new out-of-town sites of all kinds have been developed while inner-city industrial areas have decayed, and employment near the centre has become irregular and poorly rewarded. These structural factors have been fundamental to other political and social processes tending towards polarization and exclusion (Moulaert, 1994). As competition between cities has intensified, and employment declined, local authorities have primarily aimed to attract industries and services of all kinds. They have been willing to give priority to projects that promise jobs, irrespective of their impact on the social composition of districts, or the environmental balance of the urban community. This has been particularly obvious in those cities, such as Cork in Ireland, which used relatively relaxed laws on planning and pollution to attract multi-national companies to their sites (O'Sullivan, 1994).

Thus local authorities are forced to react to changes in household living and working strategies, and in the global location of productive resources, rather than planning proactively to balance communities or maximize tax returns and minimize social costs. Furthermore, the local planning process in most countries does not encourage a rational strategic approach to the latter task. On the one hand, local councils can attract industry, build roads or gain other discretionary aid from central government or the European Union according to benefits (tax breaks, investment grants, etc.) that pay no heed to such considerations. On the other, many of the social costs associated with polarization and concentrations of deprivation do not fall directly on local councils in most governmental systems – for instance, the costs associated with criminal justice, and especially imprisonment, are borne by central government instead. Hence it does not pay local authorities to take account of the costs of crime and social disintegration. Finally, the committee structure of local councils, and their post-war traditions of resource-building and expansionism, tend towards the growth of budgets for all forms of social provision, even when these are inefficient and inequitable, and reflect a growth in transaction and enforcement costs, rather than any genuine increase in welfare among the population. Examples of this are increased expenditures on workfare schemes and other systems of social control, such as psychiatric clinics or treatment centres for drug and alcohol abuse.

However, the social costs associated with polarization are also driven up by the action of managers within the social services themselves, who respond to the new environment of cost-consciousness by using club-like criteria for admission to or rejection from service units. The example of British state education has already been given in chapter 4 (see pp. 134–41). As governors and head teachers have been drawn into competition to enrol those pupils who attract the highest contributions and require the lowest expenditures, schools in high-income residential districts have key advantages over those in districts with concentrations of social deprivation. As a result, schools in intermediate districts, with mixed populations, may find themselves in a position where it is advantageous to become selective in their intake, rather than to include the whole range of pupils available from their area. Once some schools become selective, or parents begin to move out of a district in search of more successful schools (in terms of exam results), or to opt for private education, those that continue to recruit according to inclusive, comprehensive principles find themselves at an escalating disadvantage, with lower returns and higher costs.

Research in Britain has shown that one characteristic way in which governors and head teachers have tried to minimize costs is to exclude children with special needs, or who are disruptive at school. Since the implementation of the Education Act of 1988, the numbers of such exclusions have risen steadily. The system for reporting these numbers, which probably underestimates them, recorded an increase from 2910 permanently excluded pupils in 1990–1 to 3833 in 1991–2, with Afro-Caribbean boys forming a proportion of this figure that was around four times their proportion in school rolls (Department for Education, 1993). In one south London borough in 1995, Afro-Caribbean boys made up 8 per cent of the school rolls, but nearly 70 per cent of those permanently excluded (Younge, 1995). Of those permanently excluded in 1991–2, 14 per cent were of primary school age, and 15 per cent had statements of special educational need under the provisions of the Education Act, 1981 (Department for Education, 1993). A survey based on schools inspectors' reports suggested that by 1992–3, permanent exclusions might be as high as 8000 (Younge, 1995). A BBC survey estimated this had risen to 10,000 in 1994 (BBC Radio 4, *Today* programme, 2 June 1995). In July 1995, the Metropolitan Police Commissioner claimed that most muggings were carried out by black adolescents who had been excluded from school.

Excluding special-needs and 'disruptive' children from schools ensures that numbers of high-cost/low-return pupils are mini-mized (Blyth and Milner, 1993; 1994). For schools as clubs it therefore improves their competitive position in relation to other schools, and benefits their members (other children and parents). But for the community as a whole it is likely to be inefficient. The costs of providing special education for such children are certain to be considerably higher than those of educating them in mainstream schooling. For 'disruptive' children, exclusion increases the risk that they will need to be accommodated or taken into care by the local authority (Stirling, 1992a and b; Bennathen, 1992). This in turn probably reflects other costs to the community, from delinquency, running away from home, drug abuse, or some other problematic behaviour.

A similar analysis can be applied to primary health care since the reforms of the National Health Service in Britain (National Health Service and Community Care Act, 1991). Since many general practitioners have become 'budget holders', it pays them to be more selective about their patients, treating their practices as clubs; all listed patients can benefit if a few who involve high risks and costs are struck off their lists. Accordingly, it is not surprising to find that numbers struck off by their general practitioners have risen sharply since 1991, and that these consist mainly of frail and vulnerable elderly people, those with psychiatric illnesses, and patients who make complaints about the treatment (or lack of treatment) they have received. Research by the BBC showed that in England and Wales 82,000 patients were struck off doctors' lists without explanations (BBC Radio 4, *Today* programme, 26 November 1994). Examples given included a frail, elderly couple who were removed a month after the practice became an NHS fundholder. Here again, such action by club managers is economically rational from the point of view of club members, but costly for society. Vulnerable people who are denied primary care are more likely to need expensive hospital or day care, especially those with mental health needs, who may impose other costs on wider society through disruptive behaviour.

Social exclusion through residential polarization is thus reinforced by exclusion from club-like education, health and welfare systems. Not only are residents of deprived districts forced to rely more on public agencies to meet their everyday needs; they are also least likely to get good-quality services from those agencies (compared with the standards enjoyed by residents in higher-income districts); and they are more likely to be excluded from any access to the goods supplied by these services, the greater their risks and problems, and hence the costs that they will impose on fundholders' budgets. But all these interactions generate higher social costs, because they give rise to the resistance practices by which poor people compensate themselves for exclusion, and 'tax' the better-off. Comfortable households in the suburbs ultimately contribute more, through local and national taxes, for their exclusive privileges, because they are required to pay for prisons, reformatories, special schools, psychiatric clinics, residential homes and day-care centres, many of whose inmates and users could more efficiently be included as members of a heterogeneous and pluralistic community, whose mainstream services contained a mixture of members with the full range of needs and abilities.

WOMEN, CARE AND COMMUNITY

The notion of community also refers to the voluntary activity of members who regulate each other's actions by reinforcing norms of social obligation, and offer mutual support and assistance on a reciprocal basis, without expectation of financial reward (Etzioni, 1993). This implies that social interactions within such groups can supply appropriate responses to most of the needs of individuals without recourse to professional or bureaucratic services which should represent secondary sources of assistance, standing behind the family, friendship and voluntary networks. The principle of subsidiarity is the European way of expressing the liberal notion of 'self-help' – that the minimum use of public power, and the lightest possible bureaucratic tackle, should be deployed in relation to any social need (Hood and Schuppert, 1990).

On this account, social polarization need not represent a loss in overall efficiency and welfare, or even in equity, so long as well-functioning communities can respond appropriately to social needs. The New Right is not alone in criticizing state services, and arguing that they have given diminishing or even negative returns for many years. Other, more communitarian voices have suggested that the expansion of public welfare services has weakened kinship and associative obligations, and supplied an inferior substitute for mutuality and membership (Hadley and Hatch, 1981; Walzer, 1980; Hirst, 1994). Even in the most deprived areas there have been signs of a revival of voluntary endeavour, especially in Scotland (Holman, 1993; Donnison, 1991), represented by organizations such as credit unions and tenants associations on outer-city council housing schemes. There are very respectable arguments for the view that professionals and public agencies provide better service when they encourage and support such groups, offering them facilities and infrastructural resources as *partners*, rather than trying to engineer grandiose solutions to social problems, or striving omnipotently to meet every individual need.

However there are serious problems in assessing such claims in relation to the interactions that constitute 'community' under present-day conditions. A casual glance at any of the associations and activities at work in these fields would reveal that the vast majority of the participants are women, many of them single parents, and others with more than their share of responsibility for children or other family members with dependency needs. This phenomenon seems an almost textbook case for the feminist analysis of social relations – that patriarchal assumptions about the division of labour in the domestic domain continue to spill over into the public sphere, with women developing their social and political skills, as well as networks of mutual assistance, as an extension of their social obligations for unpaid care in households.

In eagerly adopting the notions of 'community' and 'partnership' as principles of social welfare and protection, public policy simply reinforces the specific inequities of such systems of relationships, and the public authority acts as supreme patriarch, exploiting the community of women in the very manner that individual men exploit their particular partners. What we see in such interactions is therefore a graphic manifestation of the processes through which men demonstrate their arm's-length commitment to 'caring about' vulnerable individuals by giving (usually inadequate) resources to financially dependent women, who in turn are required to do the actual 'caring for' such people and themselves, at the expense of every other opportunity to develop their contributions to society's welfare, or to meet their other needs (Dalley, 1988).

This critique can be strengthened by an economic analysis of group formation and collective action. The poor (and especially the black poor) in advanced industrialized countries have never fully shared in the rents enjoyed by mainstream citizens through the comparative success of welfare states. In the US situation, the New Frontier and Great Society programmes of the 1960s, advanced by Presidents Kennedy and Johnson, gave recognition to the fact that African Americans were largely excluded from the benefits of citizenship: that is, from their share of material prosperity, as well as the civil, political and social rights enjoyed by white members. There were indeed African Americans who benefited from such programmes, and from their counterparts in Britain and the European countries. In particular, a minority of black people gained access to better education and training and, through positions in the professions and public services, were able to escape from ghetto districts and their constrained opportunities (Esping-Andersen, 1990, pp. 208–16). But this in turn contributed to polarization, and the reduced opportunities of those denied exit from such constraints.

In other words, the policies and programmes that were belatedly directed at deprived groups and districts from the 1960s onwards, *including anti-discriminatory policies*, did not benefit such groups and districts collectively. What they did provide was opportunities for strategic action by certain individuals who gained specific advantages, and were thus able to exercise their new options by exit from those collectivities, mainly through the residential mobility of households. The situation of those who remained in increasingly deprived districts, or were relocated to the bleakest outer-city developments, deteriorated because of the economic factors identified in the previous chapter, and in the earlier sections of this one. Poor people, and especially poor black people, were labour-market outsiders, who (through their location and through discrimination) were least likely to enjoy employment security, most vulnerable to redundancy and drift into long-term unemployment or irregular, low-paid work, least entitled to social insurance benefits and services, and most likely to be targeted for the more coercive and restrictive aspects of public policies.

The implications of these changes for individual resistance and collective action were briefly analysed in the final section of chapter 4, and will be more fully explored in chapter 6. At this point it is only necessary to note that property crime, hustling, drug dealing, working while claiming, and the whole range of informal economic activities that increased in the 1980s, were mainly male phenomena. They represented a response to deteriorating opportunities in the formal labour market, and increased scope for informal (cash or shadow, in-kind) transactions, involving high risks, and often requiring predatory, athletic or enforcement skills, stereotypically associated with masculinity. Although various forms of female crime and hustling have grown in recent years, these male activities were largely a rational development from men's previous roles as manual workers, sportspeople, gang members and casual pugilists during the era of welfare states.

Given the insecurity of formal work, and the risks of injury, drug-dependency and imprisonment involved in these informal activities, stable long-term relationships, and particularly marriage and the economic support of a wife and children, were scarcely feasible for many of the male residents of such deprived areas. Conversely, it was a rational economic strategy for women to rely on the public authorities for any security of income that they could supply, while using short-term relationships with men as a source of temporary economic advantage, as these became available. Indeed, there is evidence of some long-term relationships being broken for strategic reasons, so that families in such deprived districts can qualify for the £7 per week single-parent premiums (BBC Radio 4, *Today* programme, 18 July 1995). Even in relatively stable poor districts, where criminality was more likely to be associated with a stage of men's development than to become a way of life, it was rational for women to invest in networks of female support (both kinship- and friendship-based), rather than to rely solely on male partners, for the resources needed to bring up children (Finch, 1989; Jordan et al., 1992, chs 5 and 7).

In these circumstances, therefore, collective action by women takes the form of institutionalizing and formalizing such networks, reinforcing their bonds of mutual obligation and assistance wherever possible, through the resources and support available from public or voluntary agencies, and campaigning for such partnerships to be more reliable, respectful of women's abilities, and relevant to their needs and problems. Such new groups, associations and movements have been analysed in countries as diverse as Italy (de Leonardis, 1993) and Canada (Lustiger Thaler and Shragge, 1993). Poor women, and especially women from ethnic minorities, constitute the basis for 'community', and hence for social policies that try to redefine the relationship between public providers of welfare services and their clienteles in terms of 'partnership' (A. Buchanan, 1993; Ryan, 1994).

The collective-action dilemmas facing female community groups in their interactions with local authority welfare agencies are no less complex than those facing their male counterparts in their dealings with social assistance agencies and criminal justice systems. The 'partnership game' consists of strategic bargaining between agencies which seek to maintain maximum control over their resources and spheres of professional autonomy for minimum outlay, and groups of women who seek access to such resources and to professional support for their membership activities, and sometimes also as a step to wider economic opportunities through employment and the public sphere. The agencies' strategic goal is to get groups to bear as much of the costs of social care as possible, without sacrifice of professional power or significant material resources; the groups' is to gain relevant resources and influence policy (and hence to win a share of the power monopolized by councillors and professionals). Given the small-group nature of the interactions the outcomes of such games are indeterminate (J. M. Buchanan, 1968; Olson, 1965), but a very common equilibrium consists in the identification of a sphere of social care activity in which limited partnership can be pursued, with the support of a few low-status, marginal staff, but leaving the core of the agency's policy, practice and resources untouched (Williams, 1994; Jordan, forthcoming).

Just as the culture of contentment tends to relegate women to 'supportive' roles in labour markets and households (Jordan et al., 1994, chs 2, 5 and 6), so 'communities of fate' push women into collective action that supplies an infrastructure of care equally exploitable by predatory males and slippery public welfare agencies. Thus 'community' becomes a synonym for women's unpaid work, both individual and collective. While it is obvious that such work reduces social costs and increases efficiency from a local government perspective, it is clearly inequitable and inefficient (because women could contribute even more to overall social welfare on a better-organized and properly paid basis) from the standpoint of society as a whole. The poverty and social exclusion that are built into neo-Darwinian communities of fate therefore involve avoidable social costs, and wastes potentially valuable social capital.

CONCLUSIONS

In this chapter, I have analysed how social polarization through 'voting with the feet' affects the development of poverty and social exclusion, and considered some of the social costs associated with these processes. This analysis has been undertaken with special reference to the concept of 'community' – voluntary exchanges within systems of mutual obligation that include members through reciprocity, sharing and redistribution. I have argued that social polarization does not destroy community, but it leads to the formation of contrasting associative networks, with very different ways of providing their characteristic collective goods.

Communities of choice are based on household strategies for

income security and the utility associated with comfortable, convenient healthy and status-giving private environments. They tend to generate low-density residential districts, 'single-minded' public spaces, and club-like social interactions (including social welfare agencies), in which individuals of similar incomes and tastes co-operate to supply the goods associated with a private, suburban lifestyle, and to exclude the more disturbing manifestations of cultural diversity.

Communities of fate consist of residual districts whose residents are bound into long-term interdependencies because of their lack of opportunities to move, gain access to good education or health care, get decently paid formal work, or share in the cultural resources of the mainstream society. The characteristic interdependencies and collective goods of such communities arise from the sharing among young males of high-risk lifestyles, such as crime and drug use, and among females of long-term networks of reciprocal social care. Hence social relations typically involve tough requirements of exclusive loyalty, enforced through exacting sanctions, including violence. Collective action is focused on resistance to the negative spillovers from polarization, including predation on the property of mainstream organizations and households, and mobilization for demands upon public agencies.

The social exclusion associated with polarization has recently taken dramatic forms, especially in the USA. Reports describe fences and gates having been erected, both as protection for upmarket residential estates, with checks on the identities and purposes of visiting non-residents, and also to enclose 'troublesome' housing concentrations, where residents' deviant interactions are seen as threatening to spill over disruptively into surrounding districts (BBC Radio 4, *Today* programme, 15 June 1995). In these ways, club formation is made highly visible: fences and gates serve to exclude or include according to cultural standards that reflect economic realities.

The social costs of polarization consist partly in the resource use and environmental inefficiencies associated with dispersed living-patterns. Low-density cities and single-minded spaces require much land, and the consumption of wasteful quantities of non-renewable fuels for private motor transport, as well as high levels of pollution through exhaust emissions. Residual residential districts become neglected and run down, and contribute to the further deterioration of the urban environment. The public infrastructure – transport systems, parks, libraries, theatres and so on – is undervalued and becomes under-used.

But these costs also include the 'social problems' associated with concentrations of deprivation, and those expenditures of social control that are considered necessary to counter these problems. For example, the British Labour party now advocates 'exclusion orders', banning criminal families accused of terrorizing such districts from visiting them for any purpose. Such orders have already been attempted by local authorities such as those in Bestwood, Nottingham, where five families were evicted for intimidation and mayhem (BBC Radio 4, *Today* programme, 24 August 1995). So far the economics of such measures, and the politics of decision-making about them, have only been touched upon. It is to the social costs of divisions and intergroup conflicts, and the emergence of a 'politics of enforcement' among the comfortable majority, against the excluded minority, that I shall turn in the next chapter.

6

The Politics of Enforcement

A public-choice perspective on poverty and social exclusion offers the opportunity to evaluate the outcomes of social interactions from an economic standpoint. Despite all that has been argued in the last two chapters, it might still be the case that polities with fairly strongly market-orientated institutions are more efficient by such standards than those with large public sectors and substantial income redistribution. It might even be possible to argue that they are more equitable (or could be made more equitable) for their citizens.

To address such questions, it is necessary to analyse the interaction between economic and political processes. In recent years, some scholars have attempted the ambitious task of evaluating and comparing the whole institutional structures of nation states. Their aim is to identify those features of the institutional mix that promote utility maximization and cost minimization, and in particular, to examine the factors that are conducive to high levels of investment, vigorous entrepreneurial activity, rapid income growth, and the efficient functioning of public agencies and the political process.

The theory of poverty and social exclusion developed in this book has analysed these in terms of collective action in exclusive groups. In chapter 2 it was argued that the institutions and organizations that make up societies can be explained in terms of such interactions, and chapters 4 and 5 were illustrations of this method of analysis. But if inclusion and exclusion are universal features of the collective life of human beings, the welfare of vulnerable individuals depends at least as much on the prosperity of the society in which they live as on the reciprocity, sharing and redistribution that occur within their primary membership group. This chapter considers how poverty and social exclusion influence the workings of economic and political institutions, and how the poor fare in various institutional regimes.

Both Olson (1982) and North (1990) argue strongly that an 'open and competitive environment' is a necessary condition for a strong economy, capable of sustained growth. Both contrast the institutional structure of the United States (and particularly that of its nineteenth-century heyday of economic expansion) with those of the socialist countries, and those of Third World, developing countries. Olson counterposes free-market efficiency with the 'top-heavy' structures of economies with centralized decision-making, protected industries and the 'perverse policy syndrome', driven by powerful distributional coalitions (1982, pp. 165–71). North similarly argues that the institutional mix adopted by the US in the early nineteenth century provided a path to economic success, because the constitution, laws and culture combined to encourage the maximization of productivity and growth, through hard work and educational investment (1990, pp. 8–9). By contrast, socialist and statist regimes favoured redistributive rather than productive activity, protected monopolies, and restricted opportunities.

In North's comparative analysis, the advantages gained by open, market-orientated institutional structures can be explained in terms of their lower transaction and enforcement costs. The most successful countries are likely to be those where political institutions and the formal and informal rules that govern interactions promote the maximum volume of low-cost voluntary exchanges between individuals. Norms of trust, and reliable systems for enforcing contracts, are equally necessary for the confidence to make long-term investments and to plan extensive projects. This combination of low transaction costs (because many aspects of exchanges can be informally agreed, without elaborate contractual safeguards) and low enforcement costs (because few contracts require arbitration, and those that do can be speedily and efficiently settled) is the ideal environment for a healthy economy (1990, chs 5–8). This contrasts with the picture in statist societies, such as the Soviet bloc countries in the years before 1989, when voluntary exchanges were largely confined to the informal 'shadow' economy, and formal processes entailed very high (bureaucratic) transaction costs and (surveillance, punishment) enforcement costs. Since 1989 the economic development of these same countries has been retarded by insecurity of property rights and uncertainty over contract compliance (Bönker, 1993); as in Third World economies, costs and risks are too high because of inadequate safeguards for investments. 'Large firms with substantial fixed capital will exist only under the umbrella of government protection, with subsidies, tariffs, and payoffs to the polity' (North, 1990, p. 67). North concludes, like Olson, that market-friendly laws and customs give liberal states important long-term advantages over such institutional traditions.

However, I shall argue in this chapter that this analysis does not tell the whole story. Transaction and enforcement costs are, as we saw in chapter 4, generated by many different features of social interaction, including general levels of rule compliance in society; the distribution of positional goods (Hirsch, 1977); the balance between 'oligarchic' and 'democratic' collective goods (Harrod, 1958); levels of interpersonal and intergroup conflict; and the political balance between democratic and authoritarian forces. The 'institutional mix' and 'institutional path' of particular societies are necessary but not sufficient conditions for efficiency. Liberal institutions that have stood the Anglo-Saxon countries in good stead since the Industrial Revolution may not serve so well under present-day conditions. Already in the 1980s, Wallis and North (1986) estimated that transaction costs accounted for 45 per cent of United States GDP compared with 25 per cent a hundred years earlier, while there were proportionately twice as many lawyers and accountants as in Japan. There may be new forces driving up these costs in liberal polities.

The most important question not answered by Olson's or North's theories is how countries or regions with superficially similar institutions have very different ratios of transaction and enforcement costs to total economic activity, as well as different rates of growth. It is clear that some enjoy a virtuous circle that consists of civic trust and active citizen engagement, high levels of economic co-operation (between individuals and firms) as well as competition, and effective democratic government, while others experience a vicious circle of suspicion, isolation, risk-avoidance, exploitation, clientelism, crime, protection rackets, corruption, authoritarian and ineffective government. The former might be described as Tocquevillian social interactions, in which the benefits of trust and co-operation in many informal exchanges spill over into the economy and the polity, keeping transaction and enforcement costs low. The latter could be seen as Hobbesian, in that third-party enforcement (by the state, or 'private' agencies such as the Mafia) alone provides the fragile order that allows low-level economic and political exchanges, because the costs of mistrust, fear, revenge and recrimination spill over from the informal into the formal sphere, producing economic backwardness and political authoritarianism (Putnam, 1993, ch. 6).

Anglo-Saxon political theorizing has built into it a number of rather facile assumptions about the links between liberal individualism and the former of these two scenarios. First, it assumes that 'free individuals' with typically liberal civil rights, and in rational pursuit of their own interests, are the ideal basic components of such a beneficent system. Tocqueville himself (1835–40) was careful to qualify such a notion in many ways, and to point out how easily the largely unintentional and contingent public-spiritedness of early nineteenth-century American citizens could degenerate into selfish and narrow privatism, when they 'withdraw into the circle of family and friends' (p. 652). If citizens became individualistic and materialistic, 'all powers seem to rush spontaneously to the centre. They accumulate there at an astonishing rate, and the state reaches the extreme limits of its power all at once' (p. 875). My argument in the last two chapters is designed to show how the economics of collective action in exclusive groups has brought about just such a fragmentation into the particularisms of like-income mutualities and household strategies, and an increase in central state power.

Second, it assumes that voluntary associations of all kinds are more likely to generate positive than negative externalities, because of the political skills they teach, and the norms of co-operation they foster. Such naivety would be unlikely to afflict those raised in polities that have experienced totalitarianism or civil war in this century – in other words, the inhabitants of almost all the rest of the globe, including Western Europe and the whole of Ireland. Hobbes's theory was, after all, designed to deal with English politics in the aftermath of the war between King and Parliament, and assumed that all associations were conspiracies against the public interest unless they could demonstrate their civic-minded purpose (Hobbes, 1651, ch. 22). The example of Bosnia shows how quickly a society can slide into conflictual relations, in which every association is organized for armed struggle against another. In this regard, the Oklahoma City bombing of a federal office, and the subsequent publicity given to anti-government paramilitary groups, have been timely reminders to Americans that voluntary association can be synonymous with costly intergroup antagonism.

Third, the Anglo-Saxon tradition often mentions democracy and the rule of law in the same breath, as if there existed some intimate connection between them. Yet there is increasing evidence in these very countries of a problematic relationship between democratic processes and the criminal justice system (Jordan and Arnold, 1996). Neither the policies of American populist politicians in restoring punitive regimes, the death penalty and mandatory prison sentences, nor the activities of retributionist pressure groups, encourage uncritical optimism about the democratization of law and order. Far from signalling a welcome increase in civic engagement with penal policy, this seems instead to constitute the rise in a new 'politics of enforcement' that is already driving up the costs of government, and fuelling social conflict.

In this chapter, I shall focus on the second and third elements in these processes, arguing that the economics of fragmentation and polarization can also explain the rise in transaction and enforcement costs in liberal polities, and that this threatens to become the largest barrier to economic growth in these countries. Such an analysis is a necessary element in a theory of poverty and social exclusion, since the political drive towards market-orientated social institutions resolutely ignores these costs, while focusing on the wastefulness and inefficiency of social welfare expenditure. I shall argue that liberal individualism is in greatest tension with the democratization of social interaction around these issues of intergroup relations and law enforcement, and that the public-choice perspective is an important way of clarifying this tension.

INTEGRATION AND DIFFERENTIATION IN PLURALISTIC DEMOCRACIES

The collapse of the Soviet and East European regimes has focused attention on the design of political and economic institutions. It has required social scientists in the West to question how these contribute to sustainable economic efficiency and democratic decision making (Offe, 1992). Above all, even though there is quite a strong consensus around the elements that should go to make up the constitution of a modern democratic state (Offe and Preuss, 1990), the task of designing middle-range institutions that can promote economic dynamism and good government in the former centrally planned societies has proved a challenging one, and has reflected back many questions about social and economic governance into advanced capitalist countries.

These same issues have been most acutely raised by the radical redesign of British public sector institutions under Margaret Thatcher, and her attempt to reorientate citizens towards private and voluntary organizations and the family, and away from local authorities, trade unions and the social services. But – as has been argued in chapters 4 and 5 – these reforms and restructurings have had many unintended consequences, as citizens work out new strategies for interaction within them. This, and parallel developments in the US, prompt the thought that social and political integration and differentiation are more like 'essential by-products' of institutional systems (Elster, 1985) than outcomes that can be planned or engineered. This book has argued that their explication requires an economic analysis of group inclusion and exclusion, and the externalities generated by these processes.

Two books by political scientists claim to explain interactions within these middle-range systems, and address – either indirectly or directly – the issue of whether Tocquevillian or Hobbesian outcomes are produced by particular institutions. Paul Hirst's *Associative Democracy* (1994) argues that representative democratic government and centralized, bureaucratic public administration are too unaccountable and unresponsive to the diverse, pluralistic needs of present-day societies. His is a prescriptive account, advocating voluntary, self-governing associations as the eventual replacements for such institutions. He maintains that there has been a 'failure of government' under economic liberalism as much as under Keynesian management and central planning, and his analysis is of particular interest for our purposes where he discusses the danger that a society which has been 'freed' for market interactions, and whose lesser public bodies have been regulated to achieve this (as in Britain) can fragment into antagonistic competing groups.

Hirst argues that the Thatcher programme consisted of using a remote, centralized public power, quite separate from civil society, to force every individual and collective actor to respond to price signals, for the sake of economic efficiency. This ignored those middle-range institutions through which, by negotiation and bargaining, a viable economy is sustained. These achieve the balance between competition and co-operation, by fostering trust and solidarity between groups and associations, by providing key inputs such as training, research and market information, by brokering partnerships between public bodies and voluntary associations, and by co-ordinating the actions of collective interest groups (Piore and Sabel, 1984; Scharpf, 1991; Dore, 1986).

The irony of economic liberalism is therefore that central

government has tried to do too much, both by way of deregulation and re-regulation, whereas the associative principles advocated by Hirst would make self-governing voluntary bodies, co-operatives and co-ordinating institutions the *primary* means of economic and social governance. The result is that collective action comes instead to take the form of exclusive interest groups, lobbying central government to influence public policy to their advantage; fragmentation and wasteful competition between collective actors; and the lack of long-term investment in skills and research (Hirst, 1994, pp. 123–4). He attributes the poor performances of both the US and British economies to these factors, and thus both confirms Olson's analysis and turns it on its head.

The phenomena of social fragmentation (that Hirst tries to capture in the term 'Ottomanization') are more diverse, and more problematic for his methods of analysis, because (as we saw in chapter 5) they often take the form of associations or communities. He gives the examples of divergent and violently antagonistic groups, such as gays and Christian fundamentalists, pro-life and pro-choice campaigners in the US, and attributes their hostile interactions to a thin common morality, together with mass affluence and high geographical and social mobility (pp. 65–7). On the other hand he also recognizes the existence of 'communities of fate', and especially the black ghetto communities, as examples of social relations that enclose the life of an individual, imposing an all-defining identity, demanding loyalty and prescribing action (pp. 54–5). Hirst thus recognizes that polarization produces a culture of resistance and revenge by excluded groups of poor people, and that a society that is divided in this way between mainstream and 'underclass' may not be able to use the associative principle as its basis for social governance without major structural economic and political reforms.

Robert Putnam's *Making Democracy Work* is a research study of 20 years of regional government in Italy that relates the performance of regional economies and local authorities to civic traditions over a far longer period. He traces very long-term continuities in patterns of social interaction, and shows how these correlate closely with the economic growth rates and evi-

dence of effective and responsive democratic regional government in the 1980s:

> the regions characterized by civic involvement in the late twenti-
> eth century are almost precisely the same regions where co-opera-
> tives and cultural associations and mutual aid societies were most
> abundant in the nineteenth century, and where neighbourhood
> associations and religious confraternities and guilds had con-
> tributed to flourishing communal republics in the twelfth century.
> And although those civic regions were not especially advanced
> economically a century ago, they have steadily outpaced the less
> civic regions both in economic performance and (at least since
> the advent of regional government) in the quality of government.
> (1993, p. 162)

In an analysis very similar to Hirst's, Putnam accounts for the
strengths of those regions in terms of decentralized but integrated industrial districts, combining competition over quality
with co-operation over administrative services, finance, information and research, and active partnership with local government
over training. Thus institutionalized co-ordination, drawing on
rich networks of associations and political organizations, provide
small firms with infrastructural support that they could not
afford alone (pp. 160–1).

By contrast, in those regions with low civic involvement and
few associations or mutual aid, social relations are – and have for
centuries been – characterized by mistrust and antagonism.
Social bonds are characteristically vertical, between patron and
client, rather than horizontal, between members of solidaristic
groups. Dependency and exploitation, personal contacts, lobbying and soliciting favours, and violent enforcement are all consequences of these forms of social relations. But Putnam attributes
these features of the social and economic culture of the
Mezzogiorno to the system of political authority that has prevailed
for 'at least a millennium' (p. 148), since the arrival of the
Norman kings of Naples and Sicily.

In the final chapter of his study, Putnam compares the social
capital generated by the communal civic traditions of north-
central regions with the social costs of authoritarian clientelism
in the south. Trust, reciprocity and voluntary co-operation

greatly reduce transaction costs; they build up a stock of norms and cultural practices that *increases* with use, and helps business and political actors to overcome potential prisoner's dilemmas. Networks of civic engagement reinforce these social relations, making unreliability costly (p. 176). But in the south, mistrust, suspicion and antagonism create prisoner's dilemmas in most interactions, as no party can trust another not to exploit or defect. Thus there develops a stable equilibrium around a suboptimal set of outcomes. The Hobbesian solution to these collective-action problems – authoritarian rule – was probably the first cause of these cultural traditions, but has now become the only alternative to the war of all against all (or the rule of the Mafia). It generates high transaction and enforcement costs, both because such political authorities expand their own interests, and because vertical clientelist relations give dependants no incentives to co-operate with each other, competing instead for patrons' favours.

Putnam's analysis thus postulates far longer-term stability of equilibrium solutions to collective-action dilemmas than Hirst's, with Hobbesian outcomes – which involve sub-optimal stagnation, minimal predictability and security, and outcomes that are relatively inefficient and inequitable – as the default case. He takes North's line, that institutional patterns endure because rules, norms and cultural practices all interact, giving individuals a consistent set of incentives, opportunities and sanctions that provide a cultural and historical path for development.

But Putnam's account seems too generalized to explain the middle level of social institutions and interactions in a complex society. We are invited to suppose that these are either gigantic prisoner's dilemmas that thwart all kinds of collective action, or else co-operative games that achieve integration and differentiation through decentralized self-governing bodies, running on trust and reciprocity. Neither of these fits the cases of the US and the UK. After all, the US does have the strong traditions of democratic citizenship and local voluntary action immortalized by de Tocqueville, and Britain was the cradle of working-class political associations, trade unions, friendly societies and co-operatives, so lovingly described by E. P. Thompson (1963).

There is enormous variation, both by social domain and by locality, within these two societies. Putnam's model does not sufficiently specify the collective goods and collective-action issues at stake in interactions, or how changes in the opportunities, incentives and sanctions facing individuals (either through global market forces or through political decisions) can provoke the development of new groups and strategies. In particular, I shall argue that the relation between gainful exchanges and transaction and enforcement costs is not determined by the overall nature of the political game, but can change quite quickly, and is significantly affected by the dynamics of poverty-related social exclusion.

'UNDERCLASS', CRIME AND ENFORCEMENT

The most obvious example of such a change has been the development of a politics of enforcement around issues of the 'underclass', 'dependency culture' and crime in the US and Britain in the 1980s and 1990s. I do not intend to trace the ideological roots of this movement, since this has been very well done by many scholars (Mann, 1991; Roche, 1992; Dean and Taylor Gooby, 1992; Morris, 1994). What none of these has attempted is a more systematic analysis of how the political response to rising numbers of social assistance claimants, and rising statistics of recorded crime (especially violent crime), reflects the growing social costs of social polarization, and in turn increases these still more, by further driving up transaction and enforcement costs.

While it is important to dispute whether the term 'underclass' contributes to social scientific knowledge, it is more urgent to consider whether it connotes the development of mutually antagonistic collective-action groups in these societies. Whether or not there exists a 'class' of individuals with identifiably distinctive interests, strategies and cultural practices, the very fact that influential commentators and populist politicians have been able to form public opinion and mobilize political action around such a concept suggests that 'latent groups' (Olson, 1982) existed in the 1980s, who were willing to take collective action over issues of public spending on welfare, and the tougher enforcement of criminal justice measures. What these two sections aim to do is to analyse the costs associated with higher rates of claiming, of working while claiming, of crime, and of other forms of irregular, informal economic activity, and with policies directed against these activities.

One part of this analysis has already been presented in chapter 4 (pp. 148–58), where I argued that the growth in numbers claiming social assistance and other means-tested programmes has been accompanied by a polarization of interests between taxpayers (most of whom are not eligible for such benefits) and claimants. Although in 1995 over half the households in Britain contained a member in receipt of 'targeted' assistance (BBC Radio 4, *Today* programme, 6 June 1995), the longer-term hard core of claimants were concentrated in a smaller proportion of households all of whose members relied on state services as well as benefits for their needs. In chapter 5, I showed how some of the social costs of geographical polarization through 'voting with the feet' were generated (pp. 176–81). This combination of policy-driven focusing of social benefits and services, and spatial concentration of poverty and exclusion through individual and household decisions (the flight to the suburbs), accounts for some of the direct and indirect costs, and hence the inefficiencies associated with recent social and economic change.

This section will therefore deal mainly with issues of criminal justice, and the negative externalities produced by new enforcement orientations in this sphere. The politics of enforcement developed in the US before Britain, where it appeared rather suddenly in the final quarter of 1993, with the 'back to basics' turn by the Major government. But many of the same elements apply to policy on social security fraud and single parenthood as criminality – the growth of pressure groups and political mobilizations, punctuated by moral panics in the media, contributing to new programmes of surveillance and coercion that require considerable public expenditure.

In the US, the rise in the rate of recorded crimes in the 1980s is now being outstripped by the rise in rates of imprisonment (the prison population is about one million at the time of writing) and executions. This reflects the greater responsiveness of the US criminal justice system (as compared with any other advanced industrialized country) to public opinion and political pressure; the fact that local law officers are elected is an important element in this. However, it also reflects the rise of pressure groups on criminal justice issues, and of populist politics on enforcement measures, which culminated in the Republican party's triumph in the mid-term elections of 1994. The risks of being associated with 'liberal' views on such questions have driven almost all leading state and federal politicians from both parties into strongly punitive stances.

One example of this process will suffice. In 1994, the State of California adopted a law (popularly known as 'Three Strikes and You're Out') under which a second serious felony attracted double the existing prison sentence, and a third three times the usual sentence or 25 years to life, whichever was the greater. Law AB971 also reduced the time off sentences for work or good behaviour from 50 to 20 per cent. It has been described as 'a massive experiment by the nation's largest state to see if sharply increasing sentences will have a significant deterrent effect on crime' (Pollard, 1994). One much-publicized case illustrated the outcomes – a convicted felon sentenced to 25 years for stealing sweets from a child on the beach.

What was unusual about the new law was that it was drafted by the father of a murder victim, whose daughter had been killed by a paroled offender, and who founded a pressure group for stronger enforcement. Few members of the state legislature were willing to vote against the measure, even though the Department of Corrections estimated that it would require 20 additional prisons by the turn of the century, with operating costs of $5.7 million a year, on top of the 12 new prisons already scheduled under existing sentencing policies (Erdman, 1994). It should be noted that California already spends very nearly as much on criminal justice as it does on welfare. In other words, the enforcement bandwagon, which started to roll in the 1980s, has apparently become unstoppable in the mid-1990s, and continues despite the evidence of escalating costs. Both New York State and Florida faced financial crises in 1994–5, around the costs associated with executions – the legal expenses around complex appeal procedures tipped their budgets into serious deficits.

The British case is somewhat different. In the 1980s, despite fierce rhetoric from Margaret Thatcher and her ministers, government policy on criminal justice pursued a twin-track approach. On the one hand, new efforts were made to identify, classify and contain 'dangerous' offenders (Bottoms, 1977); on the other, policy was aimed at diverting young offenders in particular from courts and custody, steeply reducing rates of incarceration for this age-group; this was accompanied by a rise in cautions and non-custodial penalties for adults, as new alternatives to prison were developed (Brown and Crisp, 1992; Home Office, 1994). In this way, the growth in reported offences and in the fear of crime that took place in these years was not reflected in a shift towards more punitive measures, despite the activities of new lobbying groups. The government remained committed to the idea that its reforms of the state, and its liberalization of the economic environment, could so increase the scope for gainful contractual and voluntary exchanges that crime rates would fall spontaneously, or at least remain reasonably stable. In this sense, the new structure of opportunities and incentives was supposed to make market transactions and household mutualities self-enforcing, and to require less, not more, coercive force. The strength of the state was reserved for restraining those collective actors (such as trade unions and local authorities) who had previously erected 'barriers' to such exchanges (Jordan and Arnold, 1996).

However, as I showed in chapter 4 (pp. 127–34), at the bottom end of the labour market wages have fallen so low that incentives for formal work have seriously weakened, while the deregulation of employment has created new opportunities for informal economic activities of all kinds. This hypercasualization has led to a vigorous 'shadow' economy, involving petty crime and trade in stolen goods, as well as various kinds of hustling; in many areas where formal employers and traders have withdrawn, more serious criminal activity, including drug-dealing and protection rackets, has filled the vacuum. The evidence for this has included the growth of gunfighting between gangs on certain notorious estates in Manchester and Liverpool (*Guardian*, 14 January 1995), and attempts by local authorities to restrain particular 'families' and gangs from terrorizing neighbourhoods through court exclusion orders (BBC Radio 4, *Today* programme, 24 August 1995).

The British government was slow to respond to these phenomena with enforcement measures, at least partly because they ran counter to its claims about the self-enforcing nature of market exchange and family bonds under its new institutional structures. But by its own analysis of criminal activity (rational-calculative opportunism or strategic action, taking account of likely costs and benefits), and in the absence of better incentives and opportunities for formal work, there was little alternative but to raise the 'price' of crime by increasing penalties. The change, when it came, was sudden, and was triggered by a series of media-driven moral panics in the summer of 1993, including accounts of escalating joy-riding and car crime, truancy, drug abuse, fear of crime, violence, begging and New Age travelling. The final push came with the murder of Jamie Bulger, a toddler who was taken from a shopping arcade by two boys aged 10 and 11, and murdered on waste ground some seven hours later. In response, the Prime Minister's 'back to basics' speech at the Conservative Party conference, and the Home Secretary's announcement of tough new measures to crack down on crime, including the amendment of a Criminal Justice Act that had been implemented only one year previously, signalled an end to the policies of the Thatcher years, and the advent of a politics of enforcement.

In the two years from November 1993 when this policy shift was announced, the British prison population rose by 20 per cent. With the cost of prison expansion running at some £80,000 a cell, the government also committed itself to a new building programme, and the privatization of some correctional services, a move that was followed by many costly and embarrassing escapes and scandals. Above all, the Home Secretary launched into a series of speeches and administrative measures, all aimed at portraying the government as giving priority to the defeat of

crime, and appealing strongly to the anxious and vengeful sentiments of suburban, comfortable Britain, against the inhabitants
of deprived areas.

Although Home Office policy still emphasizes 'value for
money' in the provision of criminal justice services, the sudden
change to a politics of enforcement has accelerated the rising
costs of law and order in British public administration. In effect,
the growth of spending in this category has wiped out all the savings on social services expenditure of the Thatcher years. By
1994, the proportion of public spending going to public order
and safety had increased from 2.6 per cent in 1979 to 5.5 per
cent (*Social Trends*, 1984 and 1994, table 6.21, p. 91). Together
with the big increase in spending on income maintenance, this
explained the Conservative government's failure to reduce public spending as a proportion of GNP despite substantial cuts,
especially in expenditure on housing.

Furthermore, although there was a slight fall in recorded
crime of many kinds in the mid-1990s, there was no evidence of a
reduction in antagonism between the police and young people
in deprived districts, or the risk of riot and destruction – a particularly costly form of disorder – by such groups. In the summer of
1995, riots by Asian youths in Bradford were closely followed by
similar disorders among white adolescents on the Marsh Farm
Estate in Luton, after the arrest of a 14–year-old boy, and by
adults in the Hyde Park district of Leeds, following a police
crackdown against drug-dealing (BBC Radio 4, *Today* programme, 20 July 95). These events showed that crime was not
confined to deviant individuals or exploitative gangs, but reflected the disaffection of a substantial group of the inhabitants
of such areas, who were capable of spontaneously collective
action (including the manufacture and use of petrol bombs)
when provoked. Thirteen buses were burnt in Leeds on the
night of 23–4 July. It also revealed that criminality was a significant part of the economy of such districts, and that – far from
being disowned by the great majority of such communities'
members – local individuals who got into trouble with the police
enjoyed widespread popular support.

Such rioting and burning echo a far earlier British tradition, and refer back specifically to the winter of 1830–1, when a wave of incendiarism signalled the end of the Speenhamland system, and the failure of the old Poor Law's attempt to contain the social forces of the early industrial revolution (Polanyi, 1944, ch. 7). In his analysis of the Swing revolt of that year, Wakefield (1831) pointed out the effectiveness of measures which caused maximum anxiety for the comfortable classes, at minimum risk and cost to those who burnt their property. Revenge, retaliation and rage were sufficient motives to drive rural paupers to this form of collective action, which triggered the collapse of the *ancien régime*, and the Reform Act of 1832. In present-day Britain, rioting and burning is unlikely to have such spectacular results, but it has proved an effective strategy for extorting major increases in public spending on community facilities in such deprived outer-city estates as North Prospect in Plymouth and Ely in Cardiff.

In this section, I have argued that social polarization has found political expression in the growth of pressure groups and populist programmes for tougher measures (in terms of policing, sentencing and prison regimes) against criminal activity. This in turn has driven up the costs of government intervention, both by increasing public spending on surveillance, prosecution and incarceration, and by provoking resistance action by groups of disaffected citizens. Yet these statistics alone do not measure the full social costs of rising crime, associated with the processes of exclusion analysed in the previous chapter. The disutilities that stem from fear of crime, the inconveniences of measures to avoid certain districts, or certain hours of travel, the installation costs of security equipment, and the rising price of insurance cover, all reflect hidden inefficiencies associated with a polarized society.

For example, there are now more private (commercial) security guards in Britain than employees of the police force. Yet these are very badly paid jobs, and often attract former criminals. An investigation by police suggested that around one-fifth of such security guards had criminal convictions, and such employees were able to commit a high proportion of crimes against companies (BBC Radio 4, *Today* programme, 7 June 1995). New experiments in enforcement can also prove extremely costly. In 1989–90, only 49 candidates for electronic tagging were found in one pilot study, of whom 80 per cent breached their orders. Over £100,000 was spent on the installation of telephones alone in this experiment. Now the policy of tagging is being reintroduced in 1995 (BBC Radio 4, *PM* programme, 16 August 1995).

Yet there has been no form of collective action to mobilize citizens against the waste of taxpayers' money associated with new prison building programmes, failed experiments with electronic tagging, or the need for private security contracts. Instead, the opportunities for mobilizing mainstream voters in support of increased spending on law and order grow, and are now exploited by the Labour party as readily as by the Conservatives.

INTEGRATION, WORKFARE AND THE 'NEW SOCIAL CONTRACT'

Enforcement costs are not confined to criminal justice issues. The movement in the US towards the 'compulsory integration' of the poor spreads such costs across a number of policy domains. This approach accepts that the poor have come to constitute an excluded underclass, but regards much of this as stemming from self-exclusion, as a response to the blandishments of public assistance. On this analysis, poor people (and in the US especially, African American women) prefer to claim welfare payments, rather than to accept responsibility for providing for themselves and their children from earnings. The only way to reintegrate them into mainstream social relations is therefore to make benefits and services more conditional upon the fulfilment of work obligations – to require them to train, to accept low-paid work, and to be responsible parents.

On this analysis, most unemployment is 'voluntary', and caused by unwillingness or inability to recognize the social obligations that accompany guarantees of income and welfare security (Mead, 1986, 1988b). Hence the provision of benefits should be more authoritative and conditional, so that applicants are made to accept work disciplines and the duty to provide for children out of earnings. In practice, because of the structure of public assistance programmes in the US, and the demography of the inner cities (see pp. 184–6), this focuses coercive policies more on African American women than the young men whom the theory describes as preferring crime and hustling to work. Lone parents from the black ghettoes are particularly likely to be the targets of training and employment programmes; yet their children require often expensive child-care facilities to enable these to be translated into jobs. This also exposes a contradiction between neo-conservative goals of enforcing work obligations, and its advocates' commitment to family values and traditional motherhood (Butler and Condratas, 1987; Roche, 1992).

In the European context, the notions of individual responsibility, work obligation and compulsory inclusion are mediated by concepts of social citizenship, social inclusion and full employment. Hence workfare as a form of conditionality and coercion is not preached or practised in the manner of the American politics of enforcement; no European politician would be likely to give voice to the slogan of the US senator who announced, 'It's time these people were made to get off the welfare wagon, and push it instead'. Programmes such as the French Revenue Minimum d'Insertion, or the active labour-market policies of Denmark and Sweden, are pursued with the goals of reintegrating the excluded, reducing unemployment and combating alienation, rather than the reduction of public expenditure.

Even so, many of the same theoretical arguments apply to US and European policies for retraining and reintegrating those receiving long-term benefits. From an economic point of view, it is efficient to provide jobs only up to the point where the marginal utility of an extra job equals the marginal cost. There is no autonomous demand for jobs – this is mediated by the demand for the products that workers produce. Hence when an economist speaks of 'full employment', he or she is likely to mean employment up to this point (Lindbeck and Snower, 1988), whereas a politician or social administrator, more concerned with such factors as the reduction of idleness, anomie, suicide or mental illness, might postulate a much larger expenditure on the creation of 'therapeutic work', or 'programmes for social inclusion'. Indeed, ambitious plans for reducing unemployment through the co-ordinated efforts of employers, trade unions and the state have been canvassed by the European Union (Delors, 1993), and put into the form of a 'New Social Contract' – the Treaty of Louvain – in Belgium (DeHane, 1994).

There are circumstances in which workfare and its various derivatives (such as 'trainfare' and 'carefare') can promote efficiency, but these are quite limited. One relates to the buoyancy of the open labour market; if there are many adequately paid jobs for those with skills, qualifications and a suitable personal profile, even quite expensive measures that require claimants to train and equip themselves for these available opportunities will be efficient, because they will overcome supply-side barriers to employment among the claimant population. Such examples can be found in many districts of the western states of the USA and Canada (Wiseman, 1993). Another set of conditions occurs when unemployment benefits are high, there is a niche in which labour-market intervention can provide training or employment without substitution or displacement, motivated applicants can learn transferable skills, and enough vacancies arise to absorb 'graduates' over time. Research in Belgium (Schatteman et al., 1994; Wuyts, Van Trier and Késenne, 1994) found that various schemes in Flanders achieved efficiency because they met these conditions.

However, as a general rule there are many reasons why it is rare for compulsory employment or training to meet efficiency criteria. In the first place, coercion is itself demotivating; those who are forced to take work or courses they would not choose are unlikely to perform well. Even a few such participants can be disruptive and reduce the productivity of others. These forms of work under coercive conditions are the ideal environment for the development of a culture of resistance, using what Scott (1985; 1990) calls the 'weapons of the weak' – petty pilfering, malingering, absenteeism, defection, shoddy workmanship and sabotage. Such practices can be well co-ordinated through underground channels of communication that cost the participants much less than open rebellion. Hence a form of collective action that is particularly damaging to efficiency thrives under conditions of forced labour, where 'groups of fate' are thrown together by unchosen circumstances, and find the means to low-cost solidarity and resistance, which has the utility associated with revenge, so readily available.

History furnishes many examples of attempts to use forced labour efficiently, from the schemes to make workhouses pay in early eighteenth-century England (Oxley, 1975); through Bentham's panopticon prisons and workhouses; the Speen-hamland system (Polanyi, 1944; Halevy, 1928); camps for the unemployed in Britain and Europe at the turn of the century (Beveridge, 1911); to the whole system of labour under the centrally planned economies of the Soviet bloc. All experienced low and falling productivity, as resistance of the kind most common in Central Europe ('we pretend to work, you pretend to pay') was consolidated. As North (1990, p. 105) points out, there were periods of history and technological development when slavery was economically efficient, but those have probably passed.

In the USA, the main targets of workfare have been lone African American mothers. Because they formed a large proportion of those claiming Aid for Families with Dependent Children, they provided a focus for the neo-Conservative mobilization against 'welfare dependence'. But it has proved difficult to reconcile the goals of enforced economic provision and enforced parental responsibility. The former demands training and placement in employment; this in turn requires child-care provision, which is expensive. Neo-Conservative emphasis on traditional family values would indicate that lone mothers should be at home with their children, not out at work. This contradiction has not been resolved, in theory or in policy implementation (Roche, 1992, chs 4–6).

In Britain, the policy dilemmas have been slightly different. The target of compulsory inclusion has been long-term unemployment, rather than single parenthood. By making benefits paid to unemployed claimants more conditional, the government has tried to drive them into low-paid work or training. From 1996, unemployment benefit will be called 'job-seekers' benefit' and paid for six months instead of a year, a fact that reflects this change to stricter enforcement. If numbers of long-term male claimants of benefits can be reduced, this will indirectly affect numbers of single-parent female claimants, the government reasons. It has sought to reduce their numbers by enforcing maintenance payments through a new Child Support Agency on the Australian model. Its first year of operations was a catastrophe, as it provoked a flurry of resistance mobilization among absent fathers of all social classes, and a whole new range of strategies for avoiding payments. Seldom can any single measure have provoked so much collective action, both in the form of protest movements and political lobbies, and in the shape of collusions between separating parents to conspire against the CSA, by making concealed allowances (which would otherwise be deducted from benefits). This was another clear example of extra-parliamentary opposition, since the Labour party broadly supported the CSA.

DEMOCRACY AND ENFORCEMENT

The compatibility of political democracy and market economics is claimed to lie in decentralized decision-making, with the electoral choices of individual voters echoing the purchasing choices of individual consumers. In this view, the active citizen in a healthy democracy is well informed about policy issues, and chooses rationally between programmes, much as the customer shopping for good-value bundles of purchases does (Elster, 1986b), and the defining democratic act is voting. Just as markets create 'spontaneous order' without commands (Hayek, 1973; 1976; 1978), so democratic governance should minimize the need for coercive enforcement. In de Tocqueville's account, the autonomy and competence that citizens gain through participation, and the self-governing activities of voluntary bodies themselves, make political authority more about establishing a framework for voluntary exchanges (the rules for social interaction) than an attempt to produce any particular outcomes, or achieve specific plans.

However, any set of institutions provides orientations for action, and moulds actors' identities as well as influencing their strategies (Offe, 1992; Offe and Preuss, 1990). Late twentieth-century neo-liberalism had its own particular models of the 'good citizen' and the dangerous, burdensome, deviant, dependent or deranged denizen. Unlike de Tocqueville's American burghers, the 'property-owning democrats' of Margaret Thatcher's Britain and Ronald Reagan's USA gave priority to the family over the political association, and carried over business skills into private charitable work, rather than carrying over local associative skills into participatory national politics. Their competences as citizens were primarily those of the bargain-hunter, the entrepreneur and the investor, not the public-spirited member of the local amenities committee, and their awareness of collective goods and the potential for collective action was correspondingly narrow. Accordingly, the scope for civic benevolence among such actors was decidedly limited.

Thus the neo-liberal claim that the institutional reforms of the 1980s in Britain and the USA would make efficient and equitable interactions self-enforcing largely neglected this collective dimension, which was odd, given the strong public-choice critique of social democratic institutions from just such a perspective. Actors were taken to respond primarily to price signals, and new institutions designed to give these signals more clearly to public-sector staff, claimants and service users. The reforms ignored perverse incentives and moral hazard of a collective kind – the discrepancy between the payoffs for broad, inclusive communal solidarity on the one hand, and narrow, snobbish, exclusive mutuality on the other; or between unskilled formal employment and trade-union membership, and irregular, informal economic activity and membership of a semi-criminal network, for example.

Despite its disavowal of social engineering and planned outcomes, liberal democratic governance – even of the Hayekian kind – seeks to minimize coercion by providing a framework of rules for interactions in which citizens' individual and collective decisions produce socially desirable outcomes. It is just particularly blind to the undesirable collective consequences of rational egoism (B. Barry, 1991, p. 276). Rules are necessary because citizens have potentially conflicting interests, but socially desirable outcomes are possible only because they also have potential common interests (A. Ryan 1975, p. 54). Neo-liberal institutions have proved, if anything, less strategy-proof than social democratic ones, because they have *produced* rational egoists who are designed to be good at self-interested strategies. Whereas participatory democrats would seek to educate and mobilize citizens for collective action in the common interest (Barber, 1984; Oldfield, 1990), neo-liberals can only fall back on measures of enforcement that raise the price of selfish strategies, but often also increase the social costs of all exchanges, and hence reduce efficiency.

In the absence of opportunities for legal economic activity for the poor, or payoffs for inclusive membership and co-operation between communities and groups, it was rational for many mainstream citizens to press for increased authoritative enforcement. Property owners faced increased insurance costs and the disutility of fear of crime; firms faced rising security bills (more people are now employed as private security guards than by the police forces in Britain); taxpayers' contributions to law and order grow; victims suffer loss and pain. These conditions readily reward populist politicians who exploit social conflicts, and draw dividends from antagonism, rather than brokering co-operation.

In democratic theory, pluralism allows individuals to pursue their interests through collective action in self-selecting groups, with minorities protected by a capsule of civil and political rights (Freeden, 1989). Majority governments reflect shifting coalitions of interest groups in a competitive market of political ideas and organizations (Dahl, 1961). In Hirst's (1994) model of 'associative democracy', the fundamental unit of the political community is the voluntary association, whose members act together in their interests, and are subject only to rules about rights of exit and democratic decision-making. But populism threatens participatory pluralism by mobilizing a long-term coalition of interests (in property, jobs and security) against minorities (poor people, black people, etc.), and it can become anti-democratic when it turns its attention to the very civil and political rights that guarantee individual freedom and diversity (Jordan and Arnold, 1996). The paradox of liberalism is that its fundamental values are private property and individual security as the basis for personal liberty (Holmes, 1993, p. 4), and that in defence of these it can mobilize profoundly coercive forces against impoverished minorities. The problem for democracy is that there is always a temptation for politicians to try to exploit widespread fears (on issues such as crime and 'moral degeneration') through developing movements for tougher enforcement. Populism over such issues transforms the nature of political participation by channelling intergroup antagonisms into public policy.

In Britain, despite its rhetoric of social justice and democratic community, the Labour party under Tony Blair seems more concerned with capturing a largely unreconstructed central mass of Thatcherite voters than with redefining the common good, or refurbishing institutions for collective solidarity. It appears to be quite willing to use law and order as an instrument for these purposes, and has shown little stomach for resisting the Conservative government's measures (such as the Criminal Justice Act, 1994) against minorities and protest groups. If this is so, a change of government in the mid-1990s will do little to break down the long-term coalition of comfortable interests, or change the policy drift since 1993 into greater enforcement measures and expenditures.

This has shifted the focus of participatory resistance to coercion in Britain away from parliamentary democratic processes, and towards a new form of social movement. The prototype for this was the Anti-Poll Tax movement (Hoggett and Burns, 1992), which was disowned by the Labour party because of its (largely spurious) connections with its Militant wing, but which mounted a successful resistance to the Community Charge (a regressive tax on all citizens, part of which was even imposed on social assistance claimants), and made an important contribution to the downfall of Margaret Thatcher. This movement was characterized by local mobilization of individuals, many of whom had not previously been politically active, a loose network of national organizations, with no hierarchy or permanent officials, and reliance on mass defection (non-payment) to increase transaction and enforcement costs to the point that the tax became uneconomic. While Hoggett and Burns are probably overstating their case by calling this 'the Revenge of the Poor', the strategy and the semi-coordinated collective action owed much to poor and excluded people's methods of resistance, and to their informal networks of communication.

Since then, a series of British movements have used similar methods to resist particular local programmes (such as road 'improvements'), national policies (such as the Criminal Justice Act, 1994) and entrepreneurial actions (such as the export of live animals). The core groups in such collective action are small, use computer technology for co-ordination, spurn parliamentary or local government politics, remain independent of formal political organizations and parties, and mobilize the public by appealing directly to them. They plan and execute both public relations spectaculars and street action to disrupt government of commercial activity (Grant, 1995). They borrow from the very effective action of gay groups in the USA over government policy on HIV and AIDS (O'Connor, 1994).

This kind of social movement is not only tactically shrewd and effective; it also goes with the grain of social fragmentation in British society, using single issues to mobilize local groups, rather than attempting to organize mass solidarities. It also makes much use of excluded or self-excluded groups, like New Age Travellers and homeless people, who have little stake in the institutions of comfortable society, and have often traded in their formal political rights for greater autonomy (see pp. 107–9). Indeed it draws on such 'outcast' groups as its model for co-operation in resistance, both by focusing on minority issues like rights to squat or use common land and footpaths, and in its methods of co-ordination through informal networks.

Against this form of action, the powers that be are forced to use expensive policing and unseemly coercion, thus dramaticizing the David and Goliath aspect of the contests. The risk is that public opinion, often sympathetic to the protesters, may quickly move against them. There is a danger of the dynamic of the politics of enforcement shifting towards more generalized repression and state control, as in the US in the 1994 elections. What is missing in both countries is a commitment to some broad, inclusive common good (whether in terms of social justice or some other set of values) that binds together very diverse interest groups by making common interests in shared ideals, institutions and cultural practices visible, and gives opportunities and incentives to uphold them.

The British government under John Major has already gone some way towards translating issues that were treated as ones of social justice in the previous era into ones of criminal justice (Hudson, 1993). In the US, things have gone further; John Gray (1994), an early supporter of the Thatcher reforms who emigrated to the USA, has returned with warnings of 'a comprehensive collapse . . . of trust in the institutions of government' there, because of the experiment 'of withdrawing . . . from any responsibility for the welfare of society or the protection of communities, and confining its functions to a repressive core to do with the maintenance of law and order and the inculcation of certain supposedly basic national values'.

The first duty of democratic governance is to solve collective-action problems that threaten democracy itself. Until the unintended consequences of individual actions in exclusive groups are overcome through measures to promote co-operation and risk-sharing, populist ideas of political participation are more likely to focus on enforcement that intensifies conflicts and divisions, and reinforces exclusion. A Scottish judge has urged more participation in sentencing, even if it led to floggings or brandings, because 'it is arrogant to disenfranchise the great mass of the people, . . . to deny them any effective voice in the creation of penal policy' (McCluskey, 1994). This illustrates the dilemma for democracy in a society divided between mutually antagonistic groups, where members of some of these are using strategic or illegal means to compensate for the costs of being excluded from membership of others.

CONCLUSIONS

If we regard social interactions as consisting of the totality of market and non-market exchanges between individuals, plus the totality of transactions concerned with regulating those exchanges, it makes sense to try to explain how some systems of institutional regulation promote and increase gainful exchanges, while others fail to do so, and instead generate more regulatory activities. This chapter started by reviewing some general theoretical analyses of institutional regimes' influences on the ratio of voluntary exchanges to transaction costs, and has continued by showing that poverty and social exclusion have contributed to the increase in social costs manifested in regimes with strongly liberal-individualist traditions (such as the US and UK), and which have followed a neo-liberal programme for reforming their public sectors.

The public-choice critique of social democratic institutional regime was focused on government decisions over collective goods, and on the rent-seeking behaviour of politicians and bureaucrats that led to the oversupply of public services (Buchanan, 1978; Peacock, 1979; Niskanen, 1975). It influenced attempts to improve efficiency by requiring collective decision-makers to respond to market-like signals. What has often been missing from the analysis has been a detailed evaluation of the outcomes of collective action at the intermediate level. Market forces and institutional reform have had many effects at this level, both by unleashing a Schumpeterian process of creative destruction among communities, voluntary organizations and informal groups, and by reorientating the strategies of the relevant actors.

Alternative systems of institutional regulation have different costs and benefits. A policy programme such as the neo-liberal one, aimed at reducing certain costs (associated with political rent-seeking) will also lose some of the benefits that are particular to that system. Policy makers should therefore evaluate both the positive and negative effects associated with any institutional regime, and especially the outcomes of interactions at the intermediate level, including collective action in clubs, both formal and informal (Hillman, 1992; Breuer et al., 1994; 1995).

Some externalities (both benefits and costs) arise entirely because of the technological conditions of producing goods, others from how they are consumed (Buchanan, 1968). On the cost side, most environmental pollution arises from production, while most public expenditure on the treatment of lung cancer arises from tobacco consumption. But what counts as an efficient allocation of resources always depends on the institutional structure in which decisions are taking place; it is only in this context that we can evaluate whether it is more efficient to tax factories that produce emissions, or the purchase of cigarettes, or to compensate the victims of pollution and lung damage. As Buchanan (1986c, p. 96) has pointed out, a prisoner's dilemma leads to an allocation that is presumed inefficient because (in the absence of the 'no communication' rule) the two prisoners could reach an agreement that would give each of them more utility (both refuse to talk to the police). But if one purpose of police interrogation procedures is to *prevent* prisoners from reaching such agreements, a police-station prisoner's dilemma must be considered efficient, since both confessing is the outcome society seeks.

The neo-liberal programme for institutional reform was aimed at accomplishing just such a shift in what counted as efficiency. For example, in a social democratic institutional regime, the regulation of labour markets was designed to facilitate the employment of the maximum number of employees at protected (or subsidized) wage rates and conditions collectively agreed between employers and trade unions. Redundancy and unemployment were regarded as outcomes involving avoidable social costs (the dislocation of communities as well as poverty and insecurity for individuals) that required compensation. The neo-liberal reform programme in the US and the UK sought to enable more individual contracts to be made, promoting voluntary exchanges between employers and employees, even if many of these were short-term, irregular and involved low pay. By dismantling most of the old regulatory framework, and by reducing some social security entitlements and benefit rates, the reformers hoped to reduce the role of trade unions (seen as distributional coalitions seeking rents through political lobbying, and as colluding in the creation of barriers to potentially gainful exchanges) and to allow excluded unemployed and impoverished individuals to agree employment contracts at wages below current protected levels. They claimed that restraining collective actors would benefit the poor, by enabling their economic inclusion.

In this chapter I have argued that the subsequent hypercasualization of the labour market, and fall in opportunities and incentives for formal employment of less skilled workers, has led to an increase in informal activities of many kinds, including crime. It has also generated informal clubs of various sorts, based on the acquisition, consumption and exchange of semi-legally or illegally acquired goods, the sharing of information about informal activities, and the pooling of risks associated with illegality. In this way, poor and excluded people have sought to compensate themselves for the inequities of market-based outcomes, to 'tax' the better-off for the unjustified gains they have made, and to gain revenge on the various authorities that oppress them, as well as on the mainstream population who despise and exclude them.

The political response of governments, parties and electorates in the Anglo-Saxon, liberal polities has been to raise the price of crime, by increasing the tariff of punishment, and to attempt measures of compulsory integration into the labour market by enhancing the conditionality of income maintenance benefits. In the US, this has taken the most extreme forms – executions of mentally handicapped people, large-scale prison construction, the reintroduction of chain gangs and archaic prison uniforms, and the whole workfare movement – but in the UK (and even to a lesser extent in Europe) there has also been a tendency towards increased enforcement measures, in criminal justice and in welfare-to-work schemes.

These developments introduce a fundamental ambiguity into the neo-liberal policy agenda, and hence confuse the attempt to evaluate the outcomes of institutional reforms. This ambiguity was signalled by the turn in British government policies since the autumn of 1993 when, in response to moral panics on a series of social issues, the Major administration went 'back to basics' (Jordan, 1995). Are the new institutions, in this case designed under Margaret Thatcher, intended to promote voluntary agreements and exchanges of all kinds (the libertarian agenda associated with government rhetoric in the 1980s)? Or are they intended to reinforce such traditional norms as the work ethic, marriage, family and community responsibility (also favoured by

Thatcher, but increasingly emphasized by her successor)?

As Buchanan (1986c, p. 94) has argued, a subjective-contractarian interpretation of efficiency in resource use is most closely approached when well-defined rights are exchanged under voluntary agreements. This view underpinned the institutional evaluations made by Olson (1982) and North (1990) which were summarized at the start of this chapter. Such an approach would see expenditure on policing, imprisonment and workfare enforcement as sheer waste. Of course measures are needed to deter force, fraud and defection, but the policies that promote efficiency are those that give opportunities and incentives for gainful exchanges, generate trust and co-operation, and encourage long-term investments. Hence the present situation in the US and the UK might suggest that future policy should seek to redefine rights and restructure institutions, so as to legitimate agreements that are currently 'informally' (but illegally) struck – for instance, between marginal employers and claimants of benefits – with appropriate compensation for any remaining externalities. This might point towards a Basic Income approach to income maintenance policy (Van Parijs, 1992; 1995; Parker, 1995), which aims to reduce institutionalized traps and barriers to labour-market participation, rather than to enforce formal work. It would involve giving *unconditional* income guarantees to all citizens, irrespective of work or marital status.

The alternative approach follows the neo-conservative agenda (Novak et al., 1987; Mead, 1986) in focusing on the supply side of the labour market, and especially on the attitudes, motives, morals, cultural practices and skills of the poor, and seeing expenditure on compulsory reintegration as a long-term investment to save escalating social assistance expenditures. In this view, crime is one part of a whole set of behaviours that are orientated towards short-term gain, the avoidance of effort, and the rejection of mainstream values in favour of hedonism, defiance and destructiveness. Thus the same issues are tackled by measures to enforce low-paid work and family responsibility (with compensation for employers who take on reluctant hands) and raise the price of illegality by increasing punishment.

The British Labour party seems increasingly to favour the

demand : supply

latter approach. The Commission for Social Justice rejected the Basic Income pathway to institutional reform, and instead proposed a whole range of supply-side measures, including welfare-to-work schemes, but without very accurate measures of the costs of these (Borrie, 1994). Of course, if one accepts the assumptions outlined in the previous paragraph, all such spending is efficiency-orientated, at least in the long run. But the suspicion remains that this kind of institutional design *creates* prisoner's dilemmas, and then goes on to punish those it thus traps, at high cost to taxpayers. A Hobbesian order, as Putnam (1993) emphasizes, is better than no order at all, but evidence from other societies suggests that the economic and political performance achieved through third-party enforcement is the equilibrium outcome of inefficient interactions that generate unnecessarily high social costs.

Whichever of these two paths is chosen, policy-makers will face two enormous problems. The first is one of implementation. The existence of large numbers of covert, risk-sharing 'informal clubs' for semi-legal or illegal activities, which generate high returns for members (through predation and cost-sharing), means that policy programmes must either offer larger inducements through formal labour-market participation than the benefits these clubs can supply to members, or break up the clubs through enforcement measures. Small rewards (a low level of Basic Income, plus low and irregular wages) or small individual punishments would not be enough to achieve either of these goals, since the payoffs to club members (for example, drugs gangs) are so high. Poverty and social exclusion have thus already driven up the costs of effective policies of any kind to reintegrate those citizens, because they have provoked them into relatively effective collective resistance.

Secondly, there is a problem of political legitimation and support. If either a market-minded or a socialist government favoured a libertarian strategy, and came round to the view that Basic Incomes represented the best solution consistent with social justice (Barry, 1994), it would still have to win political support for such a proposal. As the British Liberal Democrats discovered in 1992, Basic Incomes are not easy to explain to the public, and the economic and ethical case for libertarianism in such issues requires a long and complex process of reasoning. This is particularly the case in a polarized society, in which the press and populist politicians have had considerable success in persuading comfortable citizens that the poor are burdensome and morally degenerate; how then could unconditional benefits be legitimately given to them? This question will be briefly addressed in the final section of the book.

But the problem of enforcement measures is the opposite one; their very popularity may lead to them running away with themselves, leaving political leaders unable to contain costs or restrain anti-liberal excesses. If the poor resist compulsory inclusion, and if workfare regimes and increased incarceration actually breed more spectacular and effective networks, practices and strategies of resistance (as the evidence of historical and cross-national comparisons suggests they will), then it will be very difficult to sustain efficiency-orientated policies in the face of pressures for ever-increasing expenditures on enforcement. It will also be very hard to stop the culture of contentment rushing forward into the politics of punishment and revenge. Mutual antagonism, the organization of conflictual collective action, and the erosion of the cultural basis of the democratic politics of the common good, will all be consequences of such developments. The dangers of these tendencies will be further examined in the final chapter.

7

Conclusions: States and Social Policy

⸺⧓⸺

The theory of poverty and social exclusion that is advanced in this book explains these phenomena in terms of collective action by groups pursuing their common interests in a changing world economic environment. Although there has been no systematic analysis of globalization in the book, the context of my account has always been a world in which the mass solidarities and institutional systems for national economic management set up by the advanced industrialized First World states after the Second World War have been under increasing pressure. The reader has been invited to understand the processes of polarization, division and fragmentation into narrower mutualities in such societies as part of a wider set of changes, signalled by increases in the number and speed of transnational exchanges of all kinds, the greater interdependence of spheres of decision-making that were previously treated as separate, the collapse of the Soviet-bloc command economies and weakening of most statist regimes in Third World countries, and all the consequent dislocations (including starvation and mass migration) that these have entailed.

The book started by pointing to the similarities between these developments and the processes that followed the English Industrial Revolution. Karl Polanyi's *The Great Transformation* (1944) used the analysis of poverty and social exclusion in the rural villages of England in the Speenhamland period (1795–1834) as the focus for his account of the relationship between global economic change and local social protectionism. At that time, what he called the 'Utopian project' of creating a global self-regulating market economy – One Big Market (p. 72) – provoked a counter-movement to protect the human substance and values of traditional communities:

> the idea of a self-adjusting market implied a stark Utopia. Such an institution could not exist for any length of time without annihilating the human and natural substance of society; it would have physically destroyed man and transformed his surroundings into a wilderness. (p. 3)

Perhaps the most distinctive feature of Polanyi's analysis was this 'double movement' thesis, that the growth in market exchanges, and especially transnational exchanges, of all kinds in the nineteenth century, under the institutional systems sponsored by Britain as the hegemonic superpower, were countered by forms of collective action aimed at controlling these:

> While on the one hand markets spread all over the face of the globe and the amount of goods involved grew to unbelievable proportions, on the other hand a network of measures and policies was integrated into powerful institutions designed to check the market relative to labour, land and money. (p. 72)

It was this *second* movement, in reaction against market globalization, that from the 1870s produced a second institutional transformation, from the liberal, *laissez-faire*, free trade regimes that had characterized the era of British dominance, to imperialist and protectionist ones, and that in turn led to the dramatic shift from a hundred years of peace in Europe to fascism, communism and two world wars. Polanyi argued that the destructive effects of global markets provoked forms of collective action of very diverse kinds, which led to contrasting movements and regimes in the various European countries, but which all in combination produced a new form of *national* political economy (more autarkic, nationalist and protectionist) and new international relations (more militaristic, opportunistic and unstable). The social protectionism that gave the world

Bismarckian collective insurance and the whole range of central government and local authority regulatory institutions was thus intimately linked with the growth of totalitarian politics and international strife.

It is the explication of this dimension of transformation that is missing from most present-day analyses of institutional performance and the institutional transformation of Central and Eastern Europe. While Olson in his *Logic of Collective Action* (1965) provided the tools for a public-choice version of Polanyi's historical analysis, his later *The Rise and Decline of Nations* (1982) fails to address these underlying questions about the long-term directions of institutional change, or the possibility of rapid shifts in the political significance of collective action. Similarly North's (1990) work on institutions and path dependency considers transaction and enforcement costs, but fails to address the possibility that these relate to deeper political issues over conflicts between collective actors, as in Polanyi's account of the role of the peasantry in Central Europe, when weak liberal regimes came to depend on them as potentially violent upholders of market institutions threatened by the economic power of organized labour. The issues raised in the previous chapter demand a Polanyi-style analysis, in terms of potential crises in the whole institutional basis of the present world order (the United Nations, sovereign territorial states, welfare states, etc.), and their potential transformation into new and hitherto unknown forms. Putnam's (1993) and Hirst's (1994) theories fall short of a comprehensive exposition.

Although Polanyi was convinced that economic liberalism as a Utopian creed had collapsed, with its last great bastion, the gold standard, in the 1930s, he thought that some new synthesis would emerge, providing institutions that could deliver 'freedom in a complex society'. 'Industrial civilization will continue to exist when the Utopian experiment of a self-regulating market will be no more than a memory' (1944, p. 250). In the event, the twin systems of welfare states and centrally planned states, held in equilibrium by a balance of nuclear terror, did provide something like what he envisaged for the almost fifty years after his book was written. But it now begins to look as if the hundred-

year-long 'Polanyi waves' of transformation – market globalization followed by nationalistic protectionism – have not been transcended, but instead have simply shortened in duration. The era
of the heyday of both welfare states and centrally planned states
can, with hindsight, be seen as having lasted no more than 25–30
years, while the new wave of globalization, with its attendant
Utopian, universal, market-minded creed and political evange-
lists (the New Right) appear to be but a few steps ahead of
Nemesis. What next?

What Polanyi's analysis would lead us to seek is a theory that
shows how the regulatory institutions of an era of effective social
protectionism (in his account, the corporations, guilds, local
authorities and central government bodies of the era of mercantilism) were laid waste by market forces released through the
free-trade enthusiasms of liberal political movements, and
replaced by transnational and national regimes that upheld the
market order (the equivalents of the nineteenth-century balance
of power, the gold standard and the liberal state). We should
then try to identify the emergence of those collective actors and
programmes that sought to tame the destructiveness of market
forces, or harness them to their common interests and purposes
– the equivalents of the political movements towards socialism
and imperialism in the late nineteenth century.

This book has focused mainly on middle-order institutions,
and the collective actions of interest groups within these, including households and informal groups such as criminal gangs. In
this final chapter I shall consider whether transnational or
national regimes have been able to devise new methods of regulation that might contain some of the costlier forms of collective
action identified in chapters 4, 5 and 6, and thus repair the damage being done to efficiency and equity.

Just as Polanyi focused on the emergence of pauperism and
measures to control it in his analysis of the first institutional
transformation (globalization), so I have concentrated on the
phenomena of poverty and social exclusion as the source of
many of these social costs and wasteful allocations. But there are
those who would argue that many of the changes I have identified are quite superficial, in comparison with the continuities

and further development of effective methods of regulation, both national and international, in the past 25 years.

On this analysis, it is far too soon to be writing the obituary of the welfare state. Despite the determined attempt by neo-liberal governments in the USA and the UK, and more pragmatic conservative or centrist ones in Western Europe, to cut expenditure on social services and deregulate parts of the labour market, most of the institutional features of the post-war era are still recognizable, albeit in modified forms, and still perform the same functions (P. Pierson, 1995). Expenditure has largely been sustained, especially where the middle classes had a large stake in systems of income protection and health care (Klein, 1993; C. Pierson, 1991). Welfare states still provide the advanced industrialized countries with institutional ways of restraining both costly internal conflicts and their international spillovers. In so doing, they enable these countries to maintain their advantageous position in the world economy, and allow new transnational institutions to emerge, which in turn regulate global forces in line with the structures and interests of these states. Hence poverty and social exclusion, even though they have significantly increased as features of the social relations of these societies, are nonetheless of marginal significance, and unlikely to signal the kind of major shift implied by talk of 'new Great Transformation' (Bryant and Mokrzycki, 1994) or 'crisis of the nation state' (Held and McGrew, 1994).

This chapter will necessarily be rather more speculative than the previous ones, but I shall argue that the analysis developed in those earlier chapters implies a more radical set of changes, and points to the possibility of a fundamental institutional transformation. This is signalled in what is happening in societies outside the core First World bloc, such as the newly industrializing nation states of South-East Asia, and the emerging democracies of Central Europe. If these developments are taken together with those in the USA and the UK, they suggest that the pace of change will accelerate in the next century, rather than slow down as the optimists imply, and that traditionally regulated countries such as Germany, and transnational groupings such as the EU, may be at a key disadvantage in competing with newly industrializing or transforming ones. On the other hand, nations such as the USA and the UK, which have radically modified their old institutions without resolving underlying issues of polarization, conflict and the power of distributional coalitions, may be even further weakened, and experience accelerated relative economic decline, as social costs escalate. Thus institutional means for dealing with issues of poverty and social exclusion could become very important determinants of the relative success of national economies in the next century.

GLOBALIZATION AND WELFARE STATES

In chapter 4 I argued that welfare states were new social contracts between encompassing organizations for capital and labour and the state that allowed capitalists and trade unionists in those countries to reach relatively harmonious agreements about how to share the rents they could earn through expanding production and trade with less well-organized as well as less developed economies. But this expansion itself released new economic forces and – together with new technological and organizational developments in productive enterprises – changed the configuration of actors and interests within the advanced industrialized states. What are being addressed in this concluding chapter are the causes and consequences of greater interdependence between nation states and the closer interweaving of domestic and foreign policy, to the point where Bill Clinton, in his inaugural presidential speech, asserted that: 'There is no clear division between what is foreign and what is domestic' (Parry, 1994).

On the one hand, this seems to be the consequence of the success of advanced industrialized welfare states in expanding trade and creating new markets in new manufactured goods, which has resulted in the increase in transnational exchanges of all kinds. But on the other it has given rise to organizational forms, such as international enterprises and regulatory regimes (Keohane, 1989) and processes, such as the new international division of labour and large-scale capital movements, that transcend the closed logic of welfare states as systems of national economic management and social distribution.

It has been argued by some that welfare states have facilitated these changes, continued to sustain them, and remain necessary conditions for their future development. For instance, Rieger and Leibfried (1995) maintain that economic integration between national economies is mainly a relationship between welfare states. Effective social policies allow such states to throw themselves open to world markets. The tendency is for economic links to grow fastest between countries with similar values, institutional structures and regulatory principles – and in this case the relevant characteristics are political democracy and welfare statism, which provide interdependence and institutional integration with a stable foundation. This in turn has meant that the countries best integrated into the global economy and most involved in transnational regulatory systems have similar basic features, and that international organizations (like GATT) mirror the assumptions and rules of welfare states. Thus international politics and economic policy are 'saturated with welfare statism' (Rieger and Leibfried, 1995, p. 11); shared domestic notions of social justice and social protection influence such interactions, and contribute to globalization. Depending upon the date from which one starts measuring, it is quite plausible to argue that advanced industrialized welfare states have increased their share of trade in manufactures during the period since globalization has accelerated (roughly the mid-1960s), despite their slower growth rates. This is obviously particularly true of Germany and Japan, the two most successful of these economies. And finally, of course, the European Union illustrates this argument, by reflecting the economic and legitimation needs of its constituent welfare states, and aiming – by closer integration – to enable their economies to benefit disproportionately from globalization processes.

However, there are several problems with this interpretation. Was it really their systems for national economic management and social distribution that promoted greater economic integration and accelerated all forms of exchanges between these societies? This may work as an explanation of the European Union's institutional development, but it can scarcely explain the increasing exchanges between countries with sufficiently different institutions and interests to form themselves into rival trading blocs (such as the North American free trade area). Might it not instead be, as Polanyi argues, that the notion of self-regulating markets, increasingly promoted within the international sectors of these economies, has a logic of its own that tends towards the creation of a global order? Since this is not the first but the second era of globalization, and since the first created international institutions that reflected *laissez-faire* liberalism rather than welfare statism, this seems to imply that such domestic systems are not necessary conditions for closer integration or expanding trade. Indeed it was not until the mid-1980s that the volume of world trade exceeded that of 1913, so great had been its decline during the two world wars and the interwar period; the era of welfare states merely restored it to its previous level, rather than transcending previous possibilities.

The really important questions raised by Polanyi's analysis are whether institutions that attempt to counter the effects of self-regulating world markets will again emerge as strong features of collective action in these countries and trading blocs, and whether this will again – as in the interwar period – spark off a chain reaction of domestic political instability and conflict, followed by intensified international competition, nationalism and wars. Do welfare states guarantee the emerging systems of international relations against such outcomes, and if so how?

Clearly it is impossible to answer these questions in any authoritative way, but there are plenty of indications that welfare state institutions are not unambiguously harmonizing and conflict-restraining in their impact on these issues. One such is the continuing struggle between Britain and her EU partners over the Social Chapter of the Maastricht Treaty. It is easy to see that document, with its emphasis on the rights of *workers* to fair remuneration, working conditions, employment-related benefits, collective bargaining facilities, vocational training, equal opportunities, health protection and safety in the workplace (Community Charter of Fundamental Social Rights of Workers, 1992), as a reflection of the attempt, by Germany, Belgium and the Netherlands in particular, to install the principles and institutions of the conservative, corporatist welfare state at the heart of the European project. It is also easy to see why the Germans in particular, with their continued commitment to, and even extension of, these principles and institutions, should want to protect the EU's structures from opportunists, defectors and social dumpers *within* the ranks of its members, as well as from outside. But Britain had already, under Margaret Thatcher, moved a long way from these assumptions, and perceived its interests to be in attracting investment from America and South-East Asia, as much as in sharing in the benefits of collective European self-restraint and co-operation. In the name of 'flexibility' and a well-functioning labour market, the British government has ever since then resisted the Social Chapter, and tried to win support from other marginal members of the EU for relaxing its conditions, while making it plain that it regards the Union as having better economic prospects if it is willing to compete with other economies by reducing the social costs of employment, and forcing workers to accept internationally realistic wage rates.

A second example comes from the field of migration. The moral basis of welfare states is redistributive justice among members (Walzer, 1983, p. 31), based partly on contributions and partly on needs (see pp. 73–4). This has always made migration an awkward issue for such states, and they resolve it in different ways. Germany, for example, is more willing to give *Gastarbeiter* social rights and benefits than to grant them political citizenship, whereas Britain reserves most of its social rights for the diminishing number of immigrants who achieve full citizenship status (including political rights). The collapse of the regimes in Central and Eastern Europe, and the opening up of their borders to the West, along with the flood of asylum applications from Third World countries, has given a new urgency to issues around migration and the definition of membership and social entitlements. Here the European Union's rules and treaties sometimes act as restraints on national governments' attempts to limit entry rights or social expenditures, as where migrants from outside the Union have turned to the European Court of Justice for appeals against decisions by EU member states (Faist, 1994b).

The point about these developments is that the protection of the social rights of citizens becomes a major political motive for resisting immigration; even those most in favour of relaxing immigration controls argue that the hard-won social rights of citizens are threatened by unrestricted migration flows (Bauböck, 1991). Hence social protection becomes the 'spoilsport element' in what would otherwise be a situation that promoted free labour movement, and in which strong arguments, from efficiency and equity, could be used in favour of such policies. Far from favouring globalization in this sense, welfare states' redistributive programmes tend to block it, and collective actors turn to various back-door measures, such as the *Werkvertragsarbeitnehmer* schemes in Germany (Faist, 1995), to gain some of the benefits of cost-saving and flexibility without jeopardizing the agreements that constitute domestic social policy. Welfare states, far from being unambiguously globalization-friendly, tend to orientate governments towards measures of protectionism and nationalism, even when other factors might indicate the opposite orientation.

This falls well short of providing the basis for an apocalyptic Polanyi-style prediction of escalating international tension and strife, but it does indicate that social policies are likely to prove a major stumbling block to greater political and economic integration in Europe, especially when the applicants from Central Europe, with their more lean-burn public sector structures and lower wage costs, are absorbed into the EU. They might well prove to be enthusiastic supporters of the present British line on social policy issues, since they stand to gain from flexibility and competition on labour costs within the Union.

At the same time, immigration from North Africa and the more distant Third World countries will continue to raise painful issues for the EU and its member states. Although the various neo-fascist and extreme nationalist political parties seem to have reached their peak of recruitment, they will not be without political influence, as the French presidential election in 1995 amply illustrated. Much more significantly, these issues will increasingly be acted out through the street politics of gangs of racist thugs and self-protective actions by immigrant groups. Here the British case shows that weak political organization (in the sense that no extreme right party has broken through into national politics) does not guarantee social relations against the perils of quasi-fascist mobilization and costly street conflicts. In a climate of enforcement politics, these phenomena always threaten to spill over into repressive policies by the major parties, and hence to pollute the efficiency and ethics of democratic processes.

COLLECTIVE ACTION AND WELFARE STATES

In public-choice theory, the logic of collective action in exclusive groups requires them to compete for rents, and such distributional struggles are costly in terms of potential economic efficiency, and their outcomes are inequitable. The point of welfare states was – and remains – their capacity to overcome these inefficiencies and inequities in the collective interests of citizens. Both Olson's work, and the developments from Buchanan's theory of clubs that were discussed in chapters 2 and 4, can be used to analyse the unintended consequences of market-oriented reforms (for instance, in terms of undocumented migration, crime and working-while-claiming) in welfare states. These in turn provoke further strategic group responses, involving increased antagonism, conflict and social costs.

However, the public-choice perspective on the impact of globalization on welfare states and its manifestations in poverty and social exclusion yields other paradoxical conclusions. Within the world economic system, welfare states allowed both capitalists and workers in the First World countries to capture rents, to the long-term disadvantage of their counterparts in developing countries. From a world perspective, therefore, welfare states are rather successful 'distributional coalitions' (Olson, 1982), or 'multiproduct clubs' (Sandler and Tschirhart, 1993) that have overcome the chronic collective-action dilemmas of the interwar years, to achieve rapid growth and global economic dominance.

Conversely, however, globalization processes have significantly eroded the capacities of welfare states to capture these rents, giving important advantages to other, new forms of polity in international competition (see pp. 124–5). The 'four tigers' of

South-East Asia – Hong Kong, Singapore, Taiwan, South Korea – have achieved rapid growth, and significantly caught up on advanced welfare states in terms of income per head, with (and presumably because of) very different institutional structures. Not, of course, that they just redistribute a lower proportion of GDP; they also manage their economies quite differently from most advanced welfare states. And above all, they have not been democracies: they have not allowed distributional coalitions to divert them from their growth-orientated purposes.

Several things seem disturbing about this development. First, these advances are not reflected in the economies of other developing countries, and the international financial regime (IMF, World Bank) seems determined to impose on indebted governments in Africa and South America institutional structures and economic policies that are miles away from these successful ones. They have enforced the global logic of markets to dismantle their puny attempts at establishing regulatory systems, trade and payment controls, and expansionist domestic policies, denying them the chance to manage their development in ways that reconciled economic change with their particular social and political circumstances. First in countries like Sri Lanka, and then (in the 1980s) in South and Central America, this has resulted in the dismantling of welfare states (since then, most recently in Zimbabwe) and in the prohibition of their development in poorer African countries; but it has also meant that these countries were not free to develop *any* systems to protect themselves from global market forces. If the logic of the self-regulating market did not maximize efficiency and welfare, then they were at an increasing disadvantage in international competition.

Yet the newly industrializing countries of South-East Asia in particular were free to capture rents through their independent economic regimes, and mobilize increasingly effectively for competition in world markets. They may have been granted the freedom to do this by the advanced capitalist states because of their strategic geopolitical position, as some kind of buffer against 'communist expansion'. But their gains through this concession seem now to have transcended those available to the 'late developer', or through the social capital of Confucianism. Given the accelerated growth in trade and capital movements, their advantages were huge; thus instead of flowing to the poorest countries with lowest wage rates, international investment was concentrated in these successful, rapidly growing economies, to the great benefit of their citizens.

Furthermore, but more ambiguously, these same arguments apply to the transformation of the Central and East European economies, and the former Soviet Union. They too have been required to adopt open structures, dismantle regulations, privatize national assets, and reduce benefits and subsidies. But it is still too early to judge whether this will have the same consequences as in the Third World: I shall return to this topic later.

In addition, there is the disturbing evidence of the relative decline of some of the most generous welfare states, and especially of the collapse of the much-vaunted Scandinavian model. Finland, of course, with its unemployment rate at 18 per cent, is a special case, related to the collapse in Eastern Europe. But so too is optimistic, autonomous Norway with its oil bonanza, which can still afford to thumb its nose at the EU and subsidize its quainter lifestyle preferences. The most significant and worrying case is Sweden, where by 1990 the state redistributed some 60–70 per cent of GDP, including 35 per cent on social services, and where twice as many citizens were supported out of taxes (either by benefits or public-sector employment) as financed through markets. Between 1970 and 1993 Sweden fell from 3rd to 13th place in the international league table of GNP per head, by far the most spectacular decline among the rich countries; and, as measures start to be taken to remedy these problems, unemployment has risen to 13 per cent (Lindbeck, 1995). Whereas other relative declines (such as that of the USA) can be attributed to the 'catching-up effect' elsewhere, Sweden's now seems to reflect serious competitive disadvantages (Pfaller et al., 1991).

Globalization occurs partly spontaneously, through market processes and voluntary exchanges of all kinds (accelerating transnational interactions), and partly through the collective actions of various international actors and policies of transnational regimes. How do we assess the issues of transnational social justice raised by these changes, and the shifts in economic competitive advantage that have taken place since the 1980s began? In particular, what criteria do we apply to the simultaneous phenomena of Third World starvation and the transformation of the former communist countries, mass migration and the growth of cross-border organized crime?

In chapter 2 I analysed Olson's (1982) claim that all forms of redistributive social policy harmed the most vulnerable members of society, and work in favour of the more advantaged (see pp. 54–5). In arguing that distributional coalitions tend to increase inequalities and exclusions, whereas free markets allow capital to migrate to areas with lowest wages, and thus to contribute to wage rises for the poorest, Olson suggests that welfare states create involuntary unemployment by erecting barriers to potentially gainful exchanges of many kinds. Yet I also drew attention to the huge paradox in Olson's theory that nation states are themselves 'collusions', in so far as they successfully restrain internal competition between capital and labour, and allow one economy to trade more advantageously with another. While free trade may maximize *global* gainful exchanges, and thus benefit the poorest *in the world*, it can only do so by eroding the relative advantages of vulnerable members of hitherto successfully protected, wealthy nations, such as disabled Swedes, or young people in the Netherlands. Olson's policy-assisted globalization would thus compete away the 'artificial' protections given to the elderly, sick and unemployed of Europe, as well as the minimum wages and conditions enjoyed by low-skilled workers there. It would lead to the kind of cumulative falls in real wages that have happened in the USA and Britain – first of unskilled, then semi-skilled, and finally professional employees.

Furthermore, even if capital and commodities were free to flow world-wide, there would still remain one important barrier to the global market promoted by Olson's programme. He says nothing about the exchange of people – migration between states – or policies for restricting such movements. Logically, a world without borders or migration controls would be one of the necessary conditions for optimization through global markets, if the way to efficiency and welfare is individual pursuit of gainful exchanges. Yet this is not a policy canvassed in any country of the world.

From which standpoint should we address such issues? The question is not entirely a normative one, as the case of Central European transformation illustrates. Right up to 1994 the central question for research on transformation processes was why they had turned out to be so painful and costly (see for instance Offe, 1992; Bönker, 1993; Bryant and Mokrzycki, 1994). What had to be explained was why things changed so slowly, why growth was so delayed, poverty and unemployment so widespread, crime so rapidly growing. Now the situation is far more ambiguous. The indicators, in Poland and the Czech Republic particularly, are quite favourable, and most of German growth is concentrated in the *Neuen Länder.* It becomes harder to see how German manufacturers will compete with their Czech counterparts, or German farmers and fishermen with those in Poland. One is suddenly reminded that Germany's post-war miracle did not happen by 1950, but took till 1955 to accomplish; even then, the US and Britain looked on a trifle contemptuously as the EEC was formed (from a position of weakness, not strength). If Russia seems doomed to be the basket case, where else can equally confidently be consigned to that sad category?

Perhaps another of Olson's laws applies to Central Europe. Many commentators on the transformation have noted the absence or ineffectiveness of collective actors, within the new institutional structures (Bönker, 1993). These factors lead to political instability and hamper the development of democratic politics (Cirtautas, 1994). But Olson would argue that unstable conditions and collective-action problems are *favourable* to rapid economic growth, because the distributional struggle is reduced, or the rival coalitions cannot get their acts together. Again, the situation would be relatively advantageous for the emerging Central European economies, with their more open, less regulated structures – a kind of window of opportunity before the start of the next century, for a rapid push towards catching up in terms of incomes, and (who knows?) for developing new institutional structures that transcend the welfare state, and bind their citizens to some new social contract, more efficient and strategy-proof under twenty-first-century conditions.

If the perspective for social policy evaluation should be international, then may market-driven globalization, by its erosion of the advanced welfare state's protective advantages, be an instrument of greater efficiency *and* more equitable distributions worldwide? If not, might the success of somewhat cohesive, undemocratic newly industrializing polities spread further, at the expense of poor people in both richer and poorer economies? And should we worry about the fate of low-skilled workers in Central Europe, or about our own, who cannot possibly compete with them? Should we really be looking for ways to defend welfare states, or for new institutions to mobilize our human and material resources more effectively – and if we find success in this, who (in the world) will gain, and who will lose? Is international social justice better served by transfers (foreign aid) or by letting foreigners claim that aid for themselves, either through relaxing immigration restrictions, or turning a blind eye to illegal migration?

This section has ranged rather widely over the collective-action dilemmas for welfare states within the new global order. Perhaps these can be boiled down to one central question. If the collective good at stake is yet faster growth of *national* incomes, can this best be achieved by farming available resources and sharing out benefits through traditional post-war institutions (either nationally, or in pan-European systems, through some kind of Super-Germany, the extended EU); or does it require greater flexibility than such institutions can allow? Rieger's and Leibfried's (1995) analysis suggests they believe a positive answer to this question will sustain European welfare states well into the next century. I am not so sure.

The question is particularly interesting for the British, whose institutional transformation during the Thatcher decade has left this country ambiguously poised on one European margin; and for Central Europeans, whose still more radical transformation could give them a competitive edge for the next 50 years if Rieger and Leibfried are wrong. There seems little doubt that the latter economies will catch up in the 1990s, but might their new structures actually be more suited for the global environment of the future? I would certainly not bet against it.

What seems far less clear is how the US and the UK will fare, as compared with Western or Central Europe. The 'window of opportunity' for the Central European states may be flexibility through the temporary weakness of internal collective actors capable of forming effective distributional coalitions (as in Germany in the immediate post-war period). In the Anglo-Saxon countries, old and new collective actors can and do take strategic defensive action to resist the effects of structural change. This increases social conflicts, which in turn raise transaction and enforcement costs (Jordan, 1995). The obvious phenomenon of a 'politics of enforcement' in the US (the Republicans' 'Contract for America', Gingrichism) is echoed in right-wing populism, especially over crime and 'underclass' issues, in Britain (Jordan and Arnold, 1996a). All this costs money and reduces efficiency.

It is yet more difficult to perceive how deeply the problems of these states are running. Are the extraordinary costs of US health care (Morone, 1995) or the massive 'negative equity' in the British owner-occupied housing sector merely specific consequences of policy mistakes, which lead to a widespread 'feel bad' factor among middle-class voters? Or are they symptoms of a much deeper malaise, with club-like 'communities of choice' (pro-life versus pro-choice, gays versus straights) mobilized against each other, and a big mainstream club of comfort mobilized against the minority (poor, often black) 'communities of fate', whose resistance will manifest itself in still further rising crime, urban rioting and a deteriorating social environment?

Finally, pessimists will draw attention to the negative potential in the unstable politics of the new Central European democracies. If militant nationalism re-emerges as a major theme in these states, to match the disintegrative tendencies in the US and the UK (Oklahoma City, the problems of Northern Ireland) then Western Europe could find itself sandwiched between two regions of political instability and conflict. It would be ironic, but not entirely surprising, if the liberal individualism that saved the US and the UK from fascism proved to be the factor that made them more vulnerable to wasteful intergroup conflict in the first half of the next century, and if Central Europe again destabilized the international peace, as before the First World War. In this gloomy scenario, European welfare states would indeed have justified themselves, but not at all for the reasons that Rieger and Leibfried give. They would have provided institutions for relative domestic and regional harmony under democratic regimes, rather than economic growth; in other words, they would have served their original purpose.

THE FUTURE OF NATION STATES AND SOCIAL POLICY

If the regulatory order of welfare states has come under such pressure from global economic forces and the strategies of collective actors, can these in turn evolve into some new institutional form, through democratic processes? Might the whole system of nation states that emerged from competition between this new form of governance, and the city leagues (of northern Europe) and city states (of Italy) in the late Middle Ages, be transformed into something quite different – such as a balance between regional superstates like the EU on the one hand, and smaller, self-governing and self-selecting communities on the other?

In chapter 1 (pp. 27–33) and chapter 5 (pp. 170–81) the economics of 'voting with the feet' as the basis for the formation of 'private' communities of choice was counterposed to the politics of sovereign territorial states. On the one hand, the concept of sovereign individual, choosing where to live by selecting a bundle of collective goods, available through the development of a site by a private landlord in exchange for rent, gives rise to the ideal-type of a community based on contract, yet able to sustain a highly developed quality of life through democratic processes of governance (Foldvary, 1994). We have seen in chapter 5 that this corresponds in many ways with tendencies within welfare states, where the strategies of comfortable households have moved them in these directions, and have transformed residential districts into self-selecting homogeneous income zones. Local authorities have seldom resisted these developments; instead they have managed them by regulating and compensating the 'communities of fate' left behind or created by such interactions, and constructing an infrastructure of (rather inefficient) transport links – consisting mainly of environmentally unfriendly highways – between them.

On the other hand, as sovereign territorial states become less able to harness global economic forces, to broker agreements between internationally mobile capital and defensively organized national labour, to negotiate shares of tax burdens or redistributive benefits and services, or to protect their most vulnerable citizens from poverty, so the significance of national politics wanes, commitment to citizenship as a membership category with priority over others is diminished, and individuals follow strategies that transcend the national dimension of interaction. Increasingly both collective actors and their constituent members think globally and follow strategies that take account of international advantage, by combining transnational elements, orientated to institutions outside the nation state, with local and regional actions. This applies to business, wage negotiations and tourism; it implies that the 'feel bad factor', which confers on almost all national governments a lower popularity rating than their 1960s or 1970s predecessors, is not so much the reflection of a feeling that they could and should do better, as the acknowledgement of their impotence, and an anxious awareness of the need to make autonomous decisions on risk-management at the level of household, club, community or private welfare association.

In this view, the 'lifestyle politics' of the comfortable classes (Giddens, 1991) is the transcendence of the politics of emancipatory social movements only in so far as it recognizes the small returns now available to groups who lobby national governments for changes in regulatory regimes or distributional shares, and the greater payoffs to those who form clubs and take strategic decisions over risk-management and the advantageous development of assets and resources. However, some of these may prove collectively unsuccessful and self-defeating (see pp. 141–58). It may come to be recognized that apparently specific policy problems, like the failure of Bill Clinton's national health insurance plan or the negative equity phenomenon in the UK housing market, are symptoms of more general problems in the interactions between these strategies.

But equally, those excluded from these new, narrower mutualities and clubs, formed by the choices of those comfortable actors, in turn take strategic action to compensate themselves, to 'tax' them for their unmerited advantages, for the sake of revenge, or simply to avail themselves of new opportunities for handsome payoffs in a deregulated economic environment, where informal activities such as crime are far better rewarded than formal employment. Others still trade in their claims to political rights altogether, by becoming undocumented migrants, living in small, self-protecting groups and communities, mainly in large cosmopolitan cities, and working as the 'club servants' of welfare states (see pp. 70, 74), or by joining groups of travellers for the sake of autonomy and opportunities for informal activity.

In chapter 6 (pp. 217–21), I argued that national governments could respond in two ways to this challenge. On the one hand they could see these phenomena as the unintended consequences of a decade of economic individualism, released by rash reforms of post-war social institutions, and leading to high hidden social costs in the form of environmental depletion, the deterioration in the quality of social life, and an anti-democratic politics of enforcement. In this view, politics remains a question of upgrading social institutions so as to counter such socially undesirable consequences of individual and collective action (Barry, 1991, p. 276), and to engineer incentives and opportunities for actions with more favourable collective outcomes. It is also to educate and communicate with citizens, so as to make common interests in a good quality of civic life and democratic practices more recognizable (Oldfield, 1990). A shorthand way of saying all this, that also betrays a certain vagueness about how to achieve it, is signalled in the references of the British Labour party's leader to 'community', and the need to recreate collective responsibility among the citizenry (Blair, 1995).

There are many specific policy proposals available to national governments, all of which claim to offer ways of countering the social costs of mutually frustrating strategies, predatory exploitation, polarization, injustice and environmental depletion (Borrie, 1994). But there are two difficulties about the approach that combines a large number of these and fires them, machine-gun style, at the problems identified in this book. One is that they may work in such a way as to cancel out each other; measures that seem promising in terms of one policy domain may have unanticipated consequences in another, and thus may annul or reverse the benefits of some other policy measure. This, after all, was the fate of the neo-liberal programme, since its market-orientated deregulation drove up the costs of income maintenance and enforcement as fast as or faster than it saved other kinds of public expenditure. The second problem is that it is difficult to make very specific policies and regulations strategy-proof; they may work for a while, but then individuals and collective actors find ways round or through them. Here again, the examples given in chapters 4 and 5 of this book illustrate the fate of neo-liberal reforms as poor people devised strategic ways of turning them to their advantage.

Another whole approach to policy-making in this situation is to identify the directions taken by strategic action, and to look for the most efficient and equitable way of steering these towards more socially desirable outcomes. In this view, the high moral ground taken by opposition politicians such as Tony Blair is no more likely to be fertile than that occupied by Newt Gingrich and his neo-conservative followers in the USA. Instead of risking further increases in enforcement costs through a whole raft of 'welfare-to-work' schemes, new regulations, minimum wages and fancy tax-benefit adjustments, policy should coolly assess the actual costs of particular forms of strategic action, and how these might be gradually reduced, while offering greater opportunities and incentives for those that appear to contribute to efficiency and equity.

If this line is adopted, intelligent policy assessment eschews moral judgements and addresses economic realities. To take an extreme example, it has rather convincingly been argued that in present-day Russia, crime promotes efficiency (Luttwak, 1995). The Soviet command economy produced huge quantities of materials (more electricity per head than Italy, more steel per head than the USA, more tractors per 1000 people than Germany, and almost twice as much meat per head as Japan), yet its systems for processing raw materials into consumer goods and distributing them among its population were so inefficient and inequitable that standards of living were far lower there than in the First World. Some raw materials, such as cotton, were produced efficiently enough to sell in world markets, yet by the time they had been turned into garments they were of no utility. In this situation, *crime promotes efficiency*; stealing materials can only result in better allocations, since what passed for 'production' was in fact destruction of these, and nothing of value reached consumers. Crime can also provide the capital for enterprise, as the situation in post-war Western Europe showed. The prototype for the European businessman of the 1950s and 1960s was probably Harry Lime, the fictional racketeer, rather than some more edifying hero of post-war reconstruction.

From this perspective, problems of poverty and social exclusion should not necessarily seek to 'integrate' the poor and excluded into mainstream employment, civic responsibility or suburban culture. Policy should instead study how poor people survive (including their illegal activities) and look at ways of legitimating, enhancing or supporting these activities, while minimizing the social costs associated with them. It may mean that certain less destructive forms of drug-taking are legalized (or a blind eye turned to them), as some enforcement agents are coming to recognize. It may mean that the 'shadow' economy of working while claiming comes out into the light, being legalized through changes in the tax-benefit system that allow income guarantees or higher earnings disregards. And it may mean that some groups who are at present the targets of regulation and enforcement, such as travellers and undocumented immigrants, are allowed to pursue their purposes more freely, and even given better facilities and support services.

Paradoxically, therefore, the future of successful democratic governance (especially in the Anglo-Saxon countries) may depend on a subtle shift from the politics of traditional economic management and compulsory social inclusion, to more intelligent and counter-intuitive ways of enhancing voluntary exchanges and fostering autonomous economic co-operation. National governments may thus avoid the pitfalls of escalating social costs and the consolidation of a wasteful and anti-liberal politics of enforcement. This will require an imaginative approach to the adaptation of existing social institutions, in line with emerging cultural practices, especially among the poor.

However, such a shift will need at least tacit political support, and at this stage it is impossible to see any movement in its favour. Perhaps the best hope of change in the political climate on issues of poverty and exclusion lies in the escalating impact of globalization on middle-income households. As professionals and technicians are forced to compete with their counterparts in newly industrializing or post-communist countries, the effects on such salaries will quickly become apparent. For example, a computer software programmer in Hungary earns about a third of what is paid for comparable work in Britain, and many international companies are relocating their production sites in Central Europe (Barker, 1995). This in turn will quickly influence the strategies of middle-income households. As male careers become less secure and lucrative, and as long-term investments in pensions, perks and occupational welfare schemes give lower payoffs, women will review their 'supportive' roles, and consider that they too must seek to maximize their earnings. Since jobholders' rents should by then already have been competed away (through global competition), their reasons for rational self-restraint would have disappeared by the same processes (see pp. 139–48).

In these circumstances, it might be possible to appeal to the interests of middle-income voters in favour of tax-benefit reforms that gave greater security to individuals, so that they could train or take part in informal economic activity, such as social care or child care, during periods of time out from the labour market. Men and women, having greater incentives *both* to maximize earnings in the short run, *and* to take turns over time out, might see more reasons to support something like a Basic Income Scheme, which would guarantee them more reliable income security, on more flexible terms, than either the labour market or the traditional social insurance system could allow. This in turn could allow the gradual adaptation of other public welfare systems, to support informal activity, rather than impose formal obligations (see chapter 6, pp. 219–21).

Poor and socially excluded people would be the indirect beneficiaries of such changes, which would shift the emphasis of policy from enforcement to security and support. If it is too much to expect the emergence of new forms of mass collective solidarity in the foreseeable future (as it probably is), this might be the most practicable and feasible way of achieving a sort of inclusion – by letting them pursue their individual and collective strategies with less hindrance.

THE POSSIBILITY OF DEMOCRATIC COMMUNITY

Like those of 1789, the political upheavals of 1989 seemed to offer new promise of universal democratic community: the extension of liberty and democracy into new spheres of social life, and to previously authoritarian polities. I have argued in this book that such progressive possibilities are threatened as much by liberal governments' pursuit of inequality and enforcement as by atavistic nationalism, international crime or nuclear terrorism.

The ideal of democratic community sprang from the Enlightenment, and rested its hopes on possibilities for *abundance* and *benevolence*. Eighteenth-century political philosophers such as Hume (1745) and Godwin (1793) were able to recognize that *either* an end to material scarcity *or* concern for others' welfare would make the traditional issues of politics redundant:

> If every man had a tender regard for another, or if nature supplied abundantly for all our wants and desires . . . the jealousy of interest, which justice supposes, could no longer have place; nor would there be any occasion for those distinctions and limits of property and possession, which at present are in use among mankind . . . This we may observe with regard to air and water, tho' the most valuable of all external objects; and may easily conclude, that if men were supplied with every thing in the same abundance, or if *every one* had the same affection and tender regard for *every one* as for himself; justice and injustice would be equally unknown among mankind. (Hume, 1745, pp. 494–5)

Hume's emphasis on *universal* inclusion, like Godwin's on the abolition of property, brought out the demanding conditions for the eventual triumph of democratic community. While liberals like Mill explored the scope for extending limited benevolence through educational processes, Marx abandoned such idealism in favour of a technocratic road to material abundance. In the twentieth century, both liberal and socialist regimes pursued the paths of economic expansion that were pioneered by fascist systems. With harmonious prosperity as a distant goal, they developed heavy industrial production, with its characteristic social relations of mass organization, factory discipline, alienating work and intrusive state surveillance. Massive machines – of the administrative as well as the industrial kind – were characteristic of a century in which social engineering was the counterpart of mega-productive enterprise. Big was beautiful, and functionalist, prescriptive bureaucracy steered citizens along the polluted route to abundance.

In social policy, the age of welfare states marked the collectivist zenith of compulsory benevolence as the social aspect of industrial prosperity. As post-industrial changes sweep the First World states, and hopes of abundance fade, it is the authoritarianism rather than the inclusive collectivism that lingers on. Even as systems of solidarity fragment, politicians of left and right vie to construct new and more coercive ways to remind the poor of their economic obligations, and to ration their allowances more conditionally.

The prospects for benevolence have become detached from social engineering, and float freely in the idealistic democratic theory of Habermas (1984) or the later J. Rawls (1987; 1989; 1993). In some instances, they find expression in hostility to traditional methods of public administration and political mediation (Dryzek, 1990); in others they appeal to communitarian sentiments, while offering support for authoritarian policies (Etzioni, 1994).

The challenge for the next century is to discover forms of collective action that are suited to sovereign consumption-orientated, diverse and quarrelsome individuals, in a global environment with vastly unequal allocations of resources. If this sounds more Hobbesian than Humean, then the point is well made. As benevolence shrinks to narrower limits (the nasty, brutish, bourgeois, suburban family), social engineering becomes more necessary as well as far more difficult. Neither traditional liberal individualism nor compulsory collectivist socialism now seem feasible or attractive.

The search is therefore on for new and flexible institutions to unlock the traps identified in my analysis. Above all, the task is to avoid 'solutions' that block unexpected routes to benevolence and abundance. I have argued that most of the remedies that are touted by politicians of this decade would have both these unfortunate consequences. The trouble is that abundance *might* still happen, but definitely *not* by the routes foreseen by Marx, or pioneered by William Taylor and Henry Ford; and benevolence *might* be possible, though certainly *not* through institutional imitations of Keynes and Beveridge.

For example, it will be microtechnology, not macro, that determines the potential for economic expansion in the next century. Silicon chips will seem large and clumsy objects when 'nanotechnology' is developed, as it surely will be. A nanometer is a billionth of a meter, and this technology consists in manipulating matter, atom by atom, to make machines. Any chemically stable structure can be constructed by such methods, allowing a 'bottom up' technology that imitates biology rather than the Babylonian temples of the 'top down', big-machine age. The microchip was the first step in developments that will allow faster, cheaper and much more efficient production in invisible factories, biosensors travelling through the bloodstream to identify and repair tissue damage, and pollution to be gobbled up by nanomachines drifting through air and water (J. Marshall, 1995).

In such a Godwinian world, abundance would become possible only if human institutions were adapted to allow distribution to be detatched from production. This will be the future relevance of the Basic Income proposal – that it leaves sovereign individuals with enough liberty for personal autonomy and consumer choice, but allows the development of social obligations and negotiated collective decisions that are persuasive but not too binding. Instead of wasting resources on the imposition of irrelevant duties, societies could instead seek ways of enabling more benevolent interactions, by supplying an infrastructure for convivial social relations (Jordan, 1989).

Social policy, as it exists at present, would be a barrier to the development of such societies. New social institutions would have to move right away from compulsory inclusion, expert intervention and corrective enforcement, towards educative and supportive initiatives. But behind such programmes there would have to be systems that addressed the fundamental causes of poverty and social exclusion by redistributing income in ways that guaranteed the basic security and opportunity of members. In a global environment, this implies a multi-tiered scheme, with each level of provision appropriate for the relevant membership group. The universal (global) basic income would be internationally funded, and correspond with the resources necessary for survival in the world's poorest country, and hence be the material expression of the charter of human rights. On top of this, in each nation or region there would be a system of redistribution that guaranteed the citizen's individual welfare within that particular economic system. People who chose to move between countries or regions might be required to qualify for this by serving a waiting period.

In a world of abundance and benevolence, the economics of exclusion would be counterproductive and inefficient. But the problem has always been (as Marx recognized) how to move from institutions reflecting scarcity and competition between groups to ones that unfettered technological potential. Democratic community will probably be more technically feasible in the next century than ever before, and more politically unlikely. The compulsion to exclude the poor may risk instead excluding the possibilities of prosperity and progress.

Bibliography and Sources

Abbott, P. and Sapsford, R. 1994: 'Health and Material Deprivation in Plymouth: An Interim Replication: Research Note', *Sociology of Health and Illness*, 16(2), pp. 252–9.

Abrahamson, P. 1992: 'Poverty and Welfare in Denmark', *Scandinavian Journal of Social Welfare*, 1(1), pp. 20–7.

Adriaansens, H. and Dercksen, W. 1993: 'Labour-force Participation, Citizenship and Sustainable Welfare in the Netherlands', in H. Coenen and P. Leisink (eds), *Work and Citizenship in the New Europe*, Aldershot: Edward Elgar, pp. 191–204.

Aitken, I. 1994: 'Borrie Ducks Commission to Explore', *New Statesman and Society*, 11 November, p. 12.

Alber, J. 1982: *Vom Armhaus zum Wohlfahrtsstaat: Analysen zur Entwicklung der Sozialversicherung in Westeuropa*, Frankfurt: Campus.

Aponte, R. 1991: 'Urban Hispanic Poverty – Disaggregations and Explanations', *Social Problems*, 38(4), pp. 516–28.

Armitage, A. 1975: *Social Welfare in Canada: Ideals and Realities*, Toronto: McClelland and Stewart.

Atkinson, A. B. 1969: *Poverty in Britain and the Reform of Social Security*, Cambridge: Cambridge University Press.

Atkinson, A. B. 1989: *Poverty and Social Security*, Hemel Hempstead: Harvester Wheatsheaf.

Atkinson, A. B. 1995: *Public Economics in Action: The Basic Income/Flat Tax Proposal*, The Lindahl Lectures, Oxford: Oxford University Press.

Atkinson, J. 1984: 'The Flexible Firm Takes Shape', *Guardian*, 18 April.

Atkinson, J. and Meager, N. 1986: *Changing Work Patterns: How*

Companies Achieve Flexibility to Meet New Needs, London: National Economic Development Organization.

Auletta, K. 1983: *The Underclass*, New York: Vintage.

Axelrod, R. 1984: *The Evolution of Co-operation*, New York: Basic Books.

Bagguley, P. and Mann, K. 1992: '"Idle, Thieving Bastards"? Scholarly Representations of the "Underclass"', *Work, Employment and Society*, 6(1), pp. 113–26.

Bane, M. J. and Ellwood, D. T. 1986: 'Slipping Into and Out of Poverty: The Dynamics of Spells', *Journal of Human Resources*, 12, pp. 1–23.

Barber, B. 1984: *Strong Democracy: Participatory Politics for a New Age*, Berkeley: University of California Press.

Barclay, P. 1995: *Joseph Rowntree Inquiry into Income and Wealth*, York: Joseph Rowntree Trust.

Barker, J. 1995: 'Are Low-wage Workers a Danger?', *The Times*, 28 July.

Barr, N. (ed.) 1994: *Labour Markets and Social Policy in Central and Eastern Europe: The Transition and Beyond*, Oxford: Oxford University Press/ World Bank.

Barraclough, G. 1984: *The Origins of Modern Germany*, New York: W. W. Norton.

Barry, B. 1991: 'The Continuing Relevance of Socialism', in B. Barry, *Liberty and Justice: Essays in Political Theory 1*, Oxford: Clarendon Press, pp. 274–90.

Barry, B. 1994: 'Justice, Freedom and Basic Income', London: London School of Economics.

Barry, N. 1990: 'Markets, Citizenship and the Welfare State: Some Critical Reflections', in D. Green (ed.) *Citizenship and Rights in Thatcher's Britain*, London: Institute of Economic Affairs.

Bartley, M. 1992: *Authorities and Partisans – the Debate on Unemployment and Health*, Edinburgh: Edinburgh University Press.

Bartley, M. 1994: 'Unemployment and Ill-health: Understanding the Relationship', *Journal of Epidemiology and Community Health*, 48(4), pp. 333–7.

Bauböck, R. 1991: 'Migration and Citizenship', *New Community*, 8(1), pp. 27–48.

Bauman, Z. 1992: *Intimations of Post-modernity*, London: Routledge.

Beaumont, J., Leather, S., Lang, T. and Mucklow, C. 1995: *Nutrition Task Force: Low Income Project Team Working Group 2 – Policy*, London: Nutrition Task Force.

Beck, U. 1992: *Risk Society: Towards a New Modernity*, London: Sage.

Beckett, A. 1995: 'Power to the (Young) People', *Guardian*, 19 June.

Benabon, R. 1994: 'Theories of Persistent Inequalities – Human

Capital, Inequality and Growth: A Local Perspective', *European Economic Review*, 38, pp. 3–4.

Bennathen, M. 1992: 'The Care and Education of Troubled Urban Youth', *Young Minds Newsletter*, 10 March, pp. 1–7.

Berg, M. 1988: 'Women's Work, Mechanization and the Early Phases of Industrialization in England', in R. E. Pahl (ed.), *On Work*, Oxford: Blackwell, pp. 61–94.

Berger, S. and Piore, M. J. 1980: *Dualism and Discontinuity in Industrial Societies*, Cambridge: Cambridge University Press.

Berthoud, R. 1984: *The Reform of Supplementary Benefit*, London: Policy Studies Institute.

Berthoud, R. 1990: *The Social Fund: Is it Working?*, London: Policy Studies Institute.

Beveridge, W. 1909: *Unemployment: A Problem of Industry*, London: Longman, Green.

Beveridge, W. 1944: *Full Employment in a Free Society*, London: Allen & Unwin.

Bhabha, H. 1995: 'Bombs Away in Front-line Suburbia, *Guardian*, 8 July.

Bienefeld, M. 1991: 'Karl Polanyi and the Contradictions of the 1980s', in M. Mendell and P. Salée (eds), *The Legacy of Karl Polanyi*, New York: St Martin's Press.

Binmore, K. 1992: *Fun and Games: A Text on Game Theory*, Lexington: D. C. Heath.

Bishopp, D., Canter, D. and Stockley, D. 1992: *Young People on the Move*, Guildford: Department of Psychology, University of Surrey.

Blair, T. 1995: 'Left with No Option', *Guardian*, 27 July.

Blaug, M. 1987: *An Introduction to the Economics of Education*, London: Allen Lane.

Blyth, E. and Milner, J. 1993: 'Exclusion from School: A First Step in Exclusion from Society?', *Children and Society*, 7(3), pp. 255–68.

Blyth, E. and Milner, J. 1994: 'Unsaleable Goods and the Education Market', paper given at a conference on Changing Educational Structures: Policy and Practice, CEDAR, Warwick University, 15–17 April.

Bönker, F. 1993: 'Building Capitalism in Eastern Europe: State and Determinants of Institutional Reform in Bulgaria, Hungary, Czech Republic and Slovakia', Bremen: ZERP, Universität Bremen.

Borrie, G. 1994: *Social Justice: Strategies for National Renewal*, Report of the Commission on Social Justice, London: Vintage.

Bottoms, A. E. 1977: 'Reflections on the Renaissance of Dangerousness', *Howard Journal*, 16, pp. 70–97.

Bovenkerk, F., Miles, R. and Verbunt, G. 1990: 'Racism, Migration and the State in Western Europe: A Case for Comparative Analysis', *International Sociology*, 5(4), pp. 475–90.

Bowen, A. and Mayhew, K. 1991: *Improving Incentives for the Low Paid*, London: Macmillan/NEDO.

Bradshaw, J. 1990: *Child Poverty and Deprivation in the UK*, London: National Children's Bureau.

Bradshaw, J. 1993: *Household Budgets and Living Standards*, York: Joseph Rowntree Foundation.

Bradshaw, J. and Holmes, H. 1989: *Living on the Edge: A Study of the Living Standards of Families on Benefits in Tyne and Wear*, Newcastle: Tyneside CPAG.

Brandt, W. (chair) 1980: *North–South: A Programme for Survival*, London: Pan.

Brannen, J. and Wilson, E. 1987: *Give and Take in Families: Studies in Resource Distribution*, London: Allen & Unwin.

Breuer, M. 1995: 'Wettbewerb zwischen Sozialversicherungsclubs am Beispiel der Gesetzlichen Krankenversicherung', lecture to Social Policy Research Colloquium, University of Göttingen, May.

Breuer, M., Faist, T. and Jordan, B. 1994: 'Club Theory, Migration and Welfare States', ZeS Arbeitspapier 15/94, University of Bremen.

Breuer, M., Faist, T. and Jordan, B. 1995: 'Collective Action, Migration and Welfare States', *International Sociology*, 10(4), pp. 369–86.

Breughel, I. 1989: 'Sex and Race in the Labour Market', *Feminist Review*, 32, pp. 49–68.

Brittan, S. 1975: 'The Economic Contradictions of Democracy', *British Journal of Political Science*, 5(2), pp. 129–59.

Brittan, S. 1995: *Capitalism with a Human Face*, Aldershot: Edward Elgar.

Brown, A. and Crisp, C. 1992: 'Diverting Cases from Prosecution in the Public Interest', *British Journal of Criminology*, 14(1), pp. 63–9.

Brown, P. 1995: 'One Million Missed in 1991 Census', *Guardian*, 6 January.

Brown, S. and Riddell, S. 1992: *Class, Race and Gender in Schools*, Edinburgh: Scottish Council for Research in Education.

Bryant, C. G. A. and Mokrzycki, E. (eds) 1994: *The New Great Transformation? Change and Continuity in East-Central Europe*, London: Routledge.

Buchanan, A. (ed.) 1993: *Partnership in Practice*, Aldershot: Avebury.

Buchanan, J. M. 1965: 'An Economic Theory of Clubs', *Economica*, 32, pp. 1–14.

Buchanan, J. M. 1968: *The Demand and Supply of Public Goods*, Chicago:

Rand McNally.

Buchanan, J. M. 1978: *The Economics of Politics*, London: Institute for Economic Affairs.

Buchanan, J. M. 1986a: *Liberty, Market and State: Political Economy in the 1980s*, Brighton: Harvester Wheatsheaf.

Buchanan, J. M. 1986b: 'The Public Choice Perspective' in J. M. Buchanan, *Liberty, Market and State: Political Economy in the 1980s*, Brighton: Harvester Wheatsheaf, pp. 19–27.

Buchanan, J. M. 1986c: 'Rights, Efficiency and Exchange', in J. M. Buchanan, *Liberty, Market and State*, pp. 92–107.

Buchanan, J. M. 1986d: 'Dismantling the Welfare State' in J. M. Buchanan, *Liberty, Market and State*, pp. 178–86.

Butler, S. and Condratus, A. 1987: *Out of the Poverty Trap: A Conservative Strategy for Welfare Reform*, New York: Free Press.

Castles, F. C. 1986: *Working Class and Welfare: Reflections on the Political Development of the Welfare State in Australia and New Zealand*, London: Allen & Unwin.

Cawson, A. 1982: *Corporatism and Welfare*, London: Heinemann.

Centraalplanbureau 1993: *De Nederland in Drievoud*, The Hague: Ministry of Social Affairs.

Checkland, S. G. and Checkland, E. O. A. 1974: *The Poor Law Report of 1834*, Harmondsworth: Penguin.

Christensen, E. 1994: 'Argumenter for Bogerløn-nogle debatindaeg 1993–4', Aalborg: Institut for Økonomie, Politik of Forvaltung.

Cirtautas, A. M. 1994: 'In Pursuit of the Democratic Interest: The Institutionalization of Parties and Interests in Eastern Europe', in Bryant and Mokrzycki (eds), *The New Great Transformation?*, pp. 36–57.

Coates, K. 1993: 'The Dimensions of Recovery', in K. Coates and M. Barratt Brown (eds), *A European Recovery Programme: Restoring Full Employment*, Nottingham: Spokesman, pp. 9–19.

Coenen, H. and Leisink, P. (eds) 1993: *Work and Citizenship in the New Europe*, Aldershot: Edward Elgar.

Coleman, J. S. 1990: *Foundations of Social Theory*, Cambridge: Harvard University Press.

Corden, A. and Craig, P. 1991: *Perceptions of Family Credit*, London: HMSO.

Cornish, D. B. and Clarke R. V. 1986: *The Reasoning Criminal: Rational Choice Perspectives on Offending*, London: Allen & Unwin.

Craig, P. 1991: 'Costs and Benefits: A Review of Research on Take-up of Income-related Benefits', *Journal of Social Policy*, 20(4), pp. 537–65.

Craig, G. 1992: 'Anti-poverty Action and Research in the UK', *Social Policy and Administration*, 26(2), pp. 129–43.

Crouch, C. 1983: *State and Economy in Contemporary Capitalism*, London: Sage.

Crouch, C. 1992: 'The State of Articulated Industrial Relations Systems: A Stock-taking after a Liberal Decade', in M. Regini (ed.), *The Future of the Labour Movement*, London: Sage.

Dahl, R. A. 1961: *Who Governs? Democracy and Power in an American City*, New Haven: Yale University Press.

Dahrendorf, R. 1988: *The Modern Social Conflict: An Essay in the Politics of Liberty*, London: Weidenfeld & Nicolson.

Dahrendorf, R. 1989: *The Underclass and the Future of Britain*, Tenth Annual Lecture, St George's House, Windsor Castle, 27 April.

Dahrendorf, R. 1990: 'Decade of the Citizen: An Interview', [with J. Keane], *Guardian*, 1 August.

Dalley, G. 1988: *Ideologies of Caring, Rethinking Community and Collectivism*, Basingstoke: Macmillan.

Dean, H. and Taylor Gooby, B. 1992: *Dependency Culture: The Explosion of a Myth*, Hemel Hempstead: Harvester Wheatsheaf.

Dean, M. 1991: *Towards a Theory of Liberal Governance*, London: Routledge.

DeHane, J.-L. 1994: *Keys for Tomorrow*, Hasselt: Esopus.

Deleeck, H. 1991: *Indicators of Poverty and Social Security*, Luxembourg: Eurostat.

Deleeck, H. 1992: 'Poverty and Adequacy of Social Security in Europe', *Journal of European Social Policy*, 2(2), pp. 81–93.

de Leonardis, O. 1993: 'New Patterns of Collective Action in a "Post-welfare" Society: The Italian Case', in G. Drover and P. Kerans (eds), *New Approaches to Welfare Theory*, Aldershot: Edward Elgar, pp. 177–89.

Delors, J. 1993: 'The Scope and Limits of Community Action', in K. Coates and M. Barratt Brown (eds), *A European Recovery Programme: Restoring Full Employment*, Nottingham: Spokesman, pp. 45–52.

Department for Education 1993: *National Exclusions Reporting System*, London: HMSO.

Department of the Environment 1994: 'Index of Local Conditions and Analysis of Census Data', London: Inner Cities Directorate.

Desai, M. and Shah, A. 1988: 'An Econometric Approach to the Measurement of Poverty', *Oxford Economic Papers*, 40, pp. 505–22.

de Swaan, A. 1988: *In Care of the State: Health Care, Education and Welfare in Europe and the USA in the Modern Era*, Cambridge: Polity.

de Swaan, A. 1994: *Social Policy Beyond Borders: The Social Question in*

Transnational Perspective, Amsterdam: Amsterdam University Press.

de Vos, K. and Hagenaars, A. 1988: *A Comparison between the Poverty Concepts of Sen and Townsend*, Rotterdam: Erasmus University.

Dex, S. 1985: *The Sexual Division of Work*, Oxford: Blackwell.

Dex, S. 1988: 'Gender and the Labour Market', in D. Gallie (ed.), *Employment in Britain*, Oxford: Blackwell, pp. 281–309.

Donnison, D. 1991: *A Radical Agenda: After the New Right and the Old Left*, London: Riversdram Press.

Dore, R. 1986: *Flexible Rigidities: Industrial Policy and Structural Adjustment in the Japanese Economy, 1970–80*, London: Athlone Press.

Dryzek, J. 1990: *Discursive Democracy: Politics, Policy and Political Science*, Cambridge: Cambridge University Press.

Duboin, M. L. 1985: *L'économie libérée*, Paris: Syros.

Duncan, A. and Hobson, D. 1995: *Saturn's Children: How the State Devours Liberty, Prosperity and Virtue*, London: Sinclair-Stevenson.

Duncan, G. J. 1984: *Years of Poverty, Years of Plenty*, Ann Arbor: Institute for Social Research, University of Michigan.

Dworkin, R. 1981: 'What is Equality? Part II: Equality of Resources', *Philosophy and Public Affairs*, 10, pp. 283–345.

Eggebeen, D. J. and Lichter, D. T. 1991: 'Race, Family Structure and Changing Poverty among American Children', Pennsylvania State University, Department of Human and Developmental Studies.

Elliott, L. 1995a: 'U.S. Reaps the Unhappy Harvest of Deregulation', *Guardian*, 20 February.

Elliott, L. 1995b: 'Seventies-style Fear and Loathing Makes a Comeback', *Guardian*, 21 August.

Elster, J. 1985: *Making Sense of Marx*, Cambridge: Cambridge University Press.

Elster, J. (ed.) 1986a: *Rational Choice*, Oxford: Blackwell.

Elster, J. 1986b: 'The Market and the Forum: Three Varieties of Political Theory', in J. Elster and A. Hylland (eds), *Foundations of Social Choice Theory*, Cambridge, Cambridge University Press, pp. 103–32.

Elton, M. 1994: *The Annals of the Elton Family: Bristol Merchants and Somerset Landowners*, Dover, NH: Alan Sutton.

Engberson, G. and Van der Veen, R. 1987: *Modern Poverty*, Leiden: University of Leiden Press.

Engberson, G., Schuyt, C. and Timmer, J. 1993: *Cultures of Unemployment*, Boulder, CO: Westview Press.

Erdman, P. 1994: 'Probation Reorganized', *California Probation News*, 2(5), p. 1.

Erickson, A. L. 1993: *Women and Property in Early Modern England*, London: Routledge.

Esping-Andersen, G. 1990: *The Three Worlds of Welfare Capitalism*, Cambridge: Polity.

Etzioni, A. 1988: *The Moral Dimension: Towards a New Economics*, New York: Free Press.

Etzioni, A. 1993: *The Spirit of Community*, New York: Free Press.

Etzioni, A. 1994: 'Who Should Pay for Care?', *Independent*, 18 October.

Evanson, E. 1986: 'A Brief History of the Institute for Research on Poverty', *Focus*, 9.

Evason, E. and Wood, R. 1995: 'Poverty, Deregulation of Labour Markets and Benefit Fraud', *Social Policy and Administration*, 29(1), pp. 40–54.

Faist, T. 1994a: 'How to Define a Foreigner? The Symbolic Politics of Immigration in German Partisan Discourse', *West European Politics*, 17(2), pp. 50–71.

Faist, T. 1994b: 'Migration in Transnationalizing Labor Markets: Collectivization and Fragmentation of Social Rights in Europe', Bremen: Zentrum für Sozialpolitik, Universität Bremen, Arbeitspapier 9/94.

Faist, T. 1995: 'Ethnicization and Racialization of Welfare State Politics in Germany and the USA', *Ethnic and Racial Studies*, 18(2).

Family Budget Unit 1990: *The Work of the Family Budget Unit*, Working Paper 1, York: Faculty Budget Unit.

Farrar, C. 1992: 'Ancient Greek Political Theory as a Response to Democracy', in J. Dunn (ed.), *Democracy: The Unfinished Journey, 508 BC–AD 1993*, Oxford: Oxford University Press, pp. 17–40.

Felt, L. F. and Sinclair, P. R. 1992: '"Everyone Does It": Unpaid Work in a Rural Peripheral Region', *Work, Employment and Society*, 6(1), 43–64.

Filmer, R. 1680: *Patriarcha, or the Natural Power of Kings*.

Finch, J. 1989: *Family Obligations and Social Change*, Cambridge: Polity.

Flora, P. and Heidenheimer, A. J. (eds) 1981: *The Development of Welfare States in Europe and America*, New Brunswick and London: Transaction Press.

Foldvary, F. 1994: *Public Goods and Private Communities*, Aldershot: Edward Elgar.

Forrest, R. and Murie, A. 1988a: *Selling the Welfare State: The Privatization of Public Housing*, London: Routledge.

Forrest, R. and Murie, A. 1988b: 'The Social Division of Housing Subsidies', *Critical Social Policy*, 8(2), pp. 83–93.

Freeden, M. 1989: *Rights*, Milton Keynes, Open University Press.

Freeman, G. P. 1986: 'Migration and the Political Economy of the Welfare State', *The Annals of the American Academy of Political and Social Science*, 485, pp. 51–63.

Galbraith, J. K. 1992: *The Culture of Contentment*, Harmondsworth: Penguin.

Gallie, D., Marsh, C. and Vogler, E. (eds), 1993: *Social Change and the Experience of Unemployment*, Oxford: Oxford University Press.

Gambetta, D. 1993: *The Sicilian Mafia*, Cambridge: Harvard University Press.

Garfinkel, H. 1967: *Studies in Ethnomethodology*, Englewood Cliffs: Prentice Hall. 1984: Cambridge: Polity.

Garner, C. 1988: 'Educational Attainment in Glasgow: The Role of Neighbourhood Deprivation', in L. Bondi and M. H. Matthews (eds), *Education and Society's Studies in the Politics, Sociology and Geography of Education*, London: Routledge, pp. 226–56.

Garner, P. 1994: 'Exclusions from School: Towards a New Agenda', paper presented at 'Changing Educational Structures: Policy and Practice' conference, CEDAR, Warwick University, 15–17 April.

George, H. 1879: *Progress and Poverty* [1975], New York: Robert Schalkenbach.

Gershuny, J. 1983: *Social Innovation and the Division of Labour*, Oxford: Oxford University Press.

Giddens, A. 1991: *Modernity and Self-identity: Self and Society in the Late Modern Age*, Cambridge: Polity.

Gilder, G. 1986: *Men and Marriage*, Gretna, LA: Pelican.

Gingrich, N. 1994: [Speaker, US House of Representatives], speech during the mid-term elections, *Guardian*, 20 October.

Glasman, M. 1994: 'The Great Deformation: Polanyi, Poland and the Terrors of Planned Spontaneity', in C. G. A. Bryant and E. Mokrzycki (eds), *The New Great Transformation? Change and Continuity in East-Central Europe*, London: Routledge, pp. 191–217.

Glendinning, C. and Millar, J. (eds) 1992: *Women and Poverty in Britain: The 1990s*, Hemel Hempstead: Harvester Wheatsheaf.

Godwin, W. 1793: *An Enquiry Concerning Political Justice* [1971], ed. K. Codell Carter, Oxford: Clarendon Press.

Goffman, E. 1969: *Interaction Ritual*, New York: Doubleday Anchor.

Goldberg, G. S. and Kremen, E. 1990: *The Feminization of Poverty – Only in America*, New York: Greenwood Press.

Goldblatt, P. (ed) 1990: *Longitudinal Study: Mobility and Social Organization, England and Wales*, London: HMSO.

Gorz, A. 1988: *Critique of Economic Reason*, London: Verso.

Gough, I. 1979: *The Political Economy of the Welfare State*, London: Macmillan.

Graham, H. 1987: 'Women's Poverty and Caring', in C. Glendinning and J. Millar (eds), *Women and Poverty in Britain*, Brighton: Wheatsheaf.

Graham, H. 1993: *Hardship and Health in Women's Lives*, London: Harvester Wheatsheaf.

Grant, L. 1995: 'Just Say No', *Guardian Weekend*, 13 June, pp. 13–21.

Gray, J. 1994: 'The Great Atlantic Drift', *Guardian*, 12 December.

Gregg, P. 1995: 'Point of Entry', *Guardian*, 6 February.

Habermas, J. 1984: *The Theory of Communicative Action*, Boston: Beacon. 1991: Cambridge: Polity.

Hadley, R. and Hatch, S. 1981: *Social Policy and the Failure of the State: Centralized Social Services and Participatory Alternatives*, London: Allen & Unwin.

Hagenaars, A. J. M. 1985: *The Perception of Poverty*, Amsterdam: Offsetdrukkerij Kanters.

Hakim, C. 1980: 'Homeworking: Some New Evidence', *Employment Gazette*, 88(10), pp. 1105–10.

Hakim, C. 1984: 'Employers' Use of Homework, Outwork and Freelances', *Employment Gazette*, 92(4), pp. 144–50.

Hakim, C. 1988: 'Homeworking in Britain', in R. E. Pahl (ed.), *On Work: Historical, Comparative and Theoretical Approaches*, Oxford: Blackwell, pp. 609–32.

Halevy, E. 1928: *The Growth of Philosophical Radicalism*, London: Faber and Faber.

Hammar, T. 1990: *Democracy and the Nation State: Aliens, Denizens and Citizens in a World of International Migration*, Aldershot: Gower.

Handy, C. 1989: *The Age of Unreason*, London: Hutchinson Business Books.

Hardey, M. and Glover, J. 1991: 'Income, Employment, Day Care and Lone Parenthood', in M. Hardey and G. Crow (eds), *Lone Parenthood*, London: Harvester Wheatsheaf.

Hardin, G. 1968: 'The Tragedy of the Commons', *Science*, 162, pp. 1243–8.

Hargreaves Heap, S., Hollis, M., Lyons, B., Sugden, R. and Weale, A. 1992: *The Theory of Choice: A Critical Guide*, Oxford: Blackwell.

Harrington, M. 1962: *The Other America*, New York and London: Macmillan.

Harris, C. and Morris, L. 1986: 'Households, Labour Markets and the Position of Women', in R. Crompton and M. Mann (eds), *Gender and Stratification*, Cambridge: Polity.

Harrod, R. 1958: 'The Possibility of Satiety – Use of Economic Growth for Improving the Quality of Education and Leisure', in *Problems of US Economic Development*, New York: Committee for Economic Development, pp. 207–13.

Haveman, R. H. 1987: *Poverty Policy and Poverty Research: The Great Society and the Social Sciences*, Wisconsin: University of Wisconsin Press.

Hayek, F. A. 1973: *Rules and Order*, London: Routledge & Kegan Paul.

Hayek, F. A. 1976: *The Mirage of Social Justice*, London: Routledge & Kegan Paul.

Hayek, F. A. 1978: *New Studies in Philosophy, Politics and Economics*, London: Routledge & Kegan Paul.

Haynes, R. 1991: 'Inequalities in Health and Health Service Use: Evidence from the General Household Survey', *Social Science and Medicine*, 33(4), pp. 361–8.

Heath, A. 1991: 'Political Attitudes', in D. J. Smith (ed.), *Understanding the Underclass*, London: Policy Studies Institute.

Heath, S. 1957: *Citadel, Market and Altar*, Baltimore: Science of Society Foundation.

Hegel, G. W. F. 1807: *The Phenomenology of Mind* [1931], translated by J. B. Baillie, London: Allen & Unwin.

Hegel, G. W. F. 1821: *The Philosophy of Right* [1967], translated by T. M. Knox, Oxford: Oxford University Press.

Held, D. and McGrew, A. 1994: 'Globalization and the Liberal Democratic State', *Government and Opposition*, 28(2), pp. 261–85.

Hilbert, R. A. 1992: *The Classical Roots of Ethnomethodology: Durkheim, Weber and Garfinkel*, Chapel Hill: University of North Carolina Press.

Hill, M. 1990: *Social Security Policy in Britain*, Aldershot: Edward Elgar.

Hillman, A. 1992: 'Socialist Clubs: A Perspective on the Transition', *European Journal of Political Economy*, 9, pp. 307–19.

Hillman, M., Adams, J. and Whitelegg, J. 1991: *One False Move: A Study of Children's Independent Mobility*, London: Policy Studies Institute.

Hirsch, F. 1977: *Social Limits to Growth*, London: Routledge & Kegan Paul.

Hirst, P. 1994: *Associative Democracy: New Forms of Economic and Social Governance*, Cambridge: Polity.

Hobbes, T. 1651: *Leviathan* [1966], ed. M. Oakeshott, Oxford: Blackwell.

Hoggett, P. and Burns, D. 1992: 'The Revenge of the Poor. The Anti-Poll Tax Campaign', *Critical Social Policy*, 33, pp. 95–101.

Hollis, M. 1994: *The Philosophy of Social Science: An Introduction*, Cambridge: Cambridge University Press.

Holman, B. 1993: *A New Deal for Social Welfare*, Glasgow: Lion Publishing.

Holmes, S. 1993: *The Anatomy of Anti-liberalism*, Cambridge: Harvard University Press.

Home Office 1994: *Cautions, Court Proceedings and Sentencing: England and Wales, 1993*, London: Home Office Research and Statistics.

Hood, C. and Schuppert, G. 1990: 'Para-government Organizations in the Provision of Public Services: Three Explanations', in H. Anheier and W. Seibel (eds), *The Third Sector: Comparative Studies in Non-profit Organizations*, Berlin: de Gruyter.

Hoogenboom, E. and Roebroek, J. 1990: *Basisinkomen: Alternative Uitkering of Nieuw Paradigma*, The Hague: Ministry for Social Affairs and Employment.

House of Commons 1995: *Hansard Written Answers*, London: HMSO, 18 July.

Hudson, B. A. 1993: *Penal Policy and Social Justice*, Basingstoke: Macmillan.

Hudson, P. and Lee, W. R. 1990: 'Introduction', in Hudson and Lee (eds), *Women's Work and the Family Economy in Historical Perspective*, Manchester: Manchester University Press, pp. 2–48.

Hume, D. 1745: *A Treatise of Human Nature* [1888], ed. L. A. Selby Bigge, Oxford: Clarendon Press.

Hutton, W. 1994: *The State We're In*, London: Cape.

IFS 1995: *Poverty: Two Views*, London: Institute for Fiscal Studies.

James, S., Jordan, B. and Kay, H. 1991: 'Poor People, Council Housing and the Right to Buy', *Journal of Social Policy*, 20(1), pp. 27–40.

Jenkins, S. 1991: 'Poverty Measurement and Within-household Redistribution', *Journal of Social Policy*, 20(4), pp. 457–83.

Johnson, P. and Webb, S. 1990: 'Low-income Families, 1979–87', *Fiscal Studies*, 11(4), pp. 44–62.

Jordan, B. 1989: *The Common Good: Citizenship, Morality and Self-interest*, Oxford: Blackwell.

Jordan, B. 1995: 'Are New Right Policies Sustainable? "Back to Basics" and Public Choice', *Journal of Social Policy*, 24(3), pp. 363–84.

Jordan, B. (forthcoming) 'Partnership, Child Protection and Family Support: Trying to Square the Circle', in N. Parton (ed.), *Child Protection and Family Support*, London: Routledge.

Jordan, B. and Arnold, J. 1996a: 'Democracy and Criminal Justice', *Critical Social Policy*, forthcoming.

Jordan, B. and Arnold, J. 1996b: 'Crime, Poverty and Probation', in M. Vanstone and M. Drakeford (eds), *Beyond Offending Behaviour*,

Aldershot: Arena, pp. 45–71.

Jordan, B. and Redley, M. 1994: 'Polarization, Underclass and the Welfare State', *Work, Employment and Society*, 8(2), pp. 153–76.

Jordan, B., James, S., Kay, H. and Redley, M. 1992: *Trapped in Poverty? Labour-market Decisions in Low-income Households*, London: Routledge.

Jordan, B., Redley, M. and James, S. 1994: *Putting the Family First: Identities, Decisions, Citizenship*, London: UCL Press.

Katz, M. B. 1989: *The Undeserving Poor: From the War on Poverty to the War on Welfare*, New York: Pantheon.

Kell, M. and Wright, J. 1990: 'Benefits and the Labour Supply of Women Married to Unemployed Men', *Economic Journal*, 100(399), pp. 119–26.

Keohane, R. O. 1989: *International Institutions and State Power: Essays in International Relations Theory*, Boulder, CO: Westview Press.

Keynes, J. M. 1936: *The General Theory of Employment, Interest and Money*, London: Macmillan.

Kindleberger, C. P. 1967: *Europe's Postwar Growth: The Role of Labour Supply*, Cambridge, MA: Harvard University Press.

Kirsch, G. 1993: *Neue politische Ökonomie*, Düsseldorf: Werner Verlag.

Klein, R. 1993: 'O'Goffe's Tale', in C. Jones (ed.), *New Perspectives on the Welfare State in Europe*, London: Routledge, pp. 3–14.

Kumar, V. 1993: *Poverty and Inequality in the UK: The Effects on Children*, London: National Children's Bureau.

Larmore, C. 1987: *Patterns of Moral Complexity*, Oxford: Clarendon Press.

Leibfried, S. and Pierson, P. 1994: 'Prospects for Social Europe', in A. de Swaan (ed.), *Social Policy beyond Borders*, Amsterdam: Amsterdam University Press, pp. 15–58.

Leibfried, S. and Tennstedt, F. (eds) 1985: *Regulating Poverty and the Splitting of the German Welfare State*, Frankfurt: Suhrkamp.

Leibfried, S., Leisering, L., Buhr, P. and Ludwig, M. 1995: *Zeit der Armut: Lebensläufe im Sozialstaat*, Frankfurt: Suhrkamp.

Levy, D. 1992: *The Economic Ideas of Ordinary People: From Property to Trade*, London: Routledge.

Lewis, G. W. and Ulph, D. T. 1988: 'Poverty, Inequality and Welfare', *The Economic Journal*, 98, pp. 117–31.

Lindbeck, A. 1995: 'Objectives and Strategies in the Development of the Swedish Welfare State', workshop on Objectives and Strategies in the Development of European Welfare States, University of Bremen, 24–5 April.

Lindbeck, A. and Snower, D. 1988: *The Insider-outsider Theory of Employment and Unemployment*, Cambridge: MIT Press.

Lister, R. 1990: *The Exclusive Society: Citizenship and the Poor*, London: CPAG.

Locke, J. 1698: *Two Treatises of Government* [1967], ed. Peter Laslett, Cambridge: Cambridge University Press.

Loftager, J. 1994: 'Citizens Income and the Crisis of the Welfare State: General Reflections and a Danish Perspective', paper presented at the BIEN conference, London, 8–10 September.

Luhmann, N. 1977: 'Differentiation of Society', *Canadian Journal of Sociology*, 2, pp. 29–53.

Lustiger Thaler, H. and Shragge, E. 1993: 'Social Movements and Social Welfare: The Political Problem of Need', in Drover and Kerans (eds), *New Approaches*, pp. 161–76.

Luttwak, E. 1995: 'The Good Bad Guys', *Guardian*, 31 July.

Lyons, B. 1992: 'Game Theory', in S. Hargreaves Heap et al., *The Theory of Choice: A Critical Guide*, Oxford: Blackwell, pp. 93–129.

MacCallum, S. 1970: *The Art of Community*, Mailo Park: Institute for Humane Studies.

MacIntyre, A. 1981: *After Virtue: An Essay in Moral Theory*, London: Duckworth.

Mack, J. and Lansley, S. 1984: *Poor Britain*, London: Allen & Unwin.

Malthus, T. 1798: *An Essay on the Principle of Population as It Affects the Future Improvement of Society*, London: J. Johnson.

Mann, K. 1991: *The Making of an English Underclass*, Oxford: Oxford University Press.

March, F. and Olsen, J. 1989: *Rediscovering Institutions: The Organizational Basis of Politics*, New York: Free Press.

Marklund, S. 1988: *Paradise Lost? The Nordic Welfare States and the Recession, 1975–85*, Lund: Archiv.

Marklund, S. 1992: 'The Decomposition of Social Policy in Sweden', *Scandinavian Journal of Social Welfare*, 1(1), pp. 2–11.

Marquand, D. 1988: *The Unprincipled Society*, London: Cape.

Marquand, D. 1991: 'Civic Republicanism and Liberal Individualism', *Archives Européennes de Sociologie*, 23, pp. 329–44.

Marshall, J. 1995: 'The New Alchemy', *Holland Herald*, August, pp. 11–2.

Marshall, T. H. 1950: *Citizenship and Social Class*, Cambridge: Cambridge University Press.

Marske, C. E. 1991: *Communities of Fate: Readings in the Social Organization of Risk*, Lanham: University Press of America.

McCarthy, M. 1986: *Campaigning for the Poor: CPAG and the Politics of Welfare*, London: Methuen.

McCluskey, J. 1994: 'Our Right to Exact Revenge', *Guardian*, 3

December.

McGuire, M. 1972: 'Private Goods Clubs and Public Goods Clubs: Economic Models of Group Formation', *Swedish Journal of Economics*, 8, pp. 84–99.

McLaughlin, E., Millar, J. and Cooke, K. 1989: *Work and Welfare Benefits*, London: Gower.

McNab, R. and Ryan, P. 1989: 'Segmented Labour Markets', in D. Sapsford and Z. Tsannatos (eds), *Current Issues in Labour Economics*, London: Macmillan.

Mead, L. M. 1986: *Beyond Entitlement: The Social Obligations of Citizenship*, New York: Basic Books.

Mead, L. M. 1988a: 'The New Welfare Debate', *Commentary*, 86, pp. 44–52.

Mead, L. M. 1988b: 'The Potential for Work Enforcement', *Journal of Policy Analysis and Management*, 7(2), pp. 264–86.

Mead, L. M. 1989: 'The Logic of Workfare', *Annals of the American Academy of Political and Social Science*, 501, pp. 156–69.

Mill, J. S. 1848: *Principles of Political Economy* [1965], in J. M. Robson (ed.), *Collected Works*, London: University of Toronto Press.

Millar, J. and Glendinning, C. 1991: 'Poverty: The Forgotten Englishwoman', in M. McClean and D. Groves (eds), *Women's Issues in Social Policy*, London: Routledge, pp. 20–37.

Miller, G. 1981: *Cities by Contract*, Cambridge: MIT Press.

Mishra, R. 1984: *The Welfare State in Crisis: Social Thought and Social Change*, Brighton: Wheatsheaf.

Møller, I. H. 1989: *Society Becomes Polarized: Starting in the Labour Market, Continuing in Social Policy, and Finishing in Civil Society*, Aalborg: ATA-Forlaget.

Morone, J. 1995: 'Why Did Clinton's National Health Insurance Plan Fail?', seminar on Public Health, University of Bremen, 10 May.

Morris, J. (ed.) 1992: *Alone Together: Voices of Single Mothers*, London: Women's Press.

Morris, L. 1992: 'The Social Segregation of the Long-term Unemployed in Hartlepool', *Sociological Review*, 40(2), pp. 344–69.

Morris, L. 1994: *Dangerous Classes: The Underclass and Social Citizenship*, London: Routledge.

Morris, L. and Irwin, S. 1992: 'Unemployment and Informal Support: Dependency, Exclusion or Participation?', *Work, Employment and Society*, 6(2), pp. 185–209.

Moulaert, F. 1994: 'Measuring Socio-economic Disintegration at the Local Level', paper given at seminar on the Measurement and

Analysis of Social Exclusion, Bath University, 17–18 June.

Mueller, D. C. 1989: *Public Choice II*, Cambridge: Cambridge University Press.

Mulhall, S. and Swift, A. 1992: *Liberals and Communitarians*, Oxford: Blackwell.

Murray, C. 1984: *Losing Out: American Social Policy, 1950–1980*, New York: Basic Books.

Murray, C. 1989: 'The Underclass', *Sunday Times Magazine*, 26 November, pp. 26–45.

Murray, F. 1983: 'The Decentralization of Production – the Decline of the Mass-Collective Worker?', *Capital and Class*, 19, pp. 18–38.

Myles, J., Picot, G. and Wannell, T. 1988: *Wages and Jobs in the 1980s: The Declining Middle in Canada*, Ottawa: Statistics Canada.

Negt, O. 1985: *Lebendige Arbeit-enteignete Zeit*, Frankfurt: Suhrkamp.

Niskanen, W. A. 1975: 'Bureaucrats and Politicians', *Journal of Law and Economics*, 18, pp. 617–43.

North, D. C. 1981: *Structure and Change in Economic History*, New York: W. W. Norton.

North, D. C. 1986: 'The New Institutional Economics', *Journal of Institutional and Theoretical Economics*, 142, pp. 230–7.

North, D. C. 1990: *Institutions, Institutional Change and Economic Performance*, Cambridge: Cambridge University Press.

Novak, M. 1987: '"Welfare's New Consensus": Reply to Gilder', *The Public Interest*, 89, pp. 26–30.

Novak, M. et al. 1987: *The New Consensus on Family and Welfare*, Washington: American Enterprise Institute.

Nozick, R. 1974: *Anarchy, State and Utopia*, Oxford: Blackwell.

Nye, A. 1987: *Feminist Theory and the Philosophies of Man*, London: Routledge.

O'Connell, C. 1994: 'The Dynamics of Tenure in Ireland, 922–1994', unpublished doctoral thesis, Cork: University College, Cork.

O'Connor, W. 1994: 'Demonstrating Resistance: The Development of an Activist Response by the Lesbian and Gay Community to Government Policy on AIDS in the US', unpublished masters thesis, Cork: University College, Cork.

Offe, C. 1992: 'Designing Institutions for East European Transitions', paper given at conference on Institutional Design, Australian National University School of Social Science, December 7–8.

Offe, C. and Preuss, U. K. 1990: 'Democratic Institutions and Moral Resources', in D. Held (ed.), *Political Theory Today*, Cambridge: Polity, pp. 143–71.

O'Higgins, M. and Jenkins, S. 1990: 'Poverty in the EC; Estimates for 1975, 1980 and 1985', In R. Teekens and B. Van Praag (eds), *Analyzing Poverty in the European Community*, Luxembourg: Eurostat, ch. 11.

Oldfield, A. 1990: *Citizenship and Community: Civic Republicanism in the Modern World*, London: Routledge.

Olson, M. 1965: *The Logic of Collective Action: Public Goods and the Theory of Groups*, Cambridge: Harvard University Press.

Olson, M. 1971: *The Logic of Collective Action* (2nd edn), Cambridge, MA: Harvard University Press.

Olson, M. 1982: *The Rise and Decline of Nations: Economic Growth, Stagflation and Social Rigidities*, New Haven: Yale University Press.

Oppenheim, C. 1990: *Poverty: The Facts*, London: Child Poverty Action Group.

Ostrom, E. 1990: *Governing the Commons: The Evolution of Institutions for Collective Action*, Cambridge: Cambridge University Press.

O'Sullivan, E. 1994: 'The Economy and the Environment of Ring-a-Skiddy in Microcosm', unpublished masters thesis, Cork: University College, Cork.

Ott, N. 1992: *Intrafamily Bargaining and Household Decisions*, Berlin: Springer.

Oxley, G. W. 1975: *Poor Relief in England and Wales, 1600–1834*, Newton Abbot: David and Charles.

Pacolet, J. and Debrabander, K. 1995: 'The State of the Welfare State in Belgium – Anno 1992', paper presented to workshop on Objectives and Strategies in the Development of European Welfare States, University of Bremen, 24–5 April.

Pahl, J. 1988: *Money and Marriage*, London: Macmillan.

Pahl, R. E. 1984: *Divisions of Labour*, Oxford: Blackwell.

Parker, H. 1989: *Instead of the Dole: An Enquiry into Integration of the Tax and Benefit Systems*, London: Routledge.

Parker, H. 1995: *Taxes, Benefits and Family Life: How Government is Killing the Goose (That Lays Golden Eggs)*, London: Institute of Economic Affairs, Monograph 50.

Parkinson, M. 1994: 'Economic Competition and Social Exclusion: European Cities Towards 2000', paper given at a seminar on the Measurement and Analysis of Social Exclusion, Bath University, 17–18 June.

Parry, G. 1994: 'The Interweaving of Foreign and Domestic Policy-making', *Government and Opposition*, 28(2), pp. 143–51.

Pateman, C. 1995: 'Democracy, Freedom and Special Rights', John Rees Memorial Lecture, University of Wales, Swansea.

Payne, S. 1991: *Women's Health and Poverty: An Introduction*, Hemel Hempstead: Harvester Wheatsheaf.

Peacock, A. 1979: *The Economic Analysis of Government*, Oxford: Martin Robertson.

Pechman, J. and Timpane, T. M. 1975: *Work Incentives and Income Guarantees*, Washington DC: Brookings Institute.

Petersen, J. H. and Søndergaard, A. 1994: 'A Comprehensive Reform of the Income Transfer System: A Recent Danish Proposal', CHS Working Papers, 1994/4, Centre for Health and Social Policy, Odense University.

Pfaller, A., Gough, I. and Therborn, G. 1991: *Can the Welfare State Compete?*, Houndmills: Macmillan.

Phillimore, P. and Morris, D. 1991: 'Discrepant Legacies: Premature Mortality in Two Industrial Towns', *Social Science and Medicine Journal*, 33(2), pp. 139–52.

Piachaud, D. 1987: 'Problems in the Definition and Measurement of Poverty', *Journal of Social Policy*, 16(2), pp. 335–51.

Pierson, C. 1991: *Beyond the Welfare State? The New Political Economy of Welfare*, Cambridge: Polity.

Pierson, P. 1995: 'The New Politics of the Welfare State', ZeS Arbeitspapier 3/95, University of Bremen.

Piore, M. and Sabel, C. 1984: *The Second Industrial Divide*, New York: Basic Books.

Piven, F. F. and Cloward, R. A. 1977: *Poor People's Movements: Why They Succeed and How They Fail*, New York: Pantheon.

Plant, R. 1988: *Citizenship, Rights and Socialism*, London: Fabian Society.

Plant, R. 1990: 'Citizenship and Rights', in D. Green (ed.), *Citizenship and Rights in Thatcher's Britain: Two Views*, London: Institute of Economic Affairs, pp. 3–32.

Plant, R. 1991: *Modern Political Thought*, Oxford: Blackwell.

Plant, R. 1994: 'Free Lunches Don't Nourish: Reflections on Entitlement and Citizenship', in G. Drover and P. Kerans (eds), *New Approaches to Welfare Theory*, Aldershot, Edward Elgar, pp. 33–48.

Polanyi, K. 1944: *The Great Transformation: The Political and Economic Origins of Our Time*, Boston: Beacon Press.

Pollard, V. 1994: 'Initiative or No Initiative: "Three Strikes" is Law in California', *California Journal Weekly*, reprinted in *California Probation News*, 2(5), pp. 1–3.

Psacharopoulos, G. 1992: 'Rates of Return Studies', in *Higher Educational Encyclopaedia*, 2, pp. 999–1003.

Psacharopoulos, G. and Woodhall, M. 1985: *Education for Development:*

An Analysis of Investment Choices, Oxford: Oxford University Press.

Purdy, D. 1995: Citizenship, Basic Income and the State, *New Left Review*, 208.

Putnam, R. D. 1993: *Making Democracy Work: Civic Traditions in Modern Italy*, Princeton: Princeton University Press.

Rainwater, L., Rein, M. and Schwartz, J. 1986: *Income Packaging in the Welfare State: A Comparative Study of Family Income*, Oxford: Clarendon Press.

Rawls, A. W. 1987: 'The Interaction Order *Sui Generis*: Goffman's Contribution to Social Theory', *Sociological Theory*, 5(2), pp. 136–49.

Rawls, A. W. 1989: 'An Ethnomethodological Perspective on Social Theory', in D. T. Helm et al. (eds), *The Interaction Order*, New York: Irvington, pp. 4–20.

Rawls, J. 1970: *A Theory of Justice*, Oxford: Oxford University Press.

Rawls, J. 1987: 'The Idea of Overlapping Consensus', *Oxford Journal of Legal Studies*, 7, pp. 5–6.

Rawls, J. 1989: 'The Domain of the Political and Overlapping Consensus', *New York University Law Review*, 64, pp. 234–5.

Rawls, J. 1993: *Political Liberalism*, New York: Columbia University Press.

Rieger, E. and Leibfried, S. 1995: 'The Welfare State and Globalization: Conflicts over Germany's Competitiveness', paper presented at Summer School, ZeS, University of Bremen, 25 July–5 August.

Rimlinger, G. V. 1971: *Welfare Policy and Industrialization in America, Europe and Russia*, New York: Wiley.

Ringen, S. 1988: 'Direct and Indirect Measures of Poverty', *Journal of Social Policy*, 17(3), pp. 357–66.

Robbins, P. et al. 1980: *A Guaranteed Annual Income: Evidence from a Social Experiment*, New York: Academic Press.

Robson, G., Bradford, M. and Tye, R. 1994: 'The Development of the 1991 Local Deprivation Index', paper given at a seminar on the Measurement and Analysis of Social Exclusion, Bath University, 17–18 June.

Roche, M. 1992: *Rethinking Citizenship*, Cambridge: Polity.

Roemer, J. 1982: *A General Theory of Exploitation and Class*, Cambridge: Harvard University Press.

Rogers, R. 1995: *Reith Lectures*, BBC Radio 4, Jan–March.

Room, G. 1990: *New Poverty in the European Community*, London: Macmillan

Rowntree, S. 1901: *Poverty: A Study in Town Life*, London: Macmillan

Rowntree, S. 1918: *The Human Needs of Labour*, London: Longmans.

Ryan, A. 1975: 'Mill and Rousseau: Utility and Rights', in G. Duncan (ed.), *Democratic Theory and Practice*, Cambridge: Cambridge University Press.

Ryan, C. M. 1994: *The Children Act, 1989: Putting It into Practice*, Aldershot: Arena.

Sandel, M. 1982: *Liberalism and the Limits of Justice*, Cambridge: Cambridge University Press.

Sandler, T. and Tschirhart, J. 1993: 'Multiproduct Clubs: Membership and Sustainability', *Public Finance*, 48(2), pp. 153–70.

Scharpf, F. W. 1985: 'Beschäftigungspolitische Strategien in der Krise', *Leviathan*, 13.

Scharpf, F. W. 1991: *Crisis and Choice in European Social Democracy*, Ithaca: Cornell University Press.

Schatteman, T., Van Trier, W. and Kesenne, S. 1994: *De Kloof Dichten, Brengt het Iets Op? Een onderzoek naar de Kosten en de Baten voor de Overheid van 'Leerwerkbedrijf'*, Antwerp: SESO-UFSIA.

Schmitter, P. 1989: 'Corporatism is Dead! Long Live Corporatism!', *Government and Opposition*, 24(1), pp. 54–73.

Scott, J. C. 1975: *The Moral Economy of the Peasant: Rebellion and Subsistence in South-East Asia*, New Haven: Yale University Press.

Scott, J. C. 1985: *Weapons of the Weak: Everyday Forms of Peasant Resistance*, New Haven: Yale University Press.

Scott, J. C. 1990: *Domination and Resistance: Hidden Transcripts*, New Haven: Yale University Press.

Seeleib-Kaiser, M. 1995: 'The Development and Structure of Social Assistance and Unemployment Insurance in the Federal Republic of Germany and Japan', *Social Policy and Administration*, 29(3), pp. 269–93.

Sen, A. 1983: 'Poor, Relatively Speaking', *Oxford Economic Papers*, 35, pp. 153–69.

Sen, A. 1985a: 'A Sociological Approach to the Measurement of Poverty: A Reply to Peter Townsend', *Oxford Economic Papers*, 37, pp. 669–76.

Sen, A. 1985b: *Commodities and Capabilities*, Amsterdam: North Holland.

Singleton, S. and Taylor, M. 1992: 'Common Property, Collective Action and Community', *Journal of Theoretical Politics*, 4(3), pp. 309–24.

Skocpol, T. 1988: 'A Society without a "State"? Political Organization, Social Conflict and Welfare Provision in the United States', *Journal of Public Policy*, 7, pp. 349–71.

Smart, B. 1991: *Modern Conditions, Post-modern Controversies*, London: Routledge.

Smeeding, T. S., O'Higgins, M., Rainwater, L. and Atkinson, A. B. 1990: *Poverty, Inequality and Income Distribution in Comparative Perspective*, London: Simon & Schuster.

Solow, R. 1990: *The Labour Market as a Social Institution*, Oxford: Blackwell.

Spencer, H. 1884: *The Man versus the State* [1969], Harmondsworth: Penguin.

Spruyt, H. 1994: *The Sovereign State and Its Competitors: An Analysis of Systems Change*, Princeton: Princeton University Press.

Standing, G. 1986: 'Meshing Labour Flexibility with Security: An Answer to British Unemployment?', *International Labour Review*, 125, pp. 87–107.

Stark, M. 1988: *An A to Z of Income and Wealth*, London: Fabian Society.

Starrett, D. A. 1988: *Foundations of Public Economics*, Cambridge: Cambridge University Press.

Stewart, G. and Stewart, J. 1993: *Relieving Poverty? Use of the Social Fund by Social Work Clients and Other Agencies*, London: Association of Metropolitan Authorities.

Stirling, M. 1992a: 'How Many Pupils are being Excluded?', *British Journal of Special Education*, 19(4), pp. 128–30.

Stirling, M. 1992b: 'The Education Act and EBD Children', *Young Minds Newsletter*, 10 March, pp. 8–9.

Stitt, S. 1993: *Poverty in Britain*, Cambridge: Polity.

Stone, D. 1994: 'Health Care Insurance in the US', seminar, University of Bremen, Zentrum für Sozialpolitik, 23 May.

Stone, N. 1992: 'Probation in the 1990s: No Escaping Nemesis?', in B. Williams and P. Senior (eds), *Probation Practice After the Criminal Justice Act, 1991*, Sheffield: PAVIC Publications, pp. 1–10.

Taylor, C. 1989: *Sources of the Self: The Making of Modern Identity*, Cambridge: Harvard University Press.

Taylor, C. 1991: *Cross Purposes: The Liberal–Communitarian Debate*, in N. Rosenblum (ed.), *Liberation and the Moral Life*, Cambridge: Harvard University Press.

Taylor, D. 1992: 'A Big Idea for the Nineties? The Rise of Citizens Charters', *Critical Social Policy*, 33, pp. 87–94.

Taylor, M. 1982: *Community, Anarchy and Liberty*, Cambridge: Cambridge University Press.

Taylor, M. 1987: *The Possibility of Co-operation*, Cambridge: Cambridge University Press.

Thompson, E. P. 1963: *The Making of the English Working Class*, Harmondsworth: Penguin.

Tiebout, C. 1956: 'A Pure Theory of Local Expenditures', *Journal of Political Economy*, 64, pp. 416–24.

Titmuss, R. 1958: 'The Social Division of Welfare: Some Reflections on the Search for Equity', in R. Titmuss, *Essays on 'The Welfare State'*, London: Allen & Unwin.

Tizard, B., Blatchford, P., Burke J., Farquar C. and Pleins I. 1988: *Young Children at School in the Inner City*, London: Thomas Coram Foundation.

Tocqueville, A. de 1835–40: *Democracy in America* [1968], ed. J. P. Mayer and M. Lerner, London: Collins.

Townsend, J. 1786: *A Dissertation on the Poor Laws: By a Well Wisher To Mankind* [1817], London: Murray.

Townsend, P. 1972: 'The Needs of the Elderly and the Planning of Hospitals', in R. Canvin and N. Pearson (eds), *The Needs of the Elderly for Health and Welfare Services*, Exeter: Exeter University Press.

Townsend, P. 1979: *Poverty in the United Kingdom*, Harmondsworth: Penguin.

Townsend, P. 1993: *The International Analysis of Poverty*, Hemel Hempstead: Harvester Wheatsheaf.

Townsend, P. and Abel Smith, B. 1965: *The Poor and the Poorest*, London: Bell.

Townsend, P., Phillimore, P. and Beattie, A. 1988: *Deprivation, Equality and the North*, Newcastle: Tyneside CPAG.

Turner, R., Bostyn, A. M. and Wright, D. 1985: 'The Work Ethic in a Scottish Town with Declining Employment', in B. Roberts et al. (eds), *New Approaches to Economic Life*, Manchester: Manchester University Press.

Van der Veen, R. 1994: 'The Overqualification Game', University of Amsterdam, unpublished MS.

Van Parijs, P. 1992: 'Competing Justifications for Basic Income', in P. Van Parijs (ed.), *Arguing for Basic Income: The Ethical Foundations for a Radical Reform*, London: Verso.

Van Parijs, P. 1995: *Real Freedom for All: What (if Anything) Can Justify Capitalism?*, Oxford: Clarendon Press.

Van Praag, A. M. J. and Teekens, R. 1992: *Analysing Poverty in the European Community*, Brussels: European Commission.

Van Trier, W. 1994: 'Bestaat er Nog Bestaanszekerheid na het Einde van de Vollege Tewerkstelling?', unpublished paper presented at 'Arbeid Herdacht' conference, Sociale Hogeschool, Gent, 17 March.

Victor, C. R. 1991: 'Continuity or Change? Inequalities in Health in Later Life', *Ageing and Society*, 11, pp. 23–9.

Wakefield, E. C. 1831: *Swing Unmasked*, London: E. Wilson.

Wallis, J. J. and North, D. C. 1986: 'Measuring the Transaction Sector in the American Economy, 1870–1970', in S. L. Egerson and R. E. Gallman (eds), *Long-term Factors in American Economic Growth*, Chicago: Chicago University Press.

Walter, T. 1988: *Basic Incomes: Freedom from Poverty, Freedom to Work*, London: Marion Boyars.

Walzer, M. 1980: 'Dissatisfaction in the Welfare State', in M. Walzer, *Radical Principles: Reflections of an Unreconstructed Democrat*, New York: Basic Books, pp. 23–53.

Walzer, M. 1983: *Spheres of Justice*, Oxford: Blackwell.

Walzer, M. 1990: 'The Communitarian Critique of Liberalism', *Political Theory*, 18(1), pp. 28–43.

Ward, D. 1989: *Poverty, Ethnicity and the American City, 1840–1925: Changing Conceptions of the Slum and Ghetto*, Cambridge: Cambridge University Press.

Weber, M. 1922: *Economy and Society* [1968], ed. G. Roth and C. Wittich, New York: Bedminster Press.

White, M. 1991: *Against Unemployment*, London: Policy Studies Institute.

Whiteley, P. F. and Winyard, S. J. 1987: *Pressure for the Poor: The Poverty Lobby and Policy Making*, London: Methuen.

Wicksell, K. 1896: *Finanztheoretische Untersuchungen*, Jena: Fischer.

Williams, A. 1994: 'Contracting for Children', Social Services Management Unit, Department of Social Policy and Social Work, Birmingham University, masters thesis.

Williams, N. J., Sewell, J. and Twine, F. 1986: 'Council House Sales and Residualization', *Journal of Social Policy*, 15(3), pp. 273–92.

Wilson, T. 1985: 'The Unwithered Welfare State', in D. Greenaway (ed.), *Public Choice, Public Finance and Public Policy: Essays in Honour of Alan Peacock*, Oxford: Blackwell, pp. 78–93.

Wilson, W. J. 1987: *The Truly Disadvantaged: The Underclass, the Ghetto and Public Policy*, Chicago: Chicago University Press.

Wilson, W. J. 1989: 'The Underclass', *The Annals of the American Academy of Political and Social Science*, 501, pp. 182–92.

Wiseman, M. 1991: 'What Did the American Work-welfare Demonstrations Do? Why Should the Germans Care?', Zentrum für Sozialpolitik, University of Bremen, Arbeitspapier 9/91.

Witz, A. 1992: *Professions and Patriarchy*, London: Routledge.

Wolfe, A. 1989: *Whose Keeper? Social Science and Moral Obligation*, Berkeley and Los Angeles: University of California Press.

Wolfe, A. 1991: 'Market, State and Society as Codes of Moral

Obligation', in M. Mennell and D. Salée (eds), *The Legacy of Karl Polanyi: Market State and Society at the End of the Twentieth Century*, New York, St Martin's Press, pp. 31–49.

Wooders, M. 1978: 'Equilibria, The Cost, and Jurisdictional Structures in Economies with a Local Public Good', *Journal of Economic Theory*, 18, pp. 328–48.

Woodhall, M. 1992: 'Financial Aid: Students', in *Higher Education Encyclopaedia*, 2, pp. 1358–67.

World Health Organization, *Bridging the Gaps*, Geneva: WHO.

WRR 1985: *Safeguarding Social Security*, The Hague: Netherlands.

Wuyts, L., Van Trier, W. and Késenne, S. 1994: Onderzoek naar de Effecten van Interface-Projecten met Gevalstudie Leereiland bij Lévi-Strauss', Antwerp: SESO-UFSIA.

Young, M. and Halsey, A. H. 1995: *Family and Community Socialism*, London: Institute for Public Policy Research.

Younge, P. 1995: 'Lost Boys', *Guardian*, 1 August.

Zopf, P. E. 1989: *American Women in Poverty*, New York: Greenwood Press.

Zürn, M. 1995: 'The Challenge of Globalization and Individualization: A View from Europe', in H.-H. Holm and G. Sprensen (eds), *Whose World Order? Uneven Globalization and the End of the Cold War*, Boulder, CO: Westview Press.

Index